The Best of Wine in Ireland 1999

A & A
Farmar

© A. & A. Farmar 1998

website: www.farmarbooks.com

British Library Cataloguing in Publication data
A CIP catalogue record for this book is available from
the British Library.

ISBN 1 899047 43 3

Published by
A. & A. Farmar
Beech House
78 Ranelagh Village
Dublin 6

Contents

Publishers' preface

We are delighted to welcome Sandy O'Byrne as Editor of the fourth edition of *The Best of Wine in Ireland*. She brings a balanced expertise in both food and wine that we believe has enormously enhanced the book.

As before, the tasting panel was drawn from the wine trade, the catering industry and knowledgeable amateurs. We are grateful to all of those who gave of their expertise and time to evaluate the wines. Liam Campbell, Tony Cleary and Nigel Donnan were particularly helpful.

The book would not be possible without the contribution of the wine importers who submitted wines for tasting, and patiently answered our requests for further information about their wines. As before, Jean Smullen of the Wine Development Board was extremely helpful.

We would like to express a particular debt to the management and staff of Findlaters, who made part of their splendid vaults available for storing the wine samples in near perfect conditions, and for the actual tasting sessions. As well as being an extremely appropriate location, this facility enabled us greatly to refine the management and running of the sessions.

Anna and Tony Farmar
November 1998

Editor's choices

Editor Sandy O'Byrne makes her choices from this year's tastings.

Editor's introduction

In the foreword to the first edition of the *Best of Wine in Ireland*, T. P. Whelehan wrote: 'I believe the challenge for our ilk (wine writers) is to take the intimidation out of buying wine and encourage all to explore the kaleidoscopic world of wine.'

That remains above all the intention of this guide, now in its fourth edition, and my own first close involvement with its evolution. Nobody can tell anybody which wines they should like; everybody has a different sense of taste and everybody's taste is valid. We can however, provide information and collective experience to make personal choice and exploration more enjoyable.

As a guide to available wines, *The Best of Wine* reflects the current wine market in Ireland with all its excitement and dynamism. Not unusually for this country, though small we attract a lot of attention. At just over 8 litres per head, per annum, Irish wine consumption is the lowest in the EU. However it is growing apace and has doubled since 1990, while in producing countries consumption has dropped significantly. Part of this is the change from wine being part of daily meals in most of Europe, as it still is throughout much of the Mediterranean, to being a choice purchase among a number of alternatives.

Irish consumption follows some interesting patterns. The raw statistics as ever are slightly misleading. There are a lot of non-drinkers contributing to that 8 litre figure; those who enjoy wine, and if you have got as far as reading this you are undoubtedly such a person, account for a great deal more than a bottle a month. We are also a fussy, choosy market and rightly so. For a number of reasons, including a punitive and inequitable tax system, there has never been the pressure on rock bottom prices experienced across the pond. Ireland has been spared the overpowering influence of large chains and multiples which depend on the bargain basement of volume sales. This situation has altered in the past twelve months, chiefly with the arrival of Tesco on the Irish scene.

The wine trade has served consumers well. Supermarkets, merchants and specialist wine shops provide great variety across a very wide range of sources and prices, and increasingly the knowledge to accompany it. There is a very good range from smaller producers and individual wineries are well represented. Restaurants however, are another matter. There are far too many abysmal lists based on the resources of the local cash and carry or a lazy listing of the basics from one supplier. Though generally lower than in other countries, there is great inconsistency in markup even on wines available in the High Street. Front-of-house staff lack knowledge and even basic competence in handling wine and lists are frequently inaccurate or out of date. There are a few notable exceptions, but on the whole restaurant wine lists need a new approach—perhaps food for thought for the *Best of Wine 2000.*

Before work on the 1999 edition began, I thought I knew the wine scene pretty well. As usual a number of surprises unfolded as the tasting results became obvious.

After years in the doldrums, Spain has emerged triumphant and as if overnight. The wines provide quality, variety and at present, great value for money. They are also pleasing wines, easy to drink and appreciate but not obvious in an unsubtle way.

The ability of large-scale New World producers to achieve consistency and quality right across a range of styles and prices, also impressed. Peter Lehmann in Australia is a particularly good example, as is Concha y

Toro in Chile.

Of the classic regions, Champagne produced some of the best quality and though not exactly good value, justify the premium they command rather more than in the past. At the other end of the scale in France, the Midi has indeed turned the tables on the New World. With not a little Australian help, the region now produces wines which combine the best of modern, fruit-driven vinification with local character, especially in the ACs of Corbières, Faugères, Minervois etc.

There were also disappointments. The range shown and listed from the Loire belies the strength and variety of the region and the recent string of good vintages: importers please note. Burgundy remains expensive and unreliable. Set against the spiralling prices in Bordeaux, the top Burgundies are reasonable value. But the consistency is not there, and below this price level quality is extremely hit and miss and the wines always overpriced. Lower-priced wines from Australia and California can be extremely disappointing, over-commercialised parodies of themselves for which there seems no justification.

There are two new elements this year. First, each wine has been categorised by style. The intention is not to pigeonhole something whose essence is variety, but rather to indicate general styles and to encourage experiment within known boundaries. The second addition is of food notes. Most wine is bought to drink with food and most of us agree that the combination matters; yet the two subjects are usually treated quite separately. This year we hope to bridge the gap.

Finally, it is you, the consumers, who have driven a quality market, have forced the trade to buy better and know more and it is you who keep us scribes sniffing and slurping through the best and worst of wine. Keep up the good work, so that we can all raise our glasses to wine in the next millennium.

Sandy O'Byrne, November 1998

Wine styles

Each wine in the guide (apart from sweet and sparkling) has been broadly categorised by style as listed overleaf, according to 'weight' in the mouth.

Using the weight of wine as a system of classification means classifying primarily by structure, rather than taste, although both taste and aromas also enter into some of the classifications. The structure of the wine is the frame which carries the taste. The wine notes describe the aromas, tastes and length of the wines.

Some of the red wines are also categorised as tannic. This does not mean that they are in any way imbalanaced. It is simply drawing attention to another characteristic aspect of a particular style, that the tannins are noticeable unlike many of today's wines which have very soft tannins indeed. The wines described as tannic have firm structures.

Wine styles and typical examples

Light dry white
Light and crisp, with neutral or delicate fruit character, no oak influence, to be drunk young
Muscadet de Sèvre et Maine sur lie

Light fruity white
Ripe fruit flavours and balanced acidity, no oak influence, to be drunk young
Unoaked Chilean Chardonnay

Light fruity white, off-dry
Light, ripe fruit flavours with obvious residual sugar
German Riesling

Aromatic white
Made from a particularly aromatic grape variety, from a cool or relatively cool climate, with no apparent oak influence, usually best drunk young
Rueda

Aromatic white, classic
Highly aromatic but with restrained fruit and typical regional character, usually of a northern region
Sancerre; Mosel Riesling Kabinett

Aromatic white, fruit-driven
Fruit-driven made from an aromatic grape variety to express the exuberant qualities of the fruit in an exotic and ripe style
New Zealand Sauvignon Blanc

Full-bodied white
Full, rounded fruit and moderate to high supporting alcohol to give a rich wine
Châteauneuf-du-Pape blanc

Full-bodied white, oak
Obvious oak influence from fermentation and/or ageing in barrel usually strongest in young barrique-aged wines
Californian barrel-fermented Chardonnay

Rosé
Light, fruity, made by short maceration, either very dry or relatively fruity
Rosé de Provence

Rosé, off-dry
Light, fruity with obvious residual sugar
Rosé d'Anjou

Light fruity red
Light, with lots of typical berry fruit flavours, lively acidity and minimal, soft tannin, to be drunk young and possibly cool
Beaujolais

Medium-bodied red
Moderate weight and rich, rather than simple, fruit character with balanced acidity and some tannin to give structure and dryness, usually with oak-ageing, which may be obvious in the taste
Montepulciano d'Abruzzo

Medium-bodied red, classic
Medium weight with complexity and typical character of its origin, moderate tannin and generally well-balanced, usually with the ability to age
Volnay

Medium bodied red, fruit-driven
Moderate weight and alcohol with rich and expressive fruit character and usually oak ageing
Chilean Cabernet/Merlot

Full-bodied red
Full-bodied with ripe fruit, plenty of extract, balanced tannin and acidity, aged in oak and usually capable of further development in bottle
Rioja Gran Reserva

Full-bodied red, classic
Full and structured with firm, tightly-knit palate of well extracted but restrained fruit and oak, obvious tannin and usually considerable length in the aftertaste, will age in bottle and develop complexity of flavour
Pauillac

Full-bodied red, fruit-driven
Full and rich with extract, fruit, usually high alcohol and a weight of very ripe, warm fruit, very well flavoured and big in taste with a long finish and varying ability to age in bottle
Australian Shiraz

Matching wine and food

Sandy O'Byrne

Attitudes to matching wine and food depend on nationality. In France wine is as much a part of a meal as the sauce, in fact it is often called the 'second sauce', and appropriate combinations are taken for granted within the cuisine of the country. Drinking the 'wrong' wine would seem as extraordinary as pouring ketchup over oysters.

The didactic, traditional and highly successful French attitude to food and wine works within their own gastronomy. However, non-producing countries, where food traditions may be less defined than those of France, are really spoiled for choice.

The combination makes all the difference, and while nobody would wish to lay down rules, logical guidelines are needed for the great variety of food and wine available today.

The old rule of 'red wine for red meat and game; white wine for white meat and fish' is generally accurate though very limited advice. It is more a question of the weight or balance of a wine than its colour. Many red wines are more robust, full-bodied and structured than many whites and therefore suit more textured, substantial foods which meat and game usually are. White wines are usually lighter and better with fish and delicate meats such as chicken or veal. The theory falls down however, with textured fish like tuna or with a very light red wine. A less traditional method of cooking, such as a stir-fry of beef, changes the texture and introduces spices which are less happy with full-bodied red, while roasting cod can make it meaty and substantial enough for a middle-weight red like Pinot Noir or Chinon.

It is therefore the balance of weights between wine and food that is most important. To enjoy both, one must be able to taste both, and neither should overpower the other in weight (body) or intensity of flavour.

Apart from weight and body, other aspects of wine affect food in particular ways. Acidity is essential to all wine, it keeps it fresh, makes it appetising and produces the bouquet. Acid stimulates the palate and so cuts through fat and richness in food. A crisp fresh white wine acts like a squeeze of lemon on a buttery fish. Tannin which comes from the skins and stalks of grapes in red wine making, helps the wine to age and gives it bite. High tannin has a drying effect on the palate like cold, strong tea; in very young wines it can be quite astringent. Tannin interacts with protein and tough young reds are softened by rare lean meat which protects the palate. More moderate tannin is dry and appetising and an excellent foil to rich foods like game, casseroles and many classically cooked dishes.

Certain combinations of wine and food clash either because of something in the food, which reacts with wine, or something which affects the ability to taste.

Hot spices burn so that tasting anything is impossible. Mild spices can work with light fruity wines, but hot chilli, lots of ginger or crushed pepper are better with beer or water. Beware of horseradish and mustard which can be very hot and really spoil a fine red wine intended for the beef.

Some foods are difficult because of texture. Chocolate is notorious for coating the palate with a layer of fat which dulls all other flavours. High alcohol and sweetness in a fortified dessert wine such as Port, Banyuls, or Liqueur Muscat usually do the trick. Egg yolks in sauces like mayonnaise, have a similar effect, so can a lot of oil. For these, oak and high acidity work.

Acids are less a problem than might be thought. While I cannot think of any wine which would benefit from being drunk with grapefruit, it is principally fine and mature wines which suffer from vinaigrette sauce or the sweet sour effect of tomatoes. Such foods are best with wines which have lots of lively fruit.

Artichokes and, to a lesser extent asparagus can make wine taste metallic, while vegetable-based dishes in general need rather fresh, lively whites or soft, rich, red wines with little oak.

Sweet food is often just too sweet for even the most luscious wine. Natural fruit ripeness together with the acidity of a dessert wine are no match for a pudding based on refined sugar. The wine must be as sweet or preferably sweeter than the food it accompanies which means serving simple, fruit or nut-based puddings with the best dessert wines.

The taste of wine comes from the grape, soil, climate, winemaking, vintage and age. When considering wine and food combinations it often helps to start with the grape variety, then to decide which style of that grape might suit a particular dish or vice versa. (See the chart of major grape varieties on pages 14–15 below).

Varietals tend to have fairly direct fruit flavours, which are good with strongly flavoured dishes and relatively complex foods. Where soil and terroir dominate the grape variety, the wine is often drier and more austere and will suit more integrated flavours and richer foods and cooking methods. Hot climates give very ripe, rich flavours and plenty of alcohol as well as less obvious acidity. Such wines will go with strong flavours but with food that is less rich, less protein and dairy-based, and it can tolerate spices. Oak-ageing adds to the structure of the wine therefore needs more substantial food. Its drying effect is also good with rich and creamy sauces. Strong oak flavours respond best to char-gilled or barbecued foods. Maturity makes a wine more complex in flavour, but more fragile. An old Bordeaux will need quite simple meat with a carefully made sauce and subtle flavours. Old Burgundy is rather more robust but will still benefit from classically cooked food.

This year for the first time in the guide we have included individual food notes for most of the wines. These are intended to indicate the sort of food the wine suits through examples of successful combinations. If a wine goes well with lamb steaks it is likely also to suit beef steaks; if it works with garlic flavours, it is probably also successful with herbs; a wine which suits a tomato and pasta dish may also work with pizza. There is always more than one wine for a particular dish, and each wine suits many different foods.

Further reading: Sandy O'Byrne goes into more detail on the principles and practice of *Matching Food and Wine* in her book of that name.

Dinner party reds

Wines for formal entertaining do not have to be classics. Here are a few from all over the world which will complement carefully prepared food and good company.

AC Fleurie *Joseph Drouhin* 97 (France-Beaujolais)
AC Givry *Pierre Ducret* 96 (France-Burgundy)
Fetzer Valley Oaks Cabernet Sauvignon 96 (USA-California)
Carmen Cabernet Sauvignon Reserve 96 (Chile)
Badia a Passignani DOCG Chianti Classico 96 (Italy)
Candido Salice DOC Salentino Riserva 93 (Italy)
Ch. Meaume AC Bordeaux Supérieur 95 (France-Bordeaux)
Dom. Thalabert AC Crozes-Hermitage 92 (France-Rhône-North)
Chevalière Réserve Syrah 96 VdP d'Oc (France-South)
Muga DOC Rioja Reserva 94 (Spain)
Rouge Homme Coonawarra Cabernet Sauvigon 94 (Australia)
Rosemount Estate Shiraz 96 (Australia)

Classic Varietals and Food

Whites	Characteristics	Food Matches
Riesling	Dry to sweet, high acidity, light to medium body, fine and aromatic, ages well	Delicate foods like fish, richness in sauces, cooking methods and ingredients. Off-dry versions with spices, light aromatic fruit with rich sauces
Chardonnay	Balanced acidity, medium to full body, usually oaked though amount of oak varies, apple to peach or melon-type fruit, creamy and buttery flavours with toasted influence ripeness, medium to high alcohol level	Depends on style and amount of oak influence. Main course foods, fish with sauces, chicken and light meats, smoked foods, fruit-influenced savoury dishes, pasta with cream sauces, creamy cheeses
Sémillon	Dry or sweet and botrytized full-bodied, waxy, honeyed character with citrus-type fruit acidity when young	Dry—with textured fish, chicken andlight meats, spices and many Chinese dishes Sweet—nutty puddings, light cakes and pastries, blue cheese, foie gras and similar rich pâtés
Sauvignon Blanc	Dry, crisp acidity, medium body, very aromatic and intense, from gooseberry to green apple, citrus type fruit to limes, green peppers and grassy influences. Classically minerally, flinty overtones	Well-flavoured fish, some chicken and light meats, vegetable and tomato based pasta, smoked salmon, spicy and herb flavoured food, goats' cheese, some blue cheese and strong cheeses in general
Chenin Blanc	Dry to sweet, high acidity, medium to full-bodied, aromatic citrus, apple, floral and honeyed fruit, ages well	Dry—rich food especially fish with sauces, pâté and charcuterie, salads and some spices Sweet—depending on sweetness, some spicy savoury food, goats' cheese and strong cheeses; also fruit-based puddings

Reds	Characteristics	Food Matches
Cabernet Sauvignon	Tannin, medium acidity, full body, typically blackcurrant-type fruit with mint, cedar and cigar-like aromas, ages well	Protein, especially red meat, matches rich meats like lamb and duck, rich meat sauces and game like widgeon
Pinot Noir	Medium tannin, medium to upper acidity, elegant body, rich fruit, typically strawberry type with spicy overtones, develops gamey vegetal character, moderate to long ageing	Red meat and some cheeses, typically game or beef, also casseroles and wine-based sauces. Lighter, fruity styles with textured fish, some spices and mushroom pasta or risotto
Syrah	Tannin, acidity, high alcohol, full body, can be firm and dense in structure or rich and fruit driven, dark fruit character of brambles, dark plums, violets with very spicy peppery overtones, ages well	Depends on structure and tannin, red meat, grilled and barbecued meats, game, casseroles, substantial pasta and grain-based dishes which include meat; richer styles can match spicy food
Merlot	Low to moderate tannin, higher alcohol, medium to full body, ripe, rich fruit character typically raspberries, plums and chocolate, can be fruity and simple or layered, rich and complex, ageing depends on style, generally moderate	Depends on tannin and oak influence, meats like beef, game like quail, pasta dishes and vegetarian food if not too oaky. Sausages, salamis and pâtés with fruity versions, some cheeses

The mystery of vintages

Alan Crowley, Master of Wine

A great part of the mystique of wine is the importance of the 'vintage', and which are the better or lesser years. Unfortunately, to many consumers the concept of a vintage represents yet another unknown in the wine maze.

Put simply, a vintage is the year in which the grapes were picked and the wine was made. It is therefore an indication of how old the wine is. However, as with other agricultural products, the critical importance of the vintage lies in the variability from year to year of weather conditions during the growing season. In some regions, notably in Europe, the effect is of a particular importance on the potential quality of the final wine. Thus, in good vintage years, when there have been sufficient rainy and dry periods, with sufficient sunshine and warm temperatures at the right time, grapes can be produced of a better quality to make a superior wine, as opposed to those in lesser years when the weather is not so right for quality grape production.

The effect of the weather, and hence the reputation of the vintage, is usually more important in wine regions whose climate is more marginal for the growing of grapes. Generally such regions are in Europe—in Germany, in Burgundy and Bordeaux in France, in Spain and Italy. Wine regions with more or less regular weather conditions produce wines where vintages year to year assume less importance. Such wine regions include the New World vineyards of South Africa, California, Australia and Chile. In these cases the vintage serves the consumer simply as a reminder of how old the wine is, and hence when it should be drunk. Of course, even in these regions knowledge of the vintage and wine style is important to ensure the optimum time for drinking the wine.

Because European wines in particular are so dependent for their quality on the weather conditions of any one year, for many wine lovers the vintage is one of the keys to the quality of any particular wine. As such there is a benefit in having vintage knowledge, as it will assist in:

- Selecting wines from better years rather than lesser years.
- Ensuring a wine which is meant to be drunk young, or is better after a few years ageing, is at the correct age at the time of drinking.

Some wines are best consumed while still young. For example, Muscadet and Valpolicella are best consumed up to three years after their production or vintage as their charm lies in their fresh, youthful character.

On the other hand some wines, while generally not changing much in quality from vintage to vintage, benefit from two to three years' bottle maturation before consumption, for example, Australian Shiraz or Californian Cabernet Sauvignon.

As a very general guide, it can be said that most New World quality red wines benefit from having two to three years' maturation from the date of vintage before consumption, while most New World whites do not benefit from long maturation and are best consumed within three to four years after their vintage.

Identifying which European wines and which vintages have produced wine of superior quality depends more on detailed knowledge of the wine region than on general country classification. This can only be gained by wine education and experience. However, many regions are historically famous for producing fine 'vintage' wines such as Bordeaux, Burgundy, Barolo and Rioja, to name a few.

As a guide to the reputation of each year's vintage since 1985, a quick reference vintage chart is attached.

Region	96	95	94	93	92	91	90	89	88	87	86	85	Classic vintages
Bordeaux red	8	8	7	6	4	4	10	10	9	5	8	9	82, 78, 70, 61
Sauternes	8	8	5	5	4	3	10	10	8	5	9	7	80
Burgundy red	8	8	6	8	6	6	10	9	9	7	7	9	83, 78
Burgundy white	9	8	6	5	7	5	9	9	8	5	8	9	83, 78
Rhône	7	8	7	5	5	7	10	9	8	7	8	8	78, 67, 61
Champagne	-	8	-	8	7	6	8	8	-	-	8	9	79
Germany	7	8	8	8	7	6	10	8	7	6	6	8	76, 75
Spain	7	10	9	4	6	8	6	6	5	7	6	6	82, 64
Italy	8	7	7	8	4	5	9	7	8	6	7	9	78, 71
Port	-	-	10	-	8	8	7	-	-	-	-	9	77, 70, 66, 63
Australia	7	7	8	7	7	8	7	6	7	7	8	8	82, 79
California	6	7	7	7	8	9	8	7	7	8	7	8	74

Each region for each year is given a mark out of ten for its vintage.

Vintage Chart compiled by Alan Crowley, Master of Wine.

Of course, any vintage chart is only a general guide—the best producers can make a good wine in 'off' years, and in some years a winemaker, or part of a wine region, can experience local problems resulting in quite ordinary or inferior wines in an otherwise good year.

Wines to lay down

Buying to keep allows you to watch a wine mature and enjoy it at peak. These wines, chosen by Sandy O'Byrne, will benefit from moderate cellaring, say 3–4 years.

Penfolds Bin 128 Coonawarra Shiraz 95 (Australia)
Cape Mentelle Cabernet/Merlot 96 (Australia)
Ch. Xanadu Cabernet Sauvignon 96 (Australia)
AC Chorey-Lès-Beaune *Tollot Beaut. et Fils* 95 (France-Burgundy)
AC Chambolle Musigny 'Clos du Village' *Antonin Guyon* 94 (France-Burgundy)
Lamole di Lamole DOCG Chianti Classico 95 (Italy)
La Réserve du General AC Margaux 95 (France-Bordeaux)
Domaine Fleury Laplace 96 Madiran (France-South-West)
Domaine Tempier 94 Bandol (France-South)
Emilio Moro DO Ribera del Duero Reserva 94 (Spain)
Mastroberardino Radici DOCG Taurasi 94 (Italy)
Marqués de Grinon Dominio de Valdepusa Cabernet Sauvignon VdM Toledo 96 (Spain)

From cellar to glass

Liam Campbell

How to taste wine

The difference between drinking a wine and tasting a wine is reflection. The ordinary casual drinker might enjoy a particular bouquet, a more or less pleasant taste, a tingle of alcohol at the back of the throat, and so on, but hardly allows the wine to reveal all its character. The taster, on the other hand, looks closely at a wine to examine it, sniffs in the wine's aroma and then tastes the wine, letting it coat the palate in its entirety. At each stage the taster reflects and considers many things, looking for clues to help understand what messages the wine is giving about itself.

The three stages in tasting a wine follow a very logical sequence—look, sniff and sip.

A wine can tell you so much by its appearance and scent alone. The taste sensations (flavours) of a wine confirm the signals given by the former two. The secret of wine tasting is to sensitise all of these three senses and to train them to work together better to translate your own thoughts and impressions of a wine.

To begin, pour a relatively small amount of wine into your glass. (Incidentally, leave the cut crystal in the cabinet, and invest in ISO tasting glasses available from some specialist wine shops. These glasses are the ones professional wine tasters use, and they do make a difference by emphasising aromas and flavours.)

Swirl the wine gently in the glass. By filling your glass to no more than a quarter, you can swirl sufficiently without adding to your laundry bill. The swirling action does a number of things. Primarily, however, it increases the wine's surface area and the energy imparted by the swirling helps aerate the wine and release more rapidly its aromas. The swirling should coat the inside of the glass which slowly or rapidly forms little rivulets which run down the inside of the glass. These little streams are called 'tears' or 'legs'. As a general rule of thumb, the more pronounced the tears and the closer they run together down the glass, the more viscous the wine. This may indicate a wine high in alcohol or long ageing in bottle.

The colour of the wine is brimful of clues about itself—its likely origins, possible grape varieties, alcohol content, age, even details of the way the wine was made, for instance, what maturing vessels were used, whether new oak or some inert container such as steel or concrete. To read the signals, consider the following generalisations. White wines begin life pale and (un)interesting. With age they develop and evolve a deeper colour. Typically, a wine when bottled begins with a pale lemon or lime colour which deepens with time into straw and gold. (As so often in wine, the rule cannot totally be relied on. Exceptions occur if a wine has been aged in new oak or if the wine is a sweet dessert wine. However, a quick sniff will quickly tell you whether your glass of rich golden wine is a young oak-aged wine, a sweet wine or a very old mature wine.) Swirl the wine again to release more vapours and aromas. If a wine smells of a mature non-fruity bouquet or of oaky vanilla or of waxy honey you can begin to guess what the wine is.

Conversely, red wines grow paler with age. Because the wine's colour is derived from the grape skins, the warmer the climate, the riper the grapes and the richer and probably deeper the colour the wine. As the wine matures, the colouring matter in the skins, the *anthocyanins*, connect with the tannin in the wine like two pieces in a jigsaw, become solid matter and fall as a harmless, if astringent and bitter, sediment in the wine. This reaction explains how some quite tannic wines soften and improve by becoming smoother with age because the mouth-puckering, gum-tingling tannins literally fall from the wine.

Also in youth the colour forms right up to the edge. By tilting the glass away from you at a 45° angle and looking at the border of the wine furthest from you, a clearer impression is given. The more the colour fades from the edge of the wine the greater the age. The colour itself speaks volumes. Wine within its first year of bottling will appear a purple colour. Shortly afterwards the blue hue disappears to reveal a ruby colour. With time the ruby is transformed into mahogany and eventually a tawny orangey tinted colour with very noticeable fading from the rim to the deeper coloured core of the wine. As a red wine matured in new oak matures further in bottle, when poured a faint brick orange or yellow halo appears around the rim of the wine according to age.

Again, the bouquet will confirm much about the wine. Youthful berry fruit aromas suggest a young wine. Spice, cinnamon, clove, oak and vanilla suggest a wine matured in new oak. As the wine matures, it loses its exuberant, youthful fruitiness; it may even close up temporarily into sulky adolescence to emerge later as a mature, more complex and 'winey' bouquet.

Now start actually tasting the wine. Do not be intimidated by a fancy label or a grand image. First sip a little wine and swallow, just to let the brain register that it is dealing with alcohol. Next sip again, (enough this time to cover the whole tongue) purse the lips and suck in a little air. This aeration has a similar effect as swirling the wine in the glass to open up the bouquet. Then, with lips closed, roll the wine all over and around your tongue. Think of your tongue as an antenna picking up signals. Finally, either spit into a spittoon or swallow depending on the occasion. Wait a few seconds to let the signals register on your palate. The length of time the memory of the flavours on the centre of the palate remain, the better the quality of the wine. To quantify the length count from 1001, 1002, 1003 etc. Up to 1010 is a fair to good length. 1015 is even better and over 1020 is worth stocking up on providing you actually like the wine.

Your tongue has several hundred tastebuds, so do not deprive any of them when tasting wine. Different parts of the tongue and palate are affected by different substances in a wine. For instance, the tip of the tongue senses any sweetness, while the sides of the tongue detect the acidity and make you salivate. Ripe fruits, oak, spice etc. and the character of a wine are sensed in the middle of the tongue. However, tannins in red wine are sensed on the teeth and gums and have a drying effect on the saliva ducts. Alcohol is felt at the back of the throat and gives a very warming sensation if alcohol content is high. If very high in alcohol the sensation is more burning.

How do you tell if a wine is immature, ready to drink or past its best? If the wine in the glass continues to improve in aroma and/or flavour over some hours it is possibly still immature. If the wine changes little it is most likely on its plateau of perfection. However, if the wine's taste disimproves over a few hours in the glass, then it is most likely past its peak and its companion bottles should be drunk soon.

It is easy to confuse some of the characteristics of a wine as the senses are assaulted by often contradictory flavours. For instance a bone-dry wine from a warm sun-ripening climate can give a misleading impression initially of being off-dry or medium sweet because of the super-ripe fruit sensed in the middle palate. However, if no sweetness is detected on the tip of the tongue, then the wine is in fact dry.

Another area of easy confusion lies in a tart wine with high acidity but little other flavour. When counting the length of the wine after spitting/swallowing concentrate on your middle palate and do not be tempted to let the shrieking acidity alone on the sides of the tongue grab all your attention. A persistent acidic finish on a wine alone is not a sign of quality if unpartnered by flavours on the centre of the tongue.

My parting advice is:

1. Remember you are the master of your own palate. But like any craft, tasting improves with practice.

2. Your opinion of a wine is perfectly valid for you. Have faith in your first impression rather than let others influence you if you disagree.

3. Keep an open mind about all wines. Your tastes, like fashion are forever changing. Remember flares? Do not deprive yourself today of a wine that may become your favourite tomorrow.

Buying wine

When buying wines for different reasons and for different occasions, one supplier usually suits better than another for that particular reason and occasion. The basic choices are: from the winemaker directly, the wholesaler/importer, the supermarket, by mail order, from a specialist wine shop, an off-licence or a grocery store.

Because of the vulnerability of wine to its conditions of storage, the same bottle of wine, handled by different suppliers could taste notably different depending on how conscientiously the bottle was handled and cared for or not. A reliably tried and tested *winemaker* will have a pride in his or her wine and an understanding for taking care of the wine when bottled. *Wholesalers* also understand about correct storage but may not have a licence to sell direct to the consumer.

Supermarkets offer a wide range of wines but untutored staff may not always appreciate that wine is a living organism that can deteriorate if exposed for prolonged periods to heat and light. White wine in clear glass is particularly vulnerable. A fast turnover of sales and a regular rotation of stock on the shelves will help prevent a wine being damaged. All too seldom does one find staff dedicated to the off-licence section with wine knowledge.

Mail order can offer good value because there is no high street rent to pay and it is very convenient for customers whose access to wine outlets is restricted. Wines offered are usually for early consumption and are usually sold by the case (12 bottles).. Recent innovations include gift presentations for special occasions. Often wines offered are from winemakers of unknown reputation thereby placing all one's trust in the reputation of the mail order company.

Specialist wine merchants offer a more limited range than a supermarket but compensate with expert advice and a knowledge of their wines. In the absence of the same economies of scale, the wines may cost a little more but reliable producers and vintages should dominate the shelves.

Off-licences vary greatly, from those who stock a range of wines rivalling a supermarket to ones whose main speciality is cans of beer. The former can offer a surprisingly good range of wines at keen prices with an occasional 'find' if you rummage around the back of the shelves.

The *grocery shop* offers convenience at a price, but is usually limited in range and wine expertise.

Taking wine home

Like all living things, wine benefits from a little love and kindness. It does not react well to noise, vibrations, strong odours and direct light. It detests sudden erratic changes in temperature. While it is more forgiving of the cold, it can be damaged and taste 'soupy' if exposed to prolonged heat above 25^0C.

It is best to transport the wine bottles upright to minimise the 'slosh-about' factor, especially if the wine has not been heavily filtered and has thrown a deposit, or is maturing and healthy but harmless sediment is present and clouds the agitated wine.

When safely home, before you are tempted to reminisce and open a bottle, allow the wine a few days' rest to recover from the journey.

Storing wine

Much is made of the correct storing and cellaring of wine. If circumstances and space dictate that you buy wine only to consume it immediately or within a few weeks or so, then wine is quite tolerant of uncomfortable surroundings, providing it is not stored near immediate heat. So do not set up your wine rack near a hot radiator, water pipes or in the airing cupboard beside the immersion heater.

Sooner or later you will be tempted to lay down some wine for rather longer, perhaps as a result of discovering some irresistible bargains or rarities never to be seen in our time again. Since monitoring the evolving quality of the wine as it ages is part of the fun, there is hardly any point in buying less than, say, a case of any one vintage. Then attention to preparing a storage area or wine cellar is vital to the health and longevity of your wine.

Golden rules for wine storage

Store the bottles horizontally on their side with the label facing upwards, for easy identification. Maintain a regular temperature hovering between 10⁰C and 15⁰C. Avoid light, noise, vibrations and strong odours.

If your house does not run to a cellar, improvise with a wardrobe or sturdy chest of drawers, ideally in a cool north-facing room. Special wine racks are widely available. Avoid hot spots such as radiators and water pipes. If an offspring or a sibling's bedroom is adjacent, with a

state-of-the-art music centre with giant speakers consider a different location for the wine—or for your offspring/ sibling. To keep the wine as cool as possible, store it against an outside wall in the room. Exclude sunlight by closing the curtains or by covering the wine with a blanket.

The finer wines, requiring long ageing, should be stored at the lowest level, and this is also the coolest part of a room. Do not be tempted to use the top of the wardrobe as the fine wine will mature less effectively at the warmer temperatures over time. Store wines intended for earliest consumption within easy reach, e.g. the top drawer or top row of a wine rack. Finally, a cautionary tale about the effects of poor wine storage. In 1994 a New York investor purchased a 1787 Chateau Margaux for £287,000 from Thomas Jefferson's cellar. The bottle was proudly displayed, upright, in a glass case under hot lights. Inevitably, the antique cork slowly shrivelled and silently sunk into the wine, thus creating the world's most expensive bottle of vinegar.

Professional wine storage

If it is not possible to store your wines at home, look into trusting your finest wines to professional storage by a specialist in wine storage who understands and appreciates a wine's preferred habitat. To protect the legal health of your wine, ensure the specialist is financially secure and that each case of wine is clearly and unambiguously marked identifying you as the owner.

Cellar records

A written record of your cellar's consumptions and replenishments greatly adds to the enjoyment of the cellar. Allow a large page per case of wine. The heading should give price, supplier, quantity bought and purchase date. As the wine gently ages, you should sample a bottle from time to time. List a tasting note for each bottle sampled with date and details of the occasion. This monitoring of a wine's progress towards maturity will indicate to you when is the optimum time to drink up according to your personal preference. Records will also help you to keep track of which wines are stored where, helping you avoid disturbing the sleeping beauties.

If professional wine storage is used then cellar records should account for where, when, which and how much wine has been stored.

Serving wine

First remove the foil using a knife or a foil cutter just below the lip of the bottle. Old bottles that have been stored in damp cellars may have a slight mould round the lip which should be wiped. (The damp helps to preserve the moisture of the cork, but at the expense of disintegrating the labels. In these conditions, labels can be protected against damp by using clingfilm or by painting with clear varnish.)

Pulling a cork from a bottle of wine can be a smooth and slick operation or one inducing a hernia operation, depending on the efficiency of the corkscrew. Old-fashioned corkscrews can be things of beauty and ingenuity, but in practice difficult to use. The 'Screwpull' is perhaps the best corkscrew for ordinary use, though professionals prefer the 'Waiter's Friend'.

Gently twist the screw into the cork, using a good quality corkscrew. Try not to penetrate the cork all the way through as bits of cork may crumble into the wine. If the cork breaks before it is fully retrieved, it may be possible very gently to re-insert the screw and pull it out; otherwise you will do the wine no harm by gently pushing the remaining cork into the bottle, taking extreme care not to spray yourself or stain the carpet.

A wine whose cork has broken should be decanted. Indeed many not-so-brilliant wines benefit from the extra oxygenation resulting from the decanting process. Decanting can help if an immature wine is a little closed and tight and needs to be opened up on the nose and palate quickly. Finally, decanters are useful if you want to separate a wine from its sediment.

When opening potentially dangerous sparkling wine and Champagne bottles, remove the wire muzzle by untwisting the little wire loop, whilst keeping the other hand pressed firmly down on the mushroom-shaped cork. Hold the bottle at a 45⁰ angle away from yourself and anyone else within firing range. The trick is to twist the *bottle* while holding the cork steady. Just before the cork is fully released tilt the cork slightly sideways to gently release the carbon dioxide gas. A soft sigh or gentle hiss should be heard and not a loud pop. It is better to keep the fizz in the wine than on the floor. This technique should be ignored by wine waiters for whom the size of their gratuity is often in direct relation to the number of decibels of the pop!

The most important aspect of serving wine is temperature. I suspect too many wines are not enjoyed to their full potential by being drunk at too cool or too warm a temperature. While most wines will perform well within a narrow range of temperatures a general guideline is 8^0–10^0C for sweet, sparkling, rosé and dull white wines. Coldness helps reduce any cloying taste in sweet wines while masking the acidity in very tart white wines and refreshing the flavour of low acidity wines. Overchilling can be a good thing in a bad wine. If a white wine is a bit brutish and you do not want to use it for cooking or for mulled wine, then chill it.

Some red wines with low tannin are structured similarly to white wines and may benefit from being cooled to 10^0–12^0C, e.g. Beaujolais, Valpolicella, Bardolino and reds from the Loire Valley.

More tannic red wines benefit from warmer temperatures of 15^0–18^0C as warmth counters the astringency of tannin. However, if tannic reds are served too warm, e.g. over 20^0C, the alcohol will begin to evaporate and dominate the wine's aroma and taste.

High quality dry whites and delicate wines show off all their subtleties and complexities at 12^0–16^0C.

The quickest way to chill a wine is to submerge it in water chilled with ice-cubes, as more surface area of the bottle is in direct contact with the coldness than using ice cubes alone. Unfortunately the result, though quick, leaves slippery bottles, often without labels. The refrigerator takes about four times longer to cool a wine. If you only wish to chill one bottle, a patent device, the 'Rapid Ice Vacu Vin', chills in minutes. It is a silver foil sleeve of liquid which slips over a bottle. It is kept frozen in the ice box until required.

To warm a wine quickly, pour it into a warmed jug or decanter. Let it rest for a few minutes before pouring back into the bottle. Alternatively pour the wine into glasses, cup your hands around the glass and gently swirl the wine. Ideally, time permitting, stand the wine in the room for several hours to gradually bring up the temperature.

Simply holding the bottle will indicate if a wine is too warm or too cold. It is better to serve a wine too cold than too warm as the wine will invariably warm up in the glass during the meal.

The order of serving wine

The order of serving wine is usually to start with the driest and lightest and finishing with the sweetest and fullest. White wines precede red wines which in turn precede sweet dessert wines or fortified liqueur wines. Exceptions exist. For instance, there are fewer more versatile aperitifs than a chilled fresh Fino Sherry (served correctly in a copita glass, of course). Or a sweet white wine partnering and contrasting with a salty starter— one defining and flattering the other. In such challenging circumstances, cleanse the palate with a piece of bread, water or a refreshing sorbet served between courses.

How to run a wine club

Liam Campbell

The subject of wine is not limited to the liquid sunshine in the bottle. The cultivation of the vine, climate, soil composition, different grape varieties' characteristics both on their native soil and abroad, the options open to the skilled winemaker, tradition versus technology, world trends, marketing, and price points are all different facets of this fascinating subject.

One of the most sociable and enjoyable ways of learning more about wine with plenty of opportunities is the wine club. Membership usually embraces little groupings such as customers of an off-licence, office workers, friends, sporting clubs etc. They delight in sharing any newly acquired information with similar wine enthusiasts.

I remember attending my first meeting of my wine club, the Noble Rotters, in 1989 and being full of apprehension that I would be out of my depth, would say something foolish, or worse still, say nothing at all. Silly me. Had I let myself be intimidated by my high expectations of everyone else's expertise and not gone to that first meeting I would have missed out on all the tastings, excursions, barbecues, wine club tasting competitions, wine dinners, presentations by the wine trade and altogether a very enriching experience with friends I would never have made otherwise.

How do you join a wine club? Enquire locally from your nearest off-licence, wine merchant or supermarket. Alternatively, contact the Wine Development Board of Ireland's Dun Laoghaire office. If there is no wine club near you, start your own. Start with your nearest circle of friends, relations, colleagues, etc. Place an advertisement in your nearest wine shop/off-licence/supermarket. The management should be most anxious to encourage you as your activities should help boost their sales. Or place a notice at work. Word of mouth and networking among friends help to generate interest and membership.

An annual fee or a per meeting fee should be charged if members are going to value their club. A venue where there is no room rental charge is ideal as precious club funds can be reserved for fine wine purchases, subsidising the annual dinner or covering charges by guest speakers and tutors' tastings. Alternatively, rotate meetings among members homes.

One plan is to taste a range of wines according to theme e.g. grape variety, region/country or wine style e.g. sparkling, fortified etc. This can be done quite cheaply. Ask each member to bring a bottle for that themed tasting 'blind' i.e. with the identity of the bottle hidden by wrapping in tin foil or a paper bag. For ease of discussion, each bottle should be given a code or number. (Take care to remove all the wine's foil if it has a brand name or any identifying marks. The cork may also be printed with a maker's name or location. If the bottle has a very distinctive shape which may give a generous clue about itself, lie—say you decanted the wine into this bottle!) By tasting the wines blind, you are judging the wine as objectively as possible and your evaluation will be an honest appraisal. For an extra challenge, try to identify price range, country/region, grape variety, alcohol content and vintage.

Each member should have at least six glasses, each to contain a different sample from the wines to be tasted, so that direct comparisons can be made. Everyone must be responsible for bringing and cleaning their own glasses. Invest in proper ISO tasting glasses available from some wine shops from about £2 per glass. Many people find it helpful to stand each glass on a paper label indicating the code of the bottle from which the sample is taken. Members should be encouraged to use standardised tasting forms to record their impressions of smell, appearance, taste and conclusion. As with all tasting sessions, provide spittoons or buckets (ordinary plastic buckets from the local DIY store are fine) also water and bread or water biscuits to help refresh the palate between each wine. Since even the soberest taster's spitting gets a little inaccurate towards the end of a session, cover the Axminister. Keep dated tasting notes identifying each wine and refer back to them when you plan your purchases.

Themed tastings help to reinforce the personality and character of that variety, region or country and they cost little. Another approach is to invite wine specialists and the wine trade to give presentations. The wine trade frequently offers special discounted prices on some tasted wines especially during a tutored tasting. Bulk buying collectively also increases your purchasing power and additional discounts may apply.

Meet on a regular basis e.g. the second Tuesday of every month. This reduces the need to advise members of the next meeting once a fixed date is agreed.

To help coordinate a schedule of topics, themes or speakers for forthcoming meetings, elect a small committee comprising of a chairperson, secretary and treasurer. Nominate non-committee members for special projects—e.g. to research a particular wine region and present a range of the wines at a future meeting—funded by club funds.

Your wine club will increase your knowledge of wines, broaden your tasting experience and help develop your tasting skills. It is fun and you are in the company of like-minded people. As the range of wines available to us has never been greater or more diverse you have plenty of material to practise on.

The tastings

For this edition of *The Best of Wine in Ireland* we conducted 25 tasting sessions between May and October 1998, handling nearly 2,000 wines submitted by 42 importers. The tasters who assessed the wines were dawn from a group representing the wine trade, the catering trade and knowledgeable amateurs holding qualifications from the Wine and Spirit Education Trust.

Each wine was tasted blind (that is, with its label concealed). The tasters assessed the wines for:

■ Nose—aroma, intensity, complexity

■ Taste—balance, structure, extract, complexity, length

■ Value—price/quality ratio.

Eeach wine was given a score for taste and value, with only those gaining 60 per cent of the available marks qualifying for inclusion. In fact some 500 wines were excluded. As a result, *every wine listed is recommended as well made and a good buy.* A number have been singled out for commendation, 'star' status, or as presenting particular value for money.

☆☆☆ —three stars indicate exceptional wines of considerable complexity and classic balance from a very good vintage which reward serious tasting. Such wines show a classic balance and are some of the best examples of their type and origin. Wines to drink, taste and enjoy for themselves.

☆☆—two stars denote elegant wines which show character and complexity above expectations, with balance, subtlety and 'typicité'; ideal to accompany carefully prepared food at a special dinner party.

☆—one star identifies wines which show character and style and are particularly good examples of their region and winemaking. The quality of these wines generally exceeds the expectations of the label and the price.

©—commendation: wines that are good, interesting and merit attention but not quite a star, including wines which are good examples of particular regional styles or which are a little young but show potential.

££—value award: wines that offer exceptional value for money in comparison with others within their type/region; these are mainly lower-priced wines but include those from classic areas which are well priced.

®—recommended: all these wines have been tasted and selected by an independent panel of experts and are considered good examples of their style and origin.

Although many of the wines included will continue to improve for some years, the tasters judged the wines as if they are to be drunk during the next twelve months. Wines submitted that were judged likely to be past their best during the lifetime of this edition (even though still acceptable at the time of tasting) were excluded.

The published tasting notes are a distilled version of those written by the members of the panel.

Each wine is listed first under its country of origin (and region in the case of France), then by colour and price band, and finally in alphabetical order by the name of the wine, as indicated on the label. In interpreting the often confusing layout of labels, we have tried to present the essential information that will enable consumers to identify particular wines on retailers' shelves.

Price bands (guide price only).

£5 or less	
£5–£6	£6 –£8
£8–£10	£10–£12
£12–£15	£15–£20
£20–£25	£25–£30
£30-35	£35–£40
Over £40	Over £60

The tasting panel

Liam Campbell works as a Product Promotions Executive in the Irish tourist industry. He lectures extensively on wine for the Wine Development Board and for off-licences and wine clubs.

Tony Cleary, who has worked for over 20 years in the wine trade is now with Barry & Fitzwilliam, specialising in Central and South Eastern Europe.

Nigel Donnan has worked for winemakers in both Provence and Burgundy during harvest time.

Sandy O'Byrne is author of *Matching Food and Wine* (1997) and wine correspondent of *The Evening Herald* and *Retail News*; she lectures on wine and food for the Wine Development Board.

Canice McCarthy is a wine manager with Tesco Ireland.

Catherine Griffith is wine consultant to Molloy's Liquor Stores and lecturer for the Wine Development Board.

David Lonergan is the manager of The Vintry Wine shop in Rathgar, Dublin 6. He lectures for The Vintry Wine Club where his particular forte is the Rhône valley.

Anne Mullin is a director of an international freight forwarding company specialising in the importation of wines and spirits; council member of the Irish Guild of Sommeliers and founder member of the Premier Cru Wine Club.

David Power worked in the wine trade in Ireland for over 30 years with Edward Dillon; he is now an independent wine consultant and educator and lectures for the Wine Development Board.

Fergal Tynan is manager of Raheny Wine Cellar. He obtained a distinction in the WSET Diploma, 1998.

Evelyn Jones is the proprietor of The Vintry Wine Shop, Rathgar, Dublin 6 and winner of the Gilbey/NOFFLA Dublin Off-licence of the Year Award, 1996. She is a member of the Champagne Academy and runs wine appreciation courses as well as a wine club.

Julie Martin is the first Irish woman sommelier; she worked for Patrick Guilbaud at Ashford Castle and is Commandeur in the Association Internationale des Maîtres Conseils en Gastronomie Francaise.

Peter Dunne is a director of Mitchell & Son Wine Merchants.

Monica Murphy of Febvre is a professional wine and cheese consultant, lecturer and writer.

Karine Chauvot-Arnold holds an MA in Viticultural and Wine Law and Business from the University of Aix en Provence

Alan Crowley MW worked in Scottish and Newcastle Breweries Wine Division, Harvey's of Bristol and with a major Burgundy house and is now Wine Development Manager with Edward Dillon. He was the first Irish Master of Wine.

Gerry Fitzsimons is a member of the Irish Guild of Sommeliers. He won the George O'Malley tasting trophy in the Diploma tasting 1993.

Breda McSweeney of Lacken House Restaurant, has won many national sommelier competitions and has represented Ireland in three world finals.

Mary O'Callaghan holds the Advanced Diploma from the Court of Master Sommeliers; she lectures on wine for the Dublin Institute of Technology and the Wine Development Board.

Matt Quigley works with Dun Laoghaire Rathdown County Coumcil.

Maureen O'Hara is a manager with Findlater Wine Merchants.

Fiona Conway works with Findlater Wine Merchants.

Mary Gaynor lectures for the Wine Development Board of Ireland.

Alan O'Toole is sales representative with Febvre since 1985 and lectures for the Wine Development Board.

Sarah Wright worked for Findlater Wine Merchants before going to California to work in wineries there.

Erik Robson works with Mitchell & Son Wine Merchants.

Andrew Tidey is the wine-buyer for Tesco-Quinnsworth.

Brian Brady is Catering Manager at a leading private club in Dublin.

Martin Moran MW is Wine Development Manager for Gilbeys of Ireland.

Emma O'Sullivan writes wine articles for *Irish Homes* and *Creative Cook*.

David Whelehan has worked in wineries in both France and the USA and lectures for the Wine Development Board.

T. P. Whelehan was *The Irish Times* Wine Correspondent 1960–88, *Sunday Press* Wine Correspondent 1989–94. Consultant to Quinnsworth 1989–96. He is Chevalier de l'Ordre du Mérite Agricole 1966, Officier de l'Ordre 1972 and has contributed to many international magazines and is author of *The Irish Wines of Bordeaux*.

The Wines

Argentina

Argentina is the largest wine-producer yet to become a major force in the world wine market. Internal political and economic instability, together with a very large home market led to an industry based on bulk production of rather rough and ready wines from local grape varieties. However, recent changes have been export driven, probably with the example of Chile as a motivating force.

The dedication of quality producers such as Nicholas Catena has raised standards and awareness of the country's potential. Outside expertise has also been attracted by Argentina's reliable climate, range of microclimates and low land and labour costs. The Lurton Brothers, are there–and everywhere— and Robin Day, of Jacob's Creek fame, has just started a new project at Bodegas Etchart. Large multiples have seen Argentina as a source of keenly-priced basic wines and own labels, and many have sent out experts to tailor wines to their own specifications, a less positive outside influence!

Cooler microclimates in areas like Mendoza and Cafayate have been especially important for white wines, and the fresh, clean beautifully aromatic wines from Argentina's own Torrontes grapes, are now some of the best the country produces. Chardonnay is also becoming important, though with the exception of Catena's wines, oak needs more careful handling and at present overshadows fruit in many wines.

Argentinean reds show a firm structure and quite refreshing dryness. The Malbec is the red workhorse of Argentina. Modern handling produces wonderfully juicy, fruity examples with pleasing dryness; while oak-ageing and lower yields have the potential to make it more interesting. Cabernet Sauvignon is capable of considerable complexity and longevity, such as the Colleccion Privada Cabernet Sauvignon from Navarro Correas. Experiments with Spanish and especially Italian varietals are proving successful and currently produce interesting, easy-drinking wines at the lower end of the price scale.

Argentina has great potential, certainly yet to be fully explored and is somewhere to watch in 1999.

White £5 - £6

Balbi Mendoza Blanc 97
Grants ®
Light fruity white
Clean, lightly aromatic nose.
Ripe and fresh with light fruit
character. Soft, easy-drinking
style.
*Good party wine or with light first
course foods*

Etchart Rio de Plata Chardonnay 97
Fitzgerald ®
Light fruity white
Fruity, perhaps a touch over-
ripe but otherwise well-
balanced in an acceptable light
style—fine for the price.
Salads and light foods

Santa Julia Sauvignon Blanc 97
Taserra ®
Aromatic white, fruit-driven
Grassy, herby aromas with a
touch of yeast. Quite fat and
fruity on the palate with good
balancing acidity. Ripe and
pleasant fruit, slightly hot on the
finish.
*Vegetable salads or filo pastries or
samosas*

Santa Julia Torrontes 97
Taserra ®
Aromatic white, fruit-driven
Clean aromatic, Muscat-style
nose. Plenty of fruit on the
palate, grapey and delicious
served cold. Off-dry with
balancing acidity. Pleasing party
wine.
*Best on its own, as a party wine or
with spicy foods*

Trapiche Chardonnay 97
United Beverages ®
Full-bodied white
Quite fruity nose, ripe and
warm aromas. Relatively full on
the palate with melon and
pineapple fruit flavours. Fat and
buttery style, well-made and
good value.
*Guacamole or avocado and pear
salad; also vegetables and
hollandaise sauce*

White £6 - £8

Etchart Torrontés 97
Fitzgerald ☆
Aromatic white, fruit-driven
Quite complex and intense
Muscat aromas. Good assertive
fruit palate with grapey, appley
fruit, nice gripping acidity and
dry, long finish. Very good
indeed.
*Asparagus salad or bruschetta of
sundried tomato*

Trapiche Chardonnay Oak Cask 97
United Beverages ®
Full-bodied white
Buttery tropical fruit on the
nose. Oak dominates the palate
though there is plenty of fruit,
otherwise well-balanced.
*Barbecued fish, especially snapper
papillotes, or chicken bake*

Red £5 or less

Chimango Tempranillo Malbec nv
Quinnsworth ££
Light fruity red
Nice rich cherry fruit on the
nose, soft, juicy palate,
winegum flavours mix with
appetising spice. Balanced

acidity and nice dry finish.
Great quaffing wine.
Spicy pasta, stir-fry or hot sausages

Parral Merlot/Malbec 97
United Beverages ££
Light fruity red
Quite a rich nose of spicy, brambly fruit. Ripe fruit flavours also with a spicy edge and refreshing backup of acidity. Nice wine with more grip than most in the price range.
Pasta with bacon, peppers etc, or casseroles, stews and minced meat dishes

Red £5 - £6

Correas Syrah/Sangiovese 96
Gilbeys ®
Medium-bodied red
Lots of ripe, peppery berry and cherry fruit; quite plummy on the palate with marked acidity and dry finish.
Robust meat, or meat and grain-based dishes; baked pasta with meat, bean stew with sausages..

Etchart Rio de Plata Cabernet Sauvignon 95
Fitzgerald ££
Medium-bodied red, fruit-driven, tannic
Ripe blackcurrant fruit on the nose, Juicy berry fruit flavours and nice refreshing acidity. Quite firm tannin gives structure. Very good value—highly drinkable Cabernet.
Red meats in general; also turkey with fruity stuffing and spicy casseroles

Etchart Rio de Plata Malbec 95
Fitzgerald ®
Medium-bodied red, fruit-driven
Quite intense nose with slight hints of gamey savouriness. Easy tannins and mouthwatering acidity together with ripe fruit and white pepper in the finish.
Grilled or barbecued meats, hamburgers, steaks, kebabs

Maranon Malbec 97
Barry & Fitzwilliam ®
Medium-bodied fruit-driven red
Slightly dusty but ripe fruit aromas; good weight of juicy berry fruit flavour with a touch of spice. Chunky but well-made and balanced.
Grills and fairly textured meat; barbecues—chops and steaks, or good hamburgers and meaty sausages

Maranon Mendoza 97
Barry & Fitzwilliam ®
Medium-bodied fruit-driven red
Lots of ripe berry and plum aromas; good weight of fresh berry fruit with a touch of cherry richness. Nicely balanced acidity and soft tannin. Well-made, easy-drinking style
Well-flavoured meat, not too rich or substantial; good for parties with casserole and rice or at a barbecue

Santa Isabel Cabernet Sauvignon 95
Dunnes Stores ®
Full-bodied red
Nice ripe blackcurrant on the nose; good weight of fruit

balanced by soft, ripe tannins and crisp acidity.
Grilled meats with zesty marinades, even fairly hot spices; beef with soy, lamb steaks with rosemary, wine and honey

Santa Julia Malbec 96
Taserra   ®
Medium-bodied red, fruit-driven
Not very intense on the nose—damson fruit dominates. Firm but not austere on the palate with a touch of coughdrop flavour in the fruit. Quite smooth and attractive.
Meat casserole or a robust bean or lentil dish

Santa Julia Sangiovese 96
Taserra   ®
Light fruity red
Stewed fruit and cold tea aromas. Cherry-type fruit flavours with firm tannin and acidity. Nice dry finish.
Meat and tomato pastas and lasagne

Trapiche Cabernet Sauvignon 95
United Beverages   ®
Medium-bodied red, fruit-driven
Cassis comes through on the nose and follows to the palate with nicely balanced tannins and lively acidity. Good long finish.
Relatively spicy meat dishes, peppery meatloaf, stir-fried steak etc

Red £6 - £8

Bodega Jacques y Francois Lurton Malbec 97
Febvre   ®
Medium-bodied red, fruit-driven, tannic
Tightly-knit aromas of coughdrops and black pepper. Firm tannins and refreshing acidity which kicks in towards the end. Chunky, dark berry fruit which should evolve further over the next year.
Definitely a wine for a warming winter stew

Correas Syrah 96
Gilbeys   ®
Full-bodied red
Plenty of brambly fruit on the nose with a touch of black pepper. Full palate with decent weight of ripe, spicy fruit and dry bite of tannin.
Robust, well-flavoured stews and casseroles, beef with beer, lamb with peppers, goulash or stroganoff-type dishes

Etchart Cafayate Cabernet Sauvignon 95
Fitzgerald   ©
Full-bodied red
Ripe berry fruit on the nose with a hint of spice. Clean, fresh fruit, berries, blackcurrants with refreshing acidty and dry tannin to give structure. A good wine and good value.
Well-flavoured meats, especially casseroles; pot roast beef, a robust stew or lamb roast with potatoes and onions

Trapiche Cabernet Sauvignon Oak Cask 94

United Beverages ®

Medium-bodied red, fruit-driven, tannic

Lovely inviting aromas of blackcurrant and cedar. Well-rounded with good weight of blackcurrant fruit, firm tannin and dry finish. A satisfying wine, rich and savoury.

Beef casseroles or charcoal-grilled meats

Vina de Santa Isabel Malbec 95

Dunnes Stores ®

Medium-bodied red

Dark fruits and cherries with a hint of chocolate on the nose. Good intensity of rather inky fruit on the palate with smooth tannins. Good weight and overall balance. Good with food.

Grilled meats and casseroles; smoky aubergine dip

Red £8 - £10

Navarro Correas Coleccion Privada Cabernet Sauvignon/ Merlot 93

Gilbeys ☆

Full-bodied red

Super rich bouquet of ripe summer berries, vanilla and spices. Good weight of ripe, almost baked fruit with very well-balanced structure of wood, firm tannin and refreshing acidity. Long and impressively complex in the finish.

Roast meat and game or meat in pastry: roast pheasant, lamb en croûte, venison fillets

Red £10 - £12

Arnaldo B. Etchart Cafayate 93

Fitzgerald ☆

Full-bodied red

Deep, rich cassis aromas with herbal tones underneath. Layers of ripe, complex fruit, very velvety but with good firm structure and long, long finish.

Roast meats and game, especially duck with a honey or fruit sauce

Red £12 - £15

Weinert Carrascal 94

Molloy's ®

Full-bodied red

Redcurrant and damson aromas with pencil shavings in the background. Good breadth of flavour, forest fruit and black pepper. Firm tannin gives backbone. A very good wine which needs time to show at its best and will benefit from ageing.

Rare roast beef, steak or a chunky casserole

Red £15 - £20

Weinert Cabernet Sauvignon 91

Molloy's ☆ ☆

Full-bodied red

Intense aromas of cassis, cedar and cigar box. Firm and rich on the palate with great concentration of fruit yet to emerge. A serious wine with layers of flavour. Should last and develop well.

Nothings beats a juicy rare T-bone with this sort of wine!

New World value

The New World provides great value through technical expertise in winemaking and the consistent ripening of more stable climates than Europe. Here is a 'case' of some of the best value encountered in the tastings.

White

Lindemans Coonawarra Semillon/Chardonnay 97 (Australia)

Montana Marlborough Chardonnay 96 (New Zealand)

Carmen Chardonnay 97 (Chile)

Villa Maria Private Bin Sauvignon Blanc 97 (New Zealand)

Etchart Cafayate Torrontes 95 (Argentina)

Red

Rio del Plata Cabernet Sauvignon 96 (Argentina)

d'Arenberg d'Arry's Original Shiraz/Grenache 92 (Australia)

Peter Lehmann Vine Vale Shiraz (Australia)

Villiera Estate Blue Ridge Rouge 96 (South Africa)

Caliterra Merlot 97 (Chile)

Long Mountain Cabernet Sauvignon 97 (South Africa)

Santa Carolina Cabernet Sauvignon Reservado 94 (Chile)

Australia

The Australian combination of climate and a highly technical approach to winemaking has led to a consistency formerly unknown in wine. The style is wonderfully approachable : big-hearted and generous, full of fruit and flavour if short on structure. Good wines at affordable prices made Australia's name and market.

Traditionally Australian wines were blended across a wide variety of grape sources, something alien to quality European wines, which are tied rigidly to their place of origin. It gave consistency and great freedom to the winemaker and many would argue is the true style of Australian wine. This sort of non-specific blending is not just at the lower end of the market. Australia's most famous and costly wine, Grange, has an origin—in fact origins—unknown to any except its makers.

Regional wines are something new, as is the concept of de-limiting areas of viticulture. Increasingly, Australian wines are labelled from an individual region, many of which, like the Coonawarra, will soon be protected in law—something of a U-turn from a country which originally scoffed at the notion of terroir! Above all, regional wines mean greater variety. While blending provided some of the great Australian wine types like South East Australia Chardonnay or Australian Shiraz, it potentially limited the country's range. Regions such as Margaret River or Clare Valley, are cool climates, at least by Australian standards, and offer a totally different style to that of , say, the Barossa or the McLaren Vale.

In this year's listing in *The Best of Wine in Ireland* there is a notable increase in wines from the middle and upper price ranges with greater variety in grapes and styles. Less oaky, and some consciously unoaked wines are appearing. Among the whites, Riesling and dry Semillon are gaining in importance along with a number of other varieties apart from Chardonnay. Western Australia has become a very important source of quite classic, long-lived reds from smaller wineries, while producers like Peter Lehmann, Rosemount and Hardys have shown an ability to produce serious complex wines of individual style as well as their bestsellers.

White £5 or less

Tesco Australian White Wine nv
Quinnsworth   Ⓡ
Aromatic white

Delightful apple and floral aromas. Clean and fruity with broad apple fruit flavours combined with waxy influences. Fresh acidity lifts the whole wine.

Good with salads of poultry or fish, even relatively spicy flavours

White £5 - £6

Cockatoo Ridge Chardonnay 97
United Beverages   ££
Full-bodied white

Very fresh aromas of green apple and a touch of white pepper. Dry and quite full with understated ripe fruit. Well balanced.

Avocado with seafood or a prawn salad

Dry Plains Semillon/Chardonnay 97
Supervalu/Centra   ££
Medium-bodied white

Ripe fruit aromas followed by a mouthwatering palate of lemon and limes with balanced acidity. Flavours last well and the finish is beautifully clean. Thoroughly well made and good value.

Light fish dishes, especially as a first course; also avocados and mayonnaise-dressed salads

Duck's Flat Dry White nv
Barry & Fitzwilliam   Ⓡ
Light dry white

Lively citrus nose with a touch of boiled sweets. Plenty of rather loose-knit fruit on the palate. Simple and easy to drink.

A good party wine with or without food; fine for the lighter side of a summer buffet

---

Geoff Merrill Owen's Estate Sauvignon Blanc/Semillon 97
United Beverages   Ⓡ
Aromatic white

Asparagus and gooseberries on the nose. Crisp, green apple fruit and brisk, dry finish.

Escalopes of pork or stir-fried chicken

Hardys Stamp of Australia Riesling/Gewürztraminer 97
Allied Drinks   Ⓡ
Aromatic white

Rather candied nose with a touch of rose petal and lime. Very dry, tart palate with green apple fruit dominant. Short finish with a twist of white pepper.

Spicy seafood appetiser

Hardys Stamp of Australia Semillon/Chardonnay 97
Allied Drinks   Ⓡ
Full-bodied white

Ripe pineapple aromas. Dry with crisp applely fruit, quite weighty mouthfeel.

Seafood mayonnaise or mild curries

Jacob's Creek Chardonnay 97
Fitzgerald ®

Full-bodied white

Assertive if uncomplicated nose of punchy fruit: gooseberry, melon, lemon. Lively palate with crisp acidity and crunchy orchard and citrus fruit wihich lasts well.

Creamy, mild curries or a not-too-hot satay

Jacob's Creek Dry Riesling 97
Fitzgerald ®

Aromatic white

Aromas of apple and typical Riesling kerosene beginning to show. Dry with a fresh citrusy tang right through to the finish.

Fish in a mildly curried sauce; kedgeree

Jacob's Creek Semillon/ Chardonnay 97
Fitzgerald ®

Full-bodied white

Rather honeyed with ripe melon-type aromas. Dry with ripe fruit and balancing acidity. Versatile party wine.

Smoked fish pie or creamy pork casserole

Lindeman's Cawarra Semillon/Chardonnay 97
Gilbeys ££

Full-bodied white

Butterscotch and a twist of lemon on the nose. Round and soft with plenty of fruit and a slightly caramel influence coming through from the nose. Well-balanced, easy-drinking and very good value.

Chinese food especially aromatic duck, chicken with cashew or noodles

McWilliams Colombard/ Chardonnay 97
TDL ®

Light fruity white

Light, fresh nose with pineapple and gooseberry tones. Flavours of lemons and limes make a refreshing palate for chilled, summer drinking.

Excellent for drinking on its own as an aperitif or with light salads

Peter Lehmann Barossa Valley Chenin Blanc 97
United Beverages ££

Light fruity white

Lemony nose with a hint of lanolin. Dry and crisp citrus fruit fleshed out with honey. Cheap and very cheerful.

Versatile with party food— canapés or a buffet

Peter Lehmann Vine Vale Chardonnay 97
United Beverages ®

Full-bodied white

Not too much on the nose, but the palate has ripe tropical fruits, slightly honeyed and with an interesting touch of smoke.

Pasta with cream and smoky bacon

Seppelt Moyston Semillon/ Chardonnay 97
Dunnes Stores ®

Light fruity white

Light aromas of tropical-type fruit. Dry and rounded but not much concentration.

Buffet food and salads

Seppelt Moyston Unoaked Chardonnay 97

Dunnes Stores ®

Light fruity white

Attractive fresh fruit on the nose; lively palate with ripe fruit—melon, dessert apple—and a touch of white pepper in the finish.

Seafood, mussels with a light curry sauce, grilled prawns; spinach and cheese

White £6 - £8

Ch. Tahbilk Marsanne (Unwooded) 96

United Beverages ©

Full-bodied white

Attractive aromas of mango and apple blossom. Dry with a tight-knit structure and ripe, firm fruit flavour lingering well to a long finish. Should develop further.

Pork in coconut milk and spices or grilled chicken with a cream sauce

Hardys Chardonnay/ Sauvignon Blanc 97

Allied Drinks ®

Light fruity white

Inviting aromas of honeyed fruit. Dry, but with very ripe fruit character and crisp, citrusy acidity. Lasts well.

Avocado salad

Hardys Mill Cellars Chardonnay 97

Allied Drinks ®

Full-bodied white, oak

Typical aromas of ripe fruit and oak. Ripe melon and kiwi fruit

flavours just about make it through heavy oakiness. If you like wood, this is for you.

Needs strong flavours like barbecued chicken or fish in a really rich sauce

Hardys Nottage Hill Chardonnay 97

Allied Drinks ©

Medium to full-bodied white

Ripe aromas of pineapple and citrus fruit. Crisp acidity with a good weight of mouthfilling kiwi fruit flavours, balanced structure and good finish. Very well made.

Fish pie or chicken in pastry, sauced fish dishes and light meat.

Hardys Nottage Hill Riesling 95

Allied Drinks ®

Aromatic white, off-dry

Light green fruit on the nose; ripe pear fruit in an off-dry style with a clean finish.

Good party drinking on its own or with a spicy Chinese meal, even a take-away

Lindeman's Bin 65 Chardonnay 97

Gilbeys ©

Full-bodied white, oak

Typical vibrant aromas of tropical fruit with plenty of warm, ripe fruit flavours, a touch heavy-handed, but big and fruity; the original of the style!

Barbecued fish or chicken; creamy pastas

McLaren Vale d'Arenberg Olive Grove Chardonnay 96

Taserra ®

Full-bodied white

Good lively nose of honey, lemon and oak. Good weight with creamy melon and lemon fruit.

Avocado salad or seafood gratin

Miranda Estates Chardonnay 96

Taserra ®

Full-bodied white

Nose of melons and lemons with a touch of peach blossom. Mouthfilling ripe fruit and quite marked alcohol. A big wine with a big finish.

Grilled chicken or a spicy coconut curry

Penfolds Koonunga Hill Chardonnay 97

Findlater ££

Medium-bodied white

Intriguing, subtle nose with hints of ripe, Golden Delicious apples and lemon meringue pie! Dry with zesty acidity perfectly balanced by apple and citrus fruit. Well-judged oak gives a clean finish. Good value.

Fish and light meat dishes; chicken or pork, especially with cumin or coriander spice

Peter Lehmann The Barossa Semillon 96

United Beverages ®

Full-bodied white

Waxy honeyed fruit on the nose. Full and dry on the palate with honeyed apple and pear. Balanced acidity and good finish.

Pork fillet cooked with fruit and cream

Richmond Grove Cowra Verdelho 96

Quinnsworth ®

Light fruity white

Green fruit on the nose, a touch of kiwi and citrus aromas. Good weight of lively green-gage fruit, well-balanced with a good finish.

Surprisingly good with seafood curry, with warm salad of poultry or spicy Indian vegetable pastries

Rosemount Estate Semillon/ Chardonnay 97

Grants ®

Medium-bodied white

Ripe, honeyed fruit on the nose with a touch of boiled sweets. Ripeness follows to the palate which is generous and pleasing. Good value.

Versatile with mixed foods especially cold food and barbecues of fish and chicken

Salisbury Victoria Chardonnay 97

Gilbeys ®

Full-bodied white, oak

Buttery with up-front oak and vanilla and a touch of white pepper. Oily, fat tropical fruit flavours and spicy finish.

Pork or chicken with fruit or mild creamy curries

Yaldara Semillon/Chardonnay 97

Barry & Fitzwilliam ®

Medium–full-bodied white

Clean, fruity aromas with a touch of buttery Chardonnay. Soft and mellow with underlying richness and a nice weight of fruit. Clean finish.

Stir-fry chicken or pasta with squid

White £8 - £10

Brown Brothers King Valley Sauvignon Blanc 96

Molloy's ®

Aromatic white, fruit-driven

Tropical fruit and a touch of honey on the nose. Full-flavoured with refreshing acidity. Nicely balanced with a good finish.

Seafood mayonnaise or asparagus salad

Carlyle Estate Victoria Marsanne/Semillon 95

Greenhills ®

Full-bodied white

Quite honeyed and floral, herbal tea aromas. Creamy weight with tropical fruit and minerally backdrop. Crisp clean finish.

Pork and pineapple or a stir-fry

Ch. Tahbilk Chardonnay 94

United Beverages ®

Full-bodied white, oak

Ripe tropical, honeyed fruit with a touch of vanilla on the nose. Quite a spicy palate with white pepper, melon and marmalade flavours. Balanced oak and a good finish.

An elegant accompaniment to a vegetable terrine or an exotic salad of lobster and mango

Hardy's Hunter Ridge Verdelho 96

Allied Drinks ®

Light fruity white

Nutty, citrusy aromas. Good weight and concentration of restrained fruit and a long finish.

Spicy Oriental food especially squid with black beans or Singapore noodles

John James McWilliams Chardonnay 96

TDL ®

Full-bodied white, oak

Tropical fruit and oak on the nose. The palate has restrained but good crisp fruit, kiwi, mango and pineapple flavours with a smoky, peppery finish. Still young, perhaps a wine for the next century

Better with chicken and light meats than fish, try it with baked chicken or roast veal

Penfolds Barossa Valley Semillon/Chardonnay 96

Findlater ®

Full-bodied white

Rich, ripe tropical fruit with an oily background; soft and buttery with caramelised pineapple coming through the flavour. Rich yet refreshing.

Barbecued pork or a stir-fry.

Peter Lehmann Clancy's Barossa Chardonnay/Semillon 96

United Beverages ®

Full-bodied white

Tropical fruit aromas especially limes. Ripe flavours on the palate of melon and mango with a twist of citrus acidity.

Peter Lehmann The Barossa Chardonnay 96

United Beverages ®

Full-bodied white, oak

Rather slow nose with light tropical fruit and nutty aromas. Dry, spicy palate with crisp fruit at present dominated by oak. Needs time.

Chicken fillets baked in pastry or with a rich mushroom sauce

Rosemount Estate Chardonnay 97

Grants ☆

Full-bodied white

Attractive aromas of ripe fruit and vanilla. Tropical fruit on the palate—mangoes, guavas—with crisp acidity and well-balanced new oak. A round, mouthfilling wine with good length in the finish.

Especially good with chicken and turkey and creamy pasta dishes

Rosemount Estate Sauvignon Blanc 97

Grants ®

Aromatic white

Clean gooseberry fruit aromas with a hint of smoke. Plenty of weight in the mouth with lean, minerally Sauvignon fruit well balanced by acidity. Long finish.

Smoked salmon, goat's cheese, grilled fish or prawns with garlic

St Hallett Barossa Chardonnay 96

Dunnes Stores ☆

Full-bodied white, oak

Nice complexity on the nose with ripe tropical fruit, smoke and vanilla well entwined. Well-integrated palate with good weight of fruit and subtle spicy and smoky overtones. Long, quite elegant finish with a touch of honey.

Excellent with richly cooked turbot or monkfish, with a shellfish or hollandaise sauce

Wakefield Clare Valley Chardonnay 96

Koala ☆

Full-bodied white, oak

Lovely smoky, shortbready aromas and flavours of ripe melon-type fruit cut through with refreshing acidity. Better balance of oak in the taste than on the nose—the fruit shines through to a long finish.

Pasta with cream and ham or a gratin of smoked fish

Wakefield Clare Valley Promised Land Riesling 96

Koala ®

Aromatic white

Floral minerally nose with shades of lemon peel. Bone dry with brisk acidity and good weight of tart fruit.

Rich, creamy gratin of fish

WHY WAKEFIELD?

Wakefield Clare Valley Promised Land Unwooded Chardonnay 97

Koala ®

Light fruity white

A notable touch of effervescence with the creamy, tropical fruit flavours. Ripe and juicy.

Handles spices well especially creamy mild curries; also chicken pie

Wolf Blass Barrel-fermented Chardonnay 97

Dillon ®

Full-bodied white

Honey and citrus aromas with slight floral notes. A big wine in the mouth with ripe fruit flavours and plenty of supporting alcohol. Something of a blockbuster all round.

Meatier varieties of fish especially when barbecued; flavoursome chicken pie and pork with pineapple

Wolf Blass Chardonnay/ Semillon 97

Dillon ££

Full-bodied white, oak

Honey and citrus aromas; impressive weight of fruit on the palate with tropical fruit ripeness well supported by alcohol and a touch of new oak. The clean finish lasts well. Jolly good for the price.

Smoked fish salads and first course pasta with cream and fish or cured meat sauce

Wyndham Estate Bin 222 Chardonnay 96

Fitzgerald ®

Full-bodied white, oak

A nice rounded, well-balanced wine with honeyed fruit, smooth texture and a long finish. Good but pricey.

Roast chicken or turkey; marinated grilled chicken or pork

Wyndham Estate Oak Cask Hunter Valley Chardonnay 95

Fitzgerald ®

Full-bodied white, oak

Very rich aromas of toast and lemon meringue pie and similar palate of ripe mango and pineapple flavours in a silky texture.

Especially good with chicken dishes containing fruit

Yaldara Reserve Chardonnay 97

Barry & Fitzwilliam ®

Full-bodied white, oak

Ripe tropical fruit with toasted, smoky aromas underneath. Full on the palate with good weight of buttery fruit and rather oaky finish.

Creamy pasta or a gratin of chicken and ham

White £10 - £12

Ch. Reynella McLaren Vale Chardonnay 95

Allied Drinks ☆ ☆

Full-bodied white, oak

Lots of tropical fruit and vanillin oak aromas. Really crisp acidity on the palate with expansive flavours of ripe tropical fruit and butterscotch. Good weight, structure and finish.

Grills of chicken or meatier fish especially with fruit or vegetable relishes

Hardys Padthaway Chardonnay 96

Allied Drinks   ☆ ☆

Full-bodied white, oak

Benchmark Chardonnay nose with vanilla, honeyed fruits and hints of spice. Dry, with beautifully integrated oak giving a creamy mouthfeel with tropical fruit and hazelnut flavours shining through. Well-balanced acidity. Exceptional!

Lobster or a fine piece of turbot especially with buttery sauces. Also roast or braised farm chicken.

Ninth Island Tasmania Chardonnay 96

Fitzgerald   ©

Full-bodied white, oak

A touch of maturity shows in the rich honeyed aromas and the ripe lemon fruit flavours, good weight and balanced acidity.

Fish gratin or smoked haddock

White £12 - £15

Pipers Brook Vineyard Riesling 97

Fitzgerald   ©

Aromatic white

Lovely floral nose with ripe peach aromas. Elegant ripe fruit developing longlasting, quite classic Riesling flavour. Crisp acidity comes out through the wine. Beautifully made and balanced.

Seabass with roasted vegetables

Rosemount Estate Reserve Hunter Valley Chardonnay 96

Grants   ☆

Full-bodied white, oak

Typical New World Chardonnay nose with spicy vanilla tones and ripe tropical fruits. Brimming with fruit and warm, rounded toasty flavour. Well-balanced with a good finish.

Needs quite strong tastes, good with sweet-spicy marinades for chicken, turkey or pork and with barbecue flavours

Wolf Blass President's Selection McLaren Vale Chardonnay Premium 96

Dillon   ©

Full-bodied white, oak

Lovely rich, smoky fruit aromas with a weight of ripe toasty fruit—mangoes, melons and citrus flavours well supported by enriching alcohol. Big and beautiful.

Chicken and mango or roast turkey

White £15 - £20

Ch. Xanadu Chardonnay 95

Mitchell   ®

Full-bodied white, oak

Young, developing nose with aromas of lemon and stewed apple. Medium weight of fruit with crisp acidity. Shows quite an elegant structure, rounded and balanced and will do more in time.

Chicken, and meatier sauced fishes such as monkfish

Ch. Xanadu Semillon 95

Mitchell ®

Full-bodied white

Rather reserved nose, honey-suckle and tropical aromas just showing. Good balance of fruit and acidity, rather floral character. Needs more time to show its true colours.

Textured fish like monkfish in a creamy sauce or pork and ginger

Hardys Eileen Hardy Chardonnay 94

Allied Drinks ©

Full-bodied white, oak

Immediate aromas of tropical fruit and vanilla. Rich ripe fruit flavours very much to the fore, spicy backdrop with balanced acidity. Typically well-made New World style.

Mild curries, chicken or pork dishes containing fruit or grill or barbecue flavours

Pipers Brook Vineyard Tasmania Chardonnay 96

Fitzgerald ®

Full-bodied white, oak

Lovely buttery, tropical fruit aromas; a really silky-textured wine with deep, rich honeyed flavour. Attractive in every-thing except the price !

Roast or baked chicken especially with lemon and herb flavours

White £25 - £30

Rosemount Estate Roxburgh Chardonnay 94

Grants ☆ ☆

Full-bodied white, oak

Elegant, well-developed nose

with honeyed fruit and vanilla. A big wine with ripe, warm fruit balanced by refreshing acidity. Stunning for those prepared to pay!

Best with poultry and rich fish dishes

Red £5 - £6

Dry Plains Shiraz/Cabernet 97

Supervalu/Centra ®

Full-bodied red, fruit-driven

Blackcurrant with a hint of green pepper on the nose. Ripe and juicy style, well-rounded with decent weight and flavour and spicy finish.

Meatloaf or shoulder of lamb with soy and mustard

Hardys Banrock Station 97

Allied Drinks ®

Medium-bodied red, fruit-driven

Fruitgums on the nose and easy-drinking flavours of juicy red fruits with a soft structure lifted by a touch of spice in the finish.

Good party drinking which will suit a variety of meat, rice and salad mixtures

Jacob's Creek Grenache/Shiraz (limited release) 97

Fitzgerald ®

Medium-bodied red, fruit-driven

Spicy aromas of plum compote with quite a good weight of ripe, generous fruit in the taste. Spicy in the finish.

Baked ham or spicy chicken pieces

McWilliams Inheritance Shiraz/Cabernet nv

TDL ©

Full-bodied red

Ripe blackberry and blackcurrant fruit in good concentration. Dry, with mouthwatering juicy blackcurrant fruit, soft tannin and lovely peppery finish.

Barbecues with marinaded and grilled meat, even spicy flavours

Miranda Opal Ridge Shiraz/Cabernet 96

Taserra ®

Full-bodied red, fruit-driven

Jammy soft fruit nose with a a touch of pepper. Plenty of enjoyable ripe fruit and enough structure to hold together. A good party wine.

Relatively spicy casseroles and minced meat dishes or pasta with highly flavoured meatballs

Peter Lehmann Barossa Valley Grenache 97

United Beverages ®

Full-bodied red, fruit-driven

Red fruits and a touch of pepper on the nose; similar palate with juicy, ripe, rich fruit well supported by alcohol. Nice for the price.

Steaks or spicy sausages

Seppelt Moyston Cabernet Shiraz 96

Dunnes Stores ®

Full-bodied red

Ripe cassis and Ribena nose with soft, ripe, juicy fruit flavours. Pleasing, easy-drinking style, very well made.

Lasagne or other meaty pastas; good party wine

Red £6 - £8

Cockatoo Ridge Cabernet Sauvignon/Merlot 96

United Beverages ®

Full-bodied red, fruit-driven

Quite complex aromas for the price—cassis and pencil shavings; not quite so good in taste but a decent weight of well-balanced plummy fruit flavours.

Pan-fried kidneys in mustard or Madeira sauce or kidneys Tobago

d'Arenberg d'Arry's Original Shiraz/Grenache 92

Taserra ®

Full-bodied red, fruit-driven

Ripe damsons on the nose with a touch of rubber and dark cane sugar. Lots of spicy fruit and warm alcohol through the palate. Can't go wrong with this one for the price.

Hot game pie or with Merguez sausages

d'Arenberg High Trellis Cabernet Sauvignon 94

Taserra ®

Full-bodied red, fruit-driven

Very pronounced nose of baked fruit with liquorice overtones.

Raspberry and blackcurrant fruit with marked alcohol and firm tannins. Nice spicy finish.

Marinated beef, steaks or kebabs; beef stir-fry or leg of lamb with mustard and soy sauce

d'Arenberg Old Vine Shiraz 95

Taserra ®

Full-bodied red, fruit-driven

Ripe cherry and blackcurrant on the nose; mixed fruit jam—typical warm-climate Shiraz with loads of jammy fruit and warm alcohol. Long finish. Very good at the price.

Highly-flavoured dishes, even chilli—try with a not-too-fiery chilli con carne

Hardys Cabernet/Shiraz/Merlot 95

Allied Drinks ®

Full-bodied red, fruit-driven

Dense nose with stewed berries and a touch of cigar aroma. A good mouthful of juicy ripe fruit with nice smoky undertones. Ripe tannin and good weight with quite a long finish.

Beef en croûte or a beef or lamb casserole with bacon, onions and herbs

Lindeman Bin 50 Shiraz 96

Gilbeys ®

Full-bodied red, fruit-driven

Complex nose with cherries, brambles and spices, even a hint of sandalwood. Plummy fruit with a touch of mint; big and full-bodied with a long finish. Good value.

Couscous, chunky meat kebabs or pigeon and chorizo casserole

Lindeman's Bin 45 Cabernet Sauvignon 96

Gilbeys ®

Full-bodied red, fruit-driven

Aromas of ripe strawberries set off a wine laden with ripe fruit—strawberries, blackcurrants, cherries. Soft but well-balanced.

Good with strong flavours and mild spices, kebabs, stir-fry, spiced minced meat

Miranda Estates Cabernet/Shiraz 96

Taserra ®

Medium-bodied red, fruit-driven

Blackcurrant sherbet on the nose; quite light, tangy fruit on the palate with a bit of spice. Medium body and length.

Chunky spicy sausages

Peter Lehmann Vine Vale Shiraz 96

United Beverages ®

Full-bodied red, fruit-driven

Lovely nose with fruit and spices and a touch of cedar. Good weight of ripe plummy, brambly fruit and a touch of

smokiness. Nice now but could improve over a year or more. Great value.

Good choice for peppered venison or game casserole

Rosemount Estate Grenache/ Shiraz 97

Grants ©

Full-bodied red

Rich cherry aromas with a touch of peppery spice, full and flavoursome with ripe dark fruits and really warm, spicy overtones.

Barbecued foods and grilled meats, kebabs etc

Seppelt Cabernet Sauvignon 95

Dunnes Stores ®

Full-bodied red, fruit-driven

Lots of ripe blackcurrant aromas with minty tones. Full-bodied with quite firm tannin and a good weight of blackcurrant fruit. Long finish.

Roast and grilled meats especially lamb

Taltarni Fiddleback Terrace Victoria Red 96

Dunnes Stores ®

Full-bodied red, fruit-driven

Berry fruit aromas; dry and firm with ripe bramble-type fruit and nice dry finish.

Roast or grilled meat or a casserole

Tesco Australian Cabernet/ Merlot nv

Quinnsworth ®

Medium-bodied red, fruit-driven

Slightly vegetal with aromas of bramble fruit and smoke. Lots

of dark brambly fruit expanding in the mouth. Ripe tannins and well-rounded structure. Very good.

Lighter casseroles such as Irish stew; simple roast meat

Yaldara Grenache Mourvèdre Cabernet 97

Barry & Fitzwilliam ©

Medium-bodied red, fruit-driven

Ripe summer fruit and a touch of white pepper on the nose. Soft tannin with plenty of ripe berry fruit and balancing acidity. Well-made, youthful style, soft and easy-drinking.

Spicy casseroles with peppers and smoked meat flavours; mild to medium chilli

Red £8 - £10

Carlyle Estate Victoria Shiraz 94

Greenhills ®

Full-bodied red, fruit driven

Ripe berry fruit aromas; broad, meaty style with dark spicy, rather earthy fruit and firm structure.

Beef casseroles or steaks

Ch. Tahbilk Cabernet Sauvignon 94

United Beverages ®

Full-bodied red, fruit-driven

Blackcurrants and Ribena with a touch of spice on the nose. Similar palate of slightly lighter fruit than the nose with a touch of mint and highish alcohol.

Grilled lamb, noisettes or rack of lamb

Ch. Tahbilk Shiraz 94
United Beverages   ®

Full-bodied red, fruit-driven

Complex nose with red fruits, tobacco and leather. Dense flavours; well-structured with lots of dark fruit and spice lingering well in the finish.

Venison, or roast goose or a stroganoff

Clancy's Red 96
United Beverages   ®

Full-bodied red, fruit driven

Rich, fruity nose jumping out of the glass, Christmas cake aromas. Plenty of dark fruit of the forest and spice flavousr. A full-bodied, firm blockbuster.

Good with the obvious peppered steak also with venison steaks or even a cheeseboard

Hardys Bankside Shiraz 96
Allied Drinks   ®

Full-bodied red, fruit-driven

Really peppery aromas. Robust, full-bodied mouthful with plenty of fruit. Soft and well-made with length of flavour. Everybody's favourite.

Lean red meats and the more robust vegetable and grain dishes. Also spicy food especially beef teriyaki.

Jamieson's Run Coonawarra 95
Gilbeys   ®

Full-bodied red, fruit-driven

Plummy nose with hints of chocolate; mouthfilling fruit, blackcurrant and spice flavours with a backup of ripe tannin.

Decent weight and length.

Lamb steaks especially with a zesty chutney or relish; robust casseroles

John James McWilliams Cabernet Sauvignon 96
TDL   ®

Full-bodied red, fruit-driven

Ripe and blackcurranty on the nose. Full-bodied with an abundance of jammy fruit flavours and good length in a dry finish.

Ribs of beef or stuffed loin of lamb

Penfolds Koonunga Hill Shiraz/Cabernet Sauvignon 96
Findlater   ®

Full-bodied red, fruit- driven

Rich blackcurrant fruit on the nose with obvious wood. Lots of chunky fruit and spice flavours, quite rich and concentrated. Dry finish.

Meat casseroles and braised shanks of lamb

Penfolds Rawson's Retreat Bin 35 Cabernet Sauvignon/Shiraz/ Ruby Cabernet 97
Findlater   ☆

Full-bodied red, fruit-driven, tannic

Pronounced nose with loads of ripe berry fruit. Big, rich, robust wine with the flavours of summer pudding. Good structure of ripe tannin and oak balances the fruit. Long, delicious finish.

Duck cooked with beer or grilled ribs of beef

Peter Lehmann The Barossa Cabernet Sauvignon 95

United Beverages ☆

Full-bodied red, fruit-driven, tannic

Blackcurrants and cigar box aromas. Lots of ripe, blackcurrant fruit well supported by alcohol with balancing tannin and acidity. Full-bodied with weight of fruit and long finish. Very good for the price.

Well flavoured meat dishes such as lamb casserole with Middle Eastern spices, guineafowl or beef casserole

Peter Lehmann The Barossa Shiraz 96

United Beverages ☆ ☆

Full-bodied red, fruit-driven

Big, jammy, cherry fruit nose. Loads of fruit in the mouth but well balanced with acidity and ripe but definite structure. Succulent flavours expand and roll around the palate to a long, long finish.

Goose or richly flavoured game or a Chateaubriand

Rosemount Estate Cabernet Sauvignon 96

Grants ©

Medium to full-bodied red

Intense aromas of blackcurrant fruit with overtones of mint. Weight of similar fruit on the palate. Ripe, juicy and very typical.

Most red meats, especially lamb leg steaks, barbecued or marinated with herbs and garlic

Rosemount Estate Merlot 95

Grants ®

Full-bodied red, fruit-driven, tannic

Ripe plummy nose with a mocha overtone. Rich and fleshy with flavours of rather warm fruit, baked plums and spice. Balanced tannin.

Beef kebabs or barbequed beef rib

Rosemount Estate Shiraz 96

Grants ☆

Full-bodied red, fruit-driven

Spicy, plummy fruit with a hint of mocha. Rich, ripe palate of blackberries, plums and chocolate with a dry tobacco-like spice in the background. Delicious wine and great value.

Peppered venison steaks or duck with green pepper sauce

Rosemount Estate Shiraz/ Cabernet Sauvignon 97

Grants ®

Full-bodied red, fruit-driven

Ripe summer fruit aromas; quite rich and warm, full and round with quite intense blackcurrant and berry fruit flavours and a good spicy finish.

Great outdoor drinking with barbecued food, robust meat pies, cold meats etc

Taltarni Victoria Cabernet Sauvignon 91

Dunnes Stores ®

Full-bodied red, fruit-driven

Classic Australian Cabernet aromas of ripe, intense blackcurrant; well-balanced, with good intensity of fruit and lasting fruity flavours.

Marinated steaks of lamb or beef; tomato or fruit-based sauces

Tesco's Coonawarra Cabernet Sauvignon 95
Quinnsworth ®

Medium-bodied red, fruit-driven

Ripe blackcurrant with a dash of peppermint on the nose. Medium-bodied with slightly herbaceous fruit character and smooth texture.

Lamb cutlets or noisettes especially with a herb/garlic sauce and garnish of roasted vegetables

Tesco's McLaren Vale Shiraz 94
Quinnsworth ®

Full-bodied red, fruit-driven

Fresh fruity nose with a touch of cinnamon spice. Really velvety mouthfeel with lots of fruit and spice and a background of ripe figs. Well-made and balanced.

Spicy foods such as couscous or a bean casserole

Wakefield Clare Valley Cabernet Sauvignon 96
Koala ☆

Full-bodied red, fruit-driven

Hints of eucalyptus mix with the blackcurrant aromas. Full-bodied with loads of ripe blackcurrant fruit. Well-balanced and delicious.

Lamb baked with herbs and garlic

Wolf Blass Cabernet Sauvignon 'Yellow Label' 96
Dillon ®

Medium to full-bodied red

Round and supple with lots of ripe, rich fruit and balancing

structure. Thoroughly enjoyable.

Red meats, not too richly cooked, especially stir-fries and grills

Wolf Blass South Australia Shiraz 96
Dillon ®

Full-bodied red, fruit-driven, tannic

Juicy fruit with hints of pepper. Easy-drinking with oodles of plummy fruit, soft tannin and balancing acidity. Well made and appealing.

Barbecued meats and spicy meat dishes

Yaldara Reserve Grenache Whitmore Old Vineyard 97
Barry & Fitzwilliam ☆

Full-bodied red, fruit-driven

Rich berry tones on the nose. Lovely mix of raspberry fruit, chocolate and spice flavours in a velvety texture. Round and mouthfilling with a nice warm finish.

Vegetable and nut bakes, sausages and lentils or chicken in walnut sauce

Yaldara Reserve Shiraz 97
Barry & Fitzwilliam ☆

Full-bodied red, fruit-driven

Dark, brambly fruit aromas with a hint of violet on the nose. The palate has a weight of ripe blackberry fruit with layers of spice and well-balanced structure. Long and lingering—lovely Shiraz.

Spicy stir-fry of duck with plum sauce, ginger and chilli; also other well-flavoured, rich meats

Red £10 - £12

Chatsfield Mount Barker Cabernet Franc 96

Mitchell ®

Light to medium-bodied red, fruity

Rich berry fruit with plenty of acidity and a slightly stalky character. Tannin is quite firm to give a youthful, nice savoury wine.

Spicy food, including ginger and pepper flavours; also mature hard cheese

Chatsfield Shiraz 94

Mitchell ☆

Medium to full-bodied red

A really stylish Shiraz with aromas of plums and damsons. Tastes of complex, cool-climate fruit. Balanced acidity brings out plenty of flavour. Elegant rather than big and gorgeous for the price!

Red meats in general, especially kebabs, steaks and chops; not so good with spicy food, though herby casseroles work

Ninth Island Tasmania Pinot Noir 97

Fitzgerald ®

Medium-bodied red

Raspberries and redcurrants on the nose; very fruit-led. A well-rounded wine with lovely weight of ripe appealing fruit and a few typical gamey nuances.

Versatile wine which works well with spicy, garlicky food; also firm fishes like salmon or monkfish appropriately cooked

Robertson's Well Coonawarra Cabernet Sauvignon 95

Gilbeys ®

Full-bodied red, fruit-driven

Blackcurrant aromas jump out of the glass. Packed with fruit and hints of vanilla spice. Lovely, long and lingering.

Red meats in general; works well with soy sauce, teriyaki, etc

Rouge Homme Coonawarra Cabernet Sauvignon 94

Findlater ☆

Full-bodied red, fruit-driven, tannic

Lots of cassis aromas with underlying spice. Opulent style with ripe blackcurrant fruit to the fore. Tannins present but in the background.

Red meats and more robust vegetable, pasta and grain-based dishes

Ch. Reynella Basket Pressed Shiraz 94

Allied Drinks ®

Full-bodied red, tannic

Deep, brooding aromas of black cherry, spice and chocolate. Dry, with ripe, sweet fruit with hints of eucalyptus and spicy black pepper. Tannin is still firm and the wine should develop further over two years.

Goose or duck with green peppercorns; also charcoal-grilled steaks

Red £12 - £15

Ch. Reynella Basket-Pressed Cabernet/Merlot 95

Allied Drinks ®

Full-bodied red, fruit-driven, tannic

Deep, rich cassis nose with hints of mint and chocolate. Punchy young fruit and plenty of it with relatively firm tannins and lingering flavour.

Hearty casseroles of beef or venison

Hardys Coonawarra Cabernet Sauvignon 94
Allied Drinks ©

Full-bodied red, tannic

Liquorice and dark fruit aromas. The firmness of the tannin gives a rather lean taste, though full and well-tructured. Good potential.

Red meats, especially roast or pan-fried lamb or fillet of beef

Jim Barry McCrae Wood Clare Valley Shiraz 94
Dunnes Stores ®

Full-bodied red, fruit-driven

Quite ripe, almost dried, fruit on the nose; fresher palate with berry fruit and spice in a full, well-rounded wine.

Roasted or grilled vegetables especially aubergines and peppers

Penfolds Kalimna Bin 28 Shiraz 94
Findlater ☆

Full-bodied red

Aromas of mint, plums and damsons with a spicy, peppery flavour and intense, plummy fruit. Still young but with a very good future.

Autumn stews of red meat or game

Penfolds Bin 128 Coonawarra Shiraz 95

Findlater ☆

Full-bodied red, tannic

Young with a lot of promise. Lovely aromas of mint, spice and plummy fruit, but youthful tannins showing distinctly on the palate. Should improve for another five years!

Young so needs robust food, especially casseroles and rare beef steaks

Seppelt Dorrien Vineyard Barossa Valley Cabernet Sauvignon 92
Dunnes Stores ®

Full-bodied red, fruit-driven

Ripe blackcurrant aromas mingle with tar, tobacco and spice. Nicely balanced and structured with mouthfilling fruit and a long finish.

Meat dishes especially roast or grilled

Seppelt Great Western Vineyard Central Victoria Shiraz 92
Dunnes Stores ®

Full-bodied red, fruit-driven

Spicy fruit compote aromas with chunky fruit flavours of blackberries, raisins and spice. Rich and soft with a warm finish.

Spicy dishes, even chilli con carne

Wolf Blass President's Selection South Australia Cabernet Sauvignon 95
Dillon ®

Full-bodied red, fruit-driven

Elegant nose with blackcurrant and spice aromas. Lots of blackcurrant and brambly fruit, quite plummy and rich with nice spicy backdrop. Medium-bodied with some length. Attractive.

Most meats, especially fillet of beef in pastry with mushroom sauce

Wolf Blass President's Selection South Australia Shiraz 94

Dillon ☆

Full-bodied red, fruit-driven

Chocolate, spice and mint aromas give richness on the nose. Full soft wine, youthful but very well-balanced in a popular style.

Red meats especially barbecue-type dishes, stir- fries and some Chinese meals

Wolf Blass Show Reserve Coonawarra Cabernet Sauvignon Premium 93

Dillon ®

Full-bodied red, tannic

Deep garnet colour with rich fruit aromas. Flavours of baked fruit with firm tannin and lean, oaky background.

Red meats, especially steaks or chops with a sauce

Wolf Blass Show Reserve Old Vine Shiraz Private Bin Release 93

Molloy's ☆☆

Full-bodied red, fruit-driven

Dark plummy fruit, tobacco and pepper on the nose. Flavours of ripe blackcurrant, raspberry and sweet pepper in a sliky texture. Long and flavoursome in the finish.

Grilled meats especially with spicy sauces or garnishes

Red £15 - £20

Cape Mentelle Cabernet/ Merlot 96

Findlater ☆☆

Full-bodied red

Inviting berry aromas with toasty richness. Ripe cassis fruit with spicy flavours and a good structure with the fruit well balanced by tannin, acidity and body.

Red meats, especially roasted or grilled lamb

Ch. Xanadu Cabernet Sauvignon 95

Mitchell ☆☆

Full-bodied red

Quite earthy nose with liquorice hints. Very full and rich with stylish fruit and good structure. Should develop and hold well.

Red meats including leg of lamb, beef ribs and steak; also pheasant and lighter game

Cullen Cabernet Sauvignon/ Merlot 94

Mitchell ☆☆

Full-bodied red

Intriguing chocolate and mint notes on the nose. Big, complex and well-structured style—not for the faint-hearted. Could age well, too.

Roast ribs of beef; leg or loin of lamb

De Bortoli Yarra Valley Shiraz 95

Febvre ®

Full-bodied red, fruit-driven

Real blockbuster quality on the nose, fruit, liquorice, spice. Velvety mouthfeel with beautifully ripe fruit flavours; big but balanced with refreshing acidity.

Steaks with a well- flavoured sauce: green peppercorn, mustard or port

Ebenezer Barossa Valley Shiraz 93

Allied Drinks ®

Full-bodied red

Rich blackcurrant fruit aromas and similar ripe fruit flavours with spice and plums. Nice mellowness to this wine with a touch of complexity.

Red meats, especially the lighter cuts of beef and lamb such as fillet

Rosemount Estate Show Reserve Shiraz 95

Grants ☆

Full-bodied red

Intense aromas of spice, pepper and plums. A big, rich Shiraz with spicy plum fruit and great ripeness extending to the wonderful chocolatey finish. Should develop further in bottle.

Red meat and lighter game dishes; spicy beef and dark reduction sauces. A natural choice for peppered steak..

St Hallett Old Block Barossa Shiraz 94

Dunnes Stores ☆

Full-bodied red fruit-driven

Oak and dark berry fruit aromas mingle on the nose. Lots of deep, complex fruit flavour with contrasting spice. Firm and tightly-knit with a long, stylish finish

Robust venison casserole or pie

Wolf Blass Black Label Cabernet Sauvignon/Shiraz/Merlot 94

Dillon ☆

Full-bodied red

Delightful aromas of chocolate, mint and blackcurrant which appear also in the taste. Complex and well- balanced with a long finish. Superb!

Red meats: roast or grilled lamb, steaks or ribs of beef, ostrich and grilled or roast venison

Red £20 - £25

Ch. Tahbilk Cabernet Sauvignon Reserve 85

Molloy's ®

Full-bodied red, fruit-driven

Soft, mature fruit aromas. Quite a tight structure but with lots of underlying fruit and subtle flavours. Still quite hard in the finish—needs a bit of time.

Steak and mushroom sauce or roast duck

Red £25 - £30

Ch. Xanadu Cabernet Reserve 94

Mitchell ☆

Full-bodied red, tannic

Intense spicy blackcurrant aromas. Layered, flavoursome palate with smoky, oaky tastes and concentrated fruit. Elegant structure with firm tannin. Complex and stylish.

Red meats and lighter game; dark, reduced meat sauces

Red £30 - £35

Hardys Eileen Hardy Shiraz 94
Allied Drinks ☆ ☆

Full-bodied red

Full, rich nose with definite hints of rosemary and underlying savoury, meaty tones. Creamy textured with layers of complex flavour and beautifully smooth tannins. Brilliant if expensive.

Red meats and lighter game, very good with beef in pastry or a fillet with pepper sauce. Also good with barbecued leg of lamb.

Jim Barry The Armagh Clare Valley Shiraz 94
Dunnes Stores ®

Full-bodied red, fruit-driven, tannic

Ripe dark fruits and pepper on the nose. Silky smooth with a weight of concentrated fruit and balanced acidity with a bite of ripe tannin. Very nice wine but very expensive.

Peppered fillet of beef or roast venison

Peter Lehmann Stonewell Barossa Shiraz 92
United Beverages ☆ ☆

Full-bodied red, fruit-driven

Hugely complex nose which develops more and more in the glass. Wonderful mouthful of fruit, spice and ripeness—impressively refined. Very long, delicious finish. A lovely wine in every way except price!

Duck and blackcurrant sauce—for a special occasion

Rosé £5 - £6

Mount Hurtle Grenache 96
United Beverages ®

Rosé

Very appealing nose, lovely ripe, rich strawberry fruit which follows through on the palate. Quite mouthfilling and well-balanced fruit with refreshing acidty. Easy-drinking and excellent value.

Chunky terrines such as rabbit and goose

Austria

The memorable wine scandal of the eighties prompted a very serious commitment to quality by Austrian winemakers which was swiftly enforced in law. As confidence is restored, the country has become an important European producer albeit with a niche market. The scale and overheads of Austrian viticulture mean that it will never be a volume supplier. High quality individual wines are what the country does best which has been recognised by a new generation of producers.

Austria shares with Germany many grape varieties and a similar, though more rigid, classification system, based on the ripeness of the grape. The style however, is different. Austrian vineyards are warmer and the wines more full-bodied. Austrian Riesling is fuller than that of the Rhine and not as austerely dry as in Alsace.

Though most Austrian wines are white, there is real potential for quality red wine production and good examples are found in this year's guide.

Sweet wines even at Beerenauslese and Trockenbeerenauslese levels, are produced more consistently than in Germany and are less expensive. In fact, from a good producer these wines are great value, stylish and unusual.

White £5 - £6

Servús Burgenland trocken Q 94

Barry & Fitzwilliam ®

Aromatic white

Grassy herbal aromas. Dry and concentrated with minerally fruit and white pepper spice. Nice balancing acidity. Good value.

Lighter seafood dishes, especially prawns

White £10 - £12

Domäne Müller Pinot Gris Kabinett Oak-aged Kabinett Fürstenstück 95

Mitchell ©

Full-bodied white

Full and rich with quite a toasty aroma. Dry with fine balance between weighty fruit and crisp acidity. Full and rounded with a long finish.

Chicken, quail and pork, with mild aromatic spices—pork with mustard, glazed quail with anise

White £12 - £15

Domäne Müller Sauvignon Blanc Oak-aged 96
Mitchell ®

Aromatic white

Broad, highly aromatic nose with grass and green apple aromas. Quite full and weighty in the mouth, a touch oily with green fruit flavours and a mineral note. Crisp finish.
River fish like trout and textured sea fish—brill, John Dory etc; matches herb and spice flavours well—trout with dill and cour- gettes, brill with mustard and saffron, John Dory with asparagus

Red £5 - £6

Weingut Norbert Blauer Sankt Laurent Q 95
TDL ®

Light fruity red, tannic

Cranberries on the nose in good concentration. Good weight on the palate with blackcurrant and redcurrant fruit. Nice frame of tannin and acidity. Quite long.
Roast pork fillet or a blanquette of veal

Red £6 - £8

Weingut Norbert Blauer Portugieser Q 95
TDL ®

Light fruity red, tannic

Concentrated dark fruit aromas with a touch of sweet peppers and spice. Dry tannins with plum-like fruit and medium weight.
Baked chicken or sauté of lamb

Wulkatal Blauer Zweigelt Trocken Q 97
TDL ®

Light fruity red

Lovely nose of ripe, brambly fruit. Dry and lively with a firm backbone and plenty of light refreshing fruit.
Casserole or beef stroganoff

Red £12 - £15

Domäne Müller Cabernet Sauvignon Oak-aged 95
Mitchell ®

Full-bodied red

Lovely nose of cedar and blackcurrant. Well-judged oak and reasonable weight of blackcurrant fruit though rather stalky—oak has the upper hand.
Grilled or roast meats, shoulder of lamb, sirloin steak

Chile

The present story of Chilean wines is expansion. Almost every winery is building or planting, probably both. Joint ventures such as Mondavi and Errazuriz, Concha y Toro and Rothschild, account for much of the investment. But there is also a very definite quality thrust within the industry; Chile established its reputation based on value for money, now it wants to show that the country can also produce great wine. In part, this comes from the market. The worst of California's problems are over and one or two big vintages have restored supplies on the home market which means a corresponding dip for Chilean sales. Argentina is also on the map as a serious competitor. Chile needs to raise the image of its wines to maintain its export success.

This year a number of flagship reds have appeared such as Montes Alpha M, a Bordeaux blend aged in French oak and destined to sell at over £30 a bottle, which is frankly overpriced. At perhaps a third or half that price, most wineries are producing high quality Reserva reds which are based on lower yields, careful use of oak and achieve impressive levels of complexity. Concha y Toro's top Chardonnays, Reservas from Carmen and Santa Carolina are examples of great value still available. Cooler, southern vineyards such as Casablanca have produced exciting white wines. Chardonnays, even at the simplest level, are now bargains in easy-drinking, fruity whites.

Chilean Merlot is also impressive producing richly fruity, lively wine while the more serious oaked versions in general need more balance and concentration but are potentially very fine.

Most interesting is the tendency to blend Cabernet and Merlot for the top wines. This seems to slightly tame the ripe, exuberant qualities of Chilean fruit and add restrained elegance to ageworthy reds.

It is a good time to buy Chilean wines as prices will certainly rise. Those with patience and interest should consider putting aside a few red Reservas which may pay exciting dividends in years to come.

White £5 or less

San Pedro Chardonnay 97
Dunnes Stores   *££*
Light fruity white

Not especially typical Chardonnay in character but very
pleasing with nice fruit and a
lemony edge. Fine at the price.
A pleasant glass on its own or
with avocado and salads in general

**Tesco's Chilean Sauvignon
Blanc nv**
Quinnsworth   ®
Aromatic white, fruit-driven

Nice crisp, aromatic nose
follows to the palate which has
plenty of green, grassy fruit
flavour. Crisp clean finish.
Good value.
Not a bad choice for good old
seafood cocktail; good with fish and
mayonnaise in general

White £5 - £6

Carmen Sauvignon Blanc 95
Dillon   ®
Aromatic white, fruit-driven

Opulent nose of ripe eating
apples. Very ripe tropical fruit
flavours mixed with citrusy
zest. Good clean finish.
Fishcakes or tomato and fish pasta

**Santa Carolina Chenin Blanc
97**
Supervalu/Centra   ®
Light fruity white

Clean ripe fruit on the nose and
ripe tropical fruit on the palate
with crisp acidity and decent
length. Typical Chenin.
Vegetarian dishes of stuffed
vegetables or tofu; mild curry

Santa Helena Chardonnay 97
Greenhills   ®
Light fruity white

Lively fruit bowl aromas with
fresh, easy-drinking fruit on the
palate and crisp refreshing
acidity.
Cold food: chicken salad, seafood
and rice

Terra Andina Chardonnay 97
Fitzgerald   ®
Light fruity white

Ripe buttery fruit on the nose
with good weight of tropical
fruit flavour and balanced
acidity. Nice long finish, too.
Chicken baked with Parmesan
crumbs or in a spicy pie

Terra Andina Semillon 96
Fitzgerald   ®
Light fruity white

Dry with nice soft, ripe fruit;
mellow warm character with
body and crisp acidity.
Milder Chinese dishes of chicken
and pork

Tesco's Chilean Chardonnay nv
Quinnsworth   ®
Full-bodied white

Hints of caramel and honey on
the nose, mellow buttery palate
with ripe tropical fruit and
lemony acidity in the finish.
Great value.
Rich fish gratin or mild chicken
and coconut curry

**Valdezaro Maule Valley
Chardonnay 96**
Barry & Fitzwilliam   *££*
Light fruity white

Light, quite elegant nose with
peach and pear aromas. Crisp

and fresh with nice weight of summery fruit and lively acidity.

Spices: spiced fish kebabs, snapper or scallops with a pineapple, ginger and coriander salsa

White £6 - £8

Caliterra Sauvignon Blanc 97
Febvre   ®

Aromatic white, fruit-driven

Bittersweet nose like apples and wild heather honey. Soft, rounded fruit attack but then zesty acidity really kicks in to give a clean, beautifully refreshing finish.

Jambalaya or pasta with peppers and tomatoes

Carmen Chardonnay 97
Dillon   ££

Medium-bodied white

Delicate citrusy nose with refreshing palate also with citrus overtones and green apple fruit. Some length in the finsih. Well made and very good value.

Fish served with butter or light cream sauce, fishcakes, smoked fish or creamy pasta

Concha y Toro Casillero del Diablo Chardonnay 97
Findlater   ©

Full-bodied white, oak

Inviting nose of tropical fruit with a touch of spice—quite exotic aromas. Good weight of fruit, well-balanced with ripeness offset by spice flavours. Long, buttery finish.

Mild to medium spices; Chinese squid or a zippy chicken stir-fry

Concha y Toro Chardonnay 97
Findlater   ££

Full-bodied white

Minerally green apple fruit aromas; dry with rich creamy texture and tropical fruit flavours with refreshing citrus. Well-rounded, easy-drinking style and well priced.

Chicken and richer fish dishes; chicken lasagne or a big fish pie

Concha y Toro Gewürztraminer 97
Findlater   ®

Aromatic white

Rose petals and spice on the nose. Fresh clean flavours of fruit and spice, citrusy with nicely balanced acidity and crisp finish.

Hummus or a mixed mezze; spicy dishes in general

Concha y Toro Sunrise Chardonnay 97
Findlater   ®

Full-bodied white

Mango and pineapple on the nose; rich and buttery palate with refreshing citrus fruit. Quite full and mouthfilling.

Quite spicy flavours, creamy curries or chicken with coconut and banana chutney

Concha y Toro Trio Chardonnay 96
Findlater   ®

Medium to full-bodied red

Slightly floral, tropical fruit aromas. Quite buttery and full with racy acidity not entirely balanced by the fruit.

Fish, chicken and cream sauces

De Martino Sauvignon Blanc 97

Febvre   ®

Aromatic white, fruit-driven

Stewed apples dominate the nose. Rich, round fruit flavours contrast with quite racy acidity and tart, green fruit finish.
Avocado salad or asparagus and hollandaise sauce

Errázuriz Chardonnay 96

Allied Drinks   ®

Medium-bodied white

Aromas of peardrops and lemon with underlying honey. Dry with fresh acidity and medium weight of ripe, melon-like fruit flavours. Youthful style for early drinking. Good at the price.
Simple fish dishes, avocado salad or chicken and fruit dishes

Errazuriz Sauvignon Blanc 97

Allied Drinks   ®

Aromatic white, fruit-driven

Elderflowers and green apples on the nose. Refreshing palate yet with underlying richness of tropical fruit flavour. Tart green apples in the finish with a nice herby twist.
Chinese food especially prawns and squid

Errázuriz Sauvignon Blanc Reserva 94

Allied Drinks   ®

Aromatic white, fruit-driven

A touch of oily oak on the nose mixed with ripe, aromatic fruit. Ripe, tropical fruit flavours with good weight and fairly long finish.

Warm salad of monkfish or spicy chicken

Luis Felipe Edwards Chardonnay 97

Quinnsworth   ®

Full-bodied white

Ripe Cox's pippins on the nose. Peachy, citrus fruit on the palate with a lovely butttery quality. Good concentration of fruit and crisp clean acidity give a refreshing finish.
Textured fish such as turbot; monkfish in rich creamy sauces and even lobster

Montes Barrel-fermented Chardonnay 97

Grants   ££

Full-bodied white

Honey, toast and vanilla aromas mingle with citrus fruit on the nose. Relatively full-bodied with ripe tropical fruit and well-integrated new oak—quite toasty and rich. Well made with quite a long finish and good value.
Well-flavoured food especially barbecued halibut and glazed chicken; also pork satay

San Pedro Barrel-fermented Chardonnay Reserva 96

Dunnes Stores   ☆

Full-bodied white, oak

Aromas of coconut and oak combine with buttery fruit. The resulting richness follows through to a surprisingly complex flavour of ripe fruit beautifully balanced by acidity and buttery tones. Lovely!
Terrific with a good Thai-style green chicken curry or a creamy pasta flavoured with smoked ham

Santa Carolina Chardonnay 97
TDL   *££*

Full-bodied white

Subtle fruit combined with light
toasty aromas and flavours.
Well made with a lot of style
for the price.
*Pan-fried chicken or grilled
salmon*

**Santa Carolina Chardonnay
Reservado 97**
TDL   *££*

Full-bodied white, oak

Fresh lemony aromas with a
warm buttery edge followed by
flavours of melon with crisp
citrusy acidity. Full, yet lively
with a longlasting taste and
quite a bargain.
*Delicious with baked trout or brill
with butter sauce*

**Santa Carolina Chardonnay
Semillon 97**
TDL   ®

Light fruity white

Clean, zesty nose with hints of
caramelized apple. Dry and
creamy-textured with citrus
and pineapple flavours and a
refreshing finish.
*Particularly successful with pork
kebabs and satay*

**Santa Carolina Sauvignon
Blanc 97**
TDL   ®

Aromatic white, fruit-driven

Touch of gooseberry on the
nose; dry, with grassy, green
fruit flavour and crisp dry
finish.
Fish salad and mayonnaise

**Santa Carolina Sauvignon
Blanc Reserva 95**
TDL   ®

Aromatic white, fruit-driven

Peardrops and lime dominate
the nose. Dry, with high acidity
and fair weight of fruit carrying
through to a crisp finish.
*Salad of tomatoes and mozzarrella
cheese*

**Santa Helena Seleccion del
Directorio oak-aged Chardon-
nay 97**
Greenhills   ☆

Medium-bodied white

Attractive aromas of peach and
passionfruit with a hint of oak.
Dry with nicely balanced ripe
fruit and refreshing acidity.
Peach and melon flavours
dominate with a simple but
cleancut structure and some
length.
*Sauced fish dishes and mild
curries*

**Santa Helena Siglo de Oro
Chardonnay 96**
Greenhills   ®

Full-bodied white

Quite toasty on the nose with
green fruit and mineral aromas.
Well-rounded wine with nice
weight of toasty fruit and ripe,
full finish.
*Barbecued or char-grilled chicken
and fish; salmon stuffed with
Parma ham and fennel*

**Undurraga Chardonnay
Reserve 96**
United Beverages   ®

Full-bodied white

Full, ripe buttery nose with rich,
fat palate of tropical fruit

balanced by refreshing acidity. *Creamy, coconut milk curry or warm avocado*

White £8 - £10

Carmen Reserve Chardonnay 95

Dillon ®

Full-bodied white

Attractive nose of new oak and ripe fruit. Smooth, honeyed texture with lots of ripe fruit and good length in a clean, crisp finish. Well made and delicious.
Roast, stuffed chicken; fish pie; caulifower cheese

Concha y Toro Marqués de Casa Concha Chardonnay 96

Findlater ☆ ☆

Medium to full-bodied white, oak

Tropical fruit, vanilla and buttery toast give quite a complex nose. Lovely fruit flavours reminiscent of pineapple, mangoes and passionfruit with a toasty edge. Well-balanced acidity, tight structure and good length. Excellent value.
Creamy fish dishes, soufflés or cauliflower cheese

White £10 - £12

Errázuriz Chardonnay Reserva 96

Allied Drinks ☆

Medium to full-bodied white, oak

Restrained, rather elegant nose with honeyed fruit and vanilla aromas. Rounded, with crisp acidity balanced by ripe fruit.

Long, very correct finish.
Chicken especially roast or grilled, roast turkey and meatier types of fish with sauce

Santa Carolina Chardonnay Gran Reserva 96

TDL ☆

Full-bodied white, oak

Aromas still of a young wine, the oak a bit overpowering, but plenty of ripe fruit on the palate and quite complex flavours developing. A lovely velvet texture in a well-made wine with classic style.
Grilled chicken or roast turkey

White £12 - £15

Montes Alpha Special Cuvée Chardonnay 95

Grants ☆

Full-bodied white, oak

Pronounced aromas of melon and citrus fruit with a touch of smokiness. Lots of ripe fruit flavours: kiwis, bananas, pineapple with an oaky edge. Elegant style with a lingering aftertaste. Should develop further.
Chicken, lobster or other textured fishes with cream or butter sauce

Santa Carolina Reserva de Familia barrel-fermented Chardonnay 95

TDL ☆ ☆

Full-bodied white

Opulent nose with ripe honeyed fruit, lemon and mineral tones; apple and lime flavours with a nice bite of oak. Silky and understated in the mouth. Lots of style.
Turbot with shellfish sauce; creamy chicken and avocado or lobster salad

Red £5 - £6

Carmen Cabernet Sauvignon 95
Dillon ££

Medium-bodied red, fruit-driven

Ripe fruit aromas show a touch of chocolatey richness which follows through to the taste. An elegant, well-balanced wine with complexity beyond its price.
Red meat dishes and richly cooked poultry

Carta Vieja Cabernet Sauvignon 95
Barry & Fitzwilliam ©

Medium-bodied red, fruit-driven

Ripe blackcurrant aromas with spicy overtones, good depth of fruit, Concentrated cassis flavours with nice touch of smokiness in the background. Quite rich fruit develops towards the end.
Stir-fry beef with shitaki mushrooms or lamb with orange and ginger

Concha y Toro Maule Valley Cabernet Sauvignon/Merlot 97
Findlater ®

Medium-bodied red, fruit-driven

Generous cassis aromas and nice weight of ripe blackcurrant and plum fruit. Soft yet balanced with good dry finish. Good value and a great crowd-pleaser!
Spicy minced meat dishes, meatballs and sausage casserole; good for parties especially barbecues

Concha y Toro Sunrise Merlot 97
Findlater ®

Light to medium-bodied red, tannic

Peppered strawberries on the nose and similar taste with some soft, ripe tannins supporting the fruit. Appealing, very easy-drinking.
Salami, pizza and pasta with tomato

Isla de Maipo Cabernet Sauvignon 96
Febvre ®

Medium-bodied red, fruit-driven

Rather dumb nose with hints of blackcurrant. Very mellow and soft and much more open on the palate with blackcurrant and damson fruit. Refreshing, slightly stalky finish.
Medallions or noisettes of lamb; duck breast with cherry or blackcurrant sauce

Santa Carolina Cabernet Sauvignon 96
TDL ®

Medium-bodied red, fruit-driven

Lots of brambly fruit come through in the aroma and flavour in an easy-drinking wine with a nice touch of spice in the finish.
Good with mixed grills, kidneys, and cold meats

Santa Carolina Merlot/ Cabernet Sauvignon 96

TDL Ⓡ

Medium-bodied red, fruit-driven, tannic

Quite a rich nose of soft berry fruit and blackcurrant leaves. Lots of berry fruit flavour nicely balanced by ripe soft tannin and a bit of length in the finish.
Pepperoni pizza or zesty tomato-based pasta

Santa Helena Gran Vino Merlot 97

Greenhills Ⓡ

Medium-bodied red

Intense plumminess in the taste with super-ripeness to give an appealing, easy mouthful.
Versatile, even with highly flavoured food and spices; especially good with ham

Terra Andina Cabernet Sauvignon 96

Fitzgerald Ⓡ

Medium-bodied red, fruit-driven, tannic

Ripe, blackcurranty nose. Full and round on the palate with balanced tannins and ripe fruit. Dry finish.
Red meats, lamb and beef, especially marinated beef kebabs or hamburgers

Tesco's Chilean Cabernet Sauvignon nv

Quinnsworth Ⓡ

Medium-bodied red, fruit-driven

Hints of blackcurrants and mint on the nose. Flavours are similar to the nose, slightly stalky but light and easy-drinking style.
Meat casserole or steak strips with herb and garlic butter

Tesco's Chilean Merlot 98

Quinnsworth Ⓡ

Light fruity red, tannic

Lots of soft fruit aromas, strawberries, plums, slightly jammy. Nice refreshing acidity and soft tannins with plenty of raspberry and cherry fruit lasting well into the finish.
Pepperoni pizza, spicy chicken wings and many Chinese foods

Tierra Arena Cabernet Sauvignon 96

Taserra ££

Medium-bodied red, fruit-driven

Smoky cassis aromas with touch of mint. Rich and soft on the palate with blackberry and blackcurrant fruit and a really minty influence. For the price it's good indeed.
Stuffed shoulder of lamb or kefte

Undurraga Cabernet Sauvignon 97

United Beverages Ⓡ

Medium-bodied red, fruit-driven

Ripe soft fruits on the nose. Good fruit and structure in the taste. Fairly simple but correct.
Meatballs or meat-filled pitta bread

Undurraga Merlot 97

United Beverages Ⓡ

Light fruity red

Ripe berries and fruitcake come through on the nose. The palate is soft and fruity with a good finish.

Mildly spicy food, such as chicken wings with soy marinade

Valdezaro Cabernet Sauvignon 96

Barry & Fitzwilliam ®

Medium-bodied red, fruit-driven

Light blackcurrant aromas; ripe Ribena and blackcurrant fruit flavours. Quite rich and warm in the finish.
Robust meat flavours, barbecued food and stir-fried meat

Villa Montes Cabernet Sauvignon 96

Grants ®

Medium-bodied red

Lean and slightly stalky but well-balanced: the juicy blackcurrant fruit offsets a firm structure in a wine with satisfying bite and depth.
Most red meats, especially lamb and duck and casseroles; avoid hot spices or soy sauce

Red £6 - £8

Caliterra Merlot 97

Febvre ®

Light fruity red

Fruit of the forest nose with a touch of minty spice. Lovely and mellow on the palate with good concentration of plummy fruit lasting through a smooth finish.
Grilled tuna fish served with black olives

Carmen Merlot 96

Dillon ©

Medium-bodied red, fruit-driven

Quite savoury aromas with spicy plums in the background. Well-flavoured chunky Merlot with good weight of dark fruit and slightly gamey tones. Nice length in the finish.
Calves' liver and mushrooms or pheasant and sweet pepper casserole

Concha y Toro Casillero del Diablo Cabernet Sauvignon 96

Findlater ££

Full-bodied red, fruit-driven

Lovely ripe blackcurrant aromas; full and smooth with good weight of rich, ripe fruit and a long finish.
Lamb with ginger and sesame or pork cooked with dried fruits; char-grilled meats

Concha y Toro Marqués Merlot 95

Findlater ®

Medium-bodied red

Ripe, intense fruit aromas with attractive spiciness. Lovely balance of fruit and oak with a peppery nuance in the background. Very tasty at the price.
Grilled meats or barbecued rib of beef

Concha y Toro Sunrise Cabernet Sauvignon 97

Findlater ®

Full-bodied red, fruit-driven

Nice ripe fruit aromas and plenty of rich cassis flavours mixed with spicy overtones; warm finish.
Meaty or rich tomato pastas or well-flavoured home-made hamburgers

Concha y Toro Trio Merlot 96
Findlater ®

Medium-bodied red, fruit-driven

Lots of dark fruit aromas and nice weight of plummy fruit with tones of rich cherry. Dry with slightly spicy overtones.
Grilled and barbecued meats, kebabs etc

Errázuriz Cabernet Sauvignon 96
Allied Drinks ®

Medium-bodied red, fruit-driven

Nice ripeness on the nose and a good depth of jammy fruit flavour, Well-balanced, pleasing style.
Quite spicy food such as stir-fried beef or lamb with mustard

Errázuriz Merlot 97
Allied Drinks ©

Light fruity red

Ripe fruity nose with a touch of pepper and slghtly burnt character: cassis and caramel. Quite a big wine with lots of fruit and some youthful tannin. Rather nice and should become richer in time.
Garlicky salami and other strong flavours, not spices though

Luis Felipe Edwards Cabernet Sauvignon 96
Quinnsworth ®

Medium-bodied red, fruit-driven

Nice concentrated blackcurrant aromas. Blackcurrants and cherries on the nose with spicy fruitcake influence. Quite rich fruit on the palate also, rounded

and rich right to the end.
Minute steak, kebabs or lamb steaks with a relish

Millaman Cabernet Sauvignon Curicó 97
Barry & Fitzwilliam ££

Full-bodied red, fruit-driven

Soft, jammy even plummy nose. Soft and rich yet balanced with intense blackcurrant fruit flavours with delicious hints of vanilla and spice. Great value and might be even better in a year's time.
Relatively spicy dishes—Chinese duck or a meat teriyaki; also roast or grilled lamb

Millaman Merlot Curicó 97
Barry & Fitzwilliam ££

Medium-bodied red, fruit-driven

Ripe blackcurrant aromas with really impressive weight of summer fruit flavour. Soft and mouthfilling with lovely fruit lingering through the finish.
Pasta and roasted vegetables or grilled tuna and olives

Montes Oak aged Reserve Merlot 96
Grants ®

Medium-bodied red, tannic

Slightly pungent nose with red fruit and a toasted edge. Soft and round yet with good concentration of fruit and some firm tannin.
Grilled or barbecued steaks, chops

Santa Carolina Cabernet Sauvignon Reservado 94
TDL ®

Full-bodied red

Attractive soft fruits on the

nose; a full-bodied, well-balanced wine with concentrated berry fruit flavours and a dry finish. Very good value.
Grilled meats, lamb, beef etc with fruit-type garnishes or glazed duck

Santa Carolina Reservado Merlot 96
TDL ®

Medium-bodied red, fruit-driven, tannic

Ripe fruit, a touch baked on the nose. Dry, with quite crisp acidity, balanced tannin and peppery fruit. Relatively short finish.
Baked or grilled tuna

Santa Helena 'Siglo di Oro' Merlot 96
Greenhills ®

Medium-bodied red

Green pepper and a touch of smokiness on the nose. More fruit on the palate: concentrated red fruits with a firm structure in the background. Well-balanced.
Mixed grills, marinated chicken

Santa Helena Selección del Directorio Cabernet Sauvignon Curicó 96
Greenhills ££

Full-bodied red, fruit-driven, tannic

Blackcurrants with a touch of sweet pepper on the nose. Nice balance of ripe tannin and crushed blackberry flavours with a long, long finish.
Especially good with lamb with herbs and peppers or with a rack of lamb with a mustard and herb crust

Tesco's Chilean Cabernet Sauvignon Reserve 96
Quinnsworth ®

Full-bodied red

Rich cassis nose. Nice concentration of ripe spicy fruit on the palate with a touch of mint. Warm and spicy in the finish.
Fillet of beef with a mustard crust or lamb with herb coating

Undurraga Cabernet Sauvignon 95
United Beverages ®

Medium-bodied red, fruit-driven, tannic

Lovely ripe, rich blackcurrant aromas. Full and rich with rather delicious fruit, balanced tannin and a long finish.
Nut roast or lentil pie or stew

Red £8 - £10

Caliterra Reserva Cabernet Sauvignon 96
Febvre ☆

Full-bodied red

Mint, creamy oak and blackcurrant all in harmony to give an inviting nose. Loads of minty, spicy ripe fruit—really mouthfilling with uplifting oak influence. Mellow and full with a very long finish.
Roast lamb or lamb couscous; casserole of meat and dried fruits

Carmen Cabernet Sauvignon Reserve 96
Dillon ☆

Medium to full-bodied red

Ripe cassis aromas with a youthful hint of raspberry.

Plenty of fruit on the palate with hints of plumminess to come.
Red meats, especially beef fillet, and lighter game

Concha y Toro Marqués de Casa Concha Maipo Valley Cabernet Sauvignon 96
Findlater ☆

Full-bodied red, fruit-driven, tannic

Nice complexity on the nose with dark autumn fruits, smoky cedarwood and spice. Firm tannin with luscious blackcurrant fruit underneath. Mouthfilling and long.
Beef in pastry or roast pheasant; good wine and lamb casserole

Santa Rita Medalla Real Cabernet Sauvignon Special Reserve 95
Gilbeys ☆ ☆

Full-bodied red, tannic

Smoky, spicy aromas mix with brambly fruit. Complex well-integrated flavours of baked fruit and earthy spice which linger in the finish. Should age well over one to two years.
Lamb casserole, lamb or duck with shallots or other strong flavours

Santa Rita Reserva Merlot 96
Gilbeys ®

Medium-bodied red, fruit-driven

Lovely ripe soft fruit on the nose. Ripe soft fruit on the palate with good structure and balance.
Lamb or calves' liver especially with a trendy sweet-sour accompaniment

Red £10 - £12

Errázuriz Cabernet Sauvignon Reserva 96
Allied Drinks

Medium-bodied red, fruit-driven, tannic

Quite a complex nose with spicy richness behind ripe berry fruit. Full and round with ripe fruit and firm, though balanced, tannin. Long, richly fruity finish.
Meat dishes, especially beef en croûte

Red £12 - £15

Santa Carolina Reserva de Familia Cabernet Sauvignon 93
TDL ®

Medium-bodied red, fruit-driven, tannic

Fruit of the forest comes through on the nose. The flavours are mellow and attractive with balancing tannins and a long, warm, rich finish.
Shoulder of lamb filled with apricots; noisettes

Red £15 - £20

Santa Rita Casa Real Cabernet Sauvignon 95
Gilbeys ☆ ☆

Full-bodied red, tannic

Intense aromas of blackcurrant and spices. Delicious weight of ripe autumn fruit well supported by tannins and alcohol with good length to the finish. A lovely expensive treat.
Roast lamb or duck at a special diinner party

France

A Touch of Magic–some memorable wines

Sometimes a wine is special—everything seems to have come together at this particular time. These are on the expensive side, but they provide that inexplicable magic of a lovely wine.

Ch. Ségur de Cabanac AC St Estèphe cru bourgeois 93 (France-Bordeaux)
Ch. Tertre Rôteboeuf AC St Emilion Grand Cru 94 (France-Bordeaux)
Baron de Chirel DOC Rioja Reserva 92 (Spain)
Antinori Tignanello VdT Tuscana 94 (Italy)
AC Vosne-Romanée 1er Cru 'Les Beau-Monts' *Dom. Daniel Rion et Fils* 92 (France-Burgundy)
Billecart Salmon Cuvée Nicholas Francois Billecart Brut 90 Champagne (Sparkling-France)

Alsace

Alsace is probably the most consumer-friendly of French regions with varietal labelling applied simply to AC Alsace or AC Alsace Grand Cru. It is also the most sadly neglected by the vast majority of consumers. The explanation seems to lie in confusion with German wines which are similar only in grape varieties. The wines of Alsace are dry, strong and very much intended for food.

This province is unique in French winemaking. Predominantly white wine is produced made from a small range of intensely aromatic grape varieties. Riesling is relatively full with high acidity and an ability to age, Tokay Pinot Gris is rich with plenty of weight, while Pinot Blanc in a ripe year can be subtle and elegant. Most famous of all, Gewürztramminer is intensely perfumed, spicy and exotic with lots of heady fruit.

Although the appellation is blissfully easy, as in Burgundy it is the maker who makes the difference. The best guarantee of quality is a known producer. Most are negociants, though the number of domaines—and negociant holdings—is increasing.

White £6 - £8

Cave de Turckheim Pinot Blanc AC Alsace 95
Brangan   ®
Light dry white

Clean and appley on the nose. Apple-type fruit flavours with minerally quality in the finish. Balanced and easy-drinking.
Quiche or omelette or light cheese soufflé

Sipp Mack Pinot Blanc AC Alsace 96
Mitchell   ££
Light dry white

Elegant nose—a very nice wine with lovely balance of refreshing acidity and ripe, weighty fruit.
Excellent aperitif and good with light dishes such as salade composée and savoury tartlets

Sipp Mack Riesling AC Alsace 96
Mitchell   ©
Aromatic white, classic

Intense nose of floral fruit and oily. petrol tones just beginning to show. Fine, lively fruit with racy acidity and good weight of long elegant floral, green fruit flavour.
Richly cooked, fish, poultry and

game; chicken in white wine and cream, pheasant with grapes or cold stuffed pheasant or duck

Tesco's Alsace Gewürztraminer AC Alsace 96

Quinnsworth ®

Aromatic white, classic

Perfumed floral aromas of rose petals and ginger. Dry with ripe, exotic fruit flavours. Well-balanced with fresh acidity.

Spicy foods, especially Chinese or red pepper salad

White £8 - £10

Alsace Willm Gewürztraminer AC Alsace 97

Allied Drinks ®

Aromatic white, classic

Flowery Turkish Delight on the nose. Plenty of fruit, fairly low acidity. Good finish.

Good on its own or with canapés of smoked salmon and horseradish

Cave Vinicole de Turckheim Muscat Réserve AC Alsace 97

Brangan ®

Aromatic white, classic

Very grapey aromas. Dry, with nice weight of grapey fruit and a touch of ginger. Fresh and quite long.

Asparagus salad or other light or fruity salads

Cave Vinicole de Turckheim Riesling Réserve AC Alsace 96

Brangan ®

Aromatic white, classic

Maturing bouquet of ripe lemons with a whiff of petrol.

Lively acidity running through minerally fruit to a dry finish.

Crab gratin or creamy quiche

Hugel Riesling AC Alsace 94

Grants ©

Aromatic white, classic

Floral aromas just beginning to show a touch of petrol as the wine matures. Lovely balance of ripe fruit and clean, mineral tones, apple blossom meets flint! Long, lingering finish.

Rich creamy pastries, poached or baked fish with butter or cream sauce, even warm salad of game; try creamy leek tart, sole with crevettes sauce, goose liver salad

Sipp Mack Tokay Pinot Gris Réserve AC Alsace 96

Mitchell ☆

Full-bodied white

Very big, full-blown style of Pinot Gris with rich, full palate balanced by acidity and great length

Terrific with spicy food, at a Chinese meal or with quail marinated in honey and five spice!

White £10 - £12

Dom. Schlumberger Les Princes Abbés Gewürztraminer AC Alsace 95

Findlater ©

Aromatic white, classic

Complex aromas of fruit and spice. Full and rich on the palate with very good balance.

Hummus, couscous salad or a terrine of sweet red peppers

Dom. Schlumberger Les Princes Abbés Pinot Gris AC Alsace 96

Findlater ☆

Full-bodied white

Quite a complex nose. Rich, full palate with deep fruit and lots of extract perfectly balanced by acidity. Long and lingering finish.

Pork, especially with juniper, mustard or cumin and strangely successful with courgette risotto

Kaefferkopf Riesling AC Alsace 95

Febvre ®

Aromatic white, classic

Fragrant nose with definite hints of petrol showing through, Quite rich but well-balanced. Expensive but good.

Crab gratin or creamy prawn dishes

Trimbach Gewürztraminer AC Alsace 94

Gilbeys ®

Aromatic white

Attractive aromatic nose and lots of fruity flavour on the palate balanced by refreshing acidity. Good finish.

The reliable choice at a Chinese meal— especially with Peking Duck!

Trimbach Pinot Blanc AC Alsace 96

Gilbeys ®

Light dry white

Not too much on the nose but good fruit on the palate balanced by crisp acidity.

Good aperitif and with light fish dishes

White £12 - £15

Sipp Mack Riesling (Rosacker) AC Alsace Grand Cru 96

Mitchell ☆

Aromatic white

Quite complex 'developing' nose with ripe fruit, honey and a touch of kerosene. Intense palate with honeyed, rich fruit and slightly oily mouthfeel balanced by really bracing acidity. A benchmark of the style and will improve.

A wine for rich food, especially fish and shellfish mixtures with classic sauces and with cold, first courses based on game: sole with prawn sauce or fish mousse with lobster sauce, also a rich 'sausage' of pheasant

White £30 - £35

Cuvée Laurence Gewürztraminer Furstentum AC Alsace Grand Cru 96

Febvre ☆ ☆

Aromatic white

Complex aromas of flowers and spices. Great depth of full, rich flavour yet elegant with lovely balance and finesse. Long spicy finish. Quite a treat although at a price.

Rich pâté of duck livers or the Christmas goose; also with smoked salmon for those who like this combination

Red £8 - £10

**Sipp Mack Pinot Noir AC
Alsace 96**

Mitchell ☆

Medium-bodied red

Lovely nose of raspberry and
strawberry fruit, very well-
balanced palate with delicate
yet persistent fruit and nice
elegant structure. A very good
example of Alsace Pinot.

*Textured fish, veal and some pork,
as well as cheese dishes: veal with
Parma ham and mushrooms,
salmon with herbs*

Beaujolais

Beaujolais is essentially a young wine which for years capital-ised on this image with Beaujolais Nouveau, an early release of the new wine in November after the vintage. For years this succeeded in a lot of quick sales for the producers and a lot of lengthy hangovers for consumers. In fact, all regions tend to drink some of the new vintage within the region. The Gamay, the Beaujolais grape, responds better than most to this treat-ment and the idea caught the imagination.

The Beaujolais style comes in part from the grape, and more from maceration carbonique, a special fermentation process designed to release colour and fruit, but not tannin. This method is now almost universal, even among the wines of Beaujolais Villages and the Crus which makes it hard to dis-tinguish one from the other. There is some still traditionally made which can be a revelation, but it did not appear in our tastings.

Straightforward Beaujolais should be drunk as young as possible, preferably within a year of harvest. Beaujolais Vil-lages has a slightly longer life, and the Crus—the designated villages entitled to their own AC are also better with youth on their side. Moulin à Vent keeps best, five years for many, twice that for the best, traditionally-made wines. Fleurie is the most famous while Juliénas and Morgon are also well-known.

Red £6 - £8

AC Beaujolais F. Colin-Barollet 97
Barry & Fitzwilliam ®
Light fruity red
Quite rich berry fruit on the nose; slightly stalky palate with good weight of ripe berry flavours. Lively and fresh.
Sausages, meatballs or steak sandwiches

AC Beaujolais-Villages *Victor Bérard* 96
Greenhills ®
Light fruity red
Quite light raspberry-type fruit on the nose, ripe and assertive. Nicely balanced wine with good intensity of lively cherry and raspberry flavours. Zappy, fresh finish.
Great with chunky home-made sausages or with salami and olives

AC Beaujolais-Villages 'Dom. de Joye' (Louis Tête) 96

Allied Drinks ®

Light fruity red

Light raspberry fruit on the nose; quite ripe and juicy on the palate with a dry background which gives balance.
Salami and charcuterie in general or a vibrant pasta

AC Fleurie Dom. de Montgénas 96

Dunnes Stores ®

Light fruity red

Red fruit and spice aromas; silky palate of ripe berry fruit and spice with a touch of balancing tannin and fresh acidity. Good length in the finish and well-priced for the region.
Spicy sausages or Peking duck

AC Moulin à Vent 'Le Vivier' Michel Brugne 96

Dunnes Stores ££

Medium-bodied red

Concentrated fruit aromas with a touch of smoke. Rich, ripe fruit with a nice touch of oak, quite firm with very impressive balance of ripe fruit and structure. A nice wine at a very nice price.
Bacon en croûte or ham steaks wIth mustard, tarragon and cream

Red £8 - £10

AC Beaujolais-Villages Edouard Delaunay et ses Fils 97

Brangan ®

Light fruity red

Good concentrated aromas of just-picked berries. Chewy texture with chunky berry fruit—fresh and satisfying right

to the end.
Salami, olives and crusty bread

AC Fleurie Ch. du Chatelard 97

Wines Direct ®

Light fruity red

Lovely fruit aromas with a touch of violet scent. Balanced fruit and ripe, light structure, smooth and polished yet very lively in the mouth. Quite long.
Roasted salmon, also vegetarian dishes especially those containing mushrooms, pulses or nuts

AC Juliénas Roland Thévenin 96

Leinster Merchant Wines ®

Light fruity red

Intense aromas of floral berry fruit with good weight in the mouth. Nicely balanced with smooth elegant structure to support the fruit. Good value in a pricey area.
Spatchcocked poussin or chicken with rich sauces

Red £10 - £12

AC Beaujolais-Villages Paul Sapin 97

Febvre ®

Light fruity red

A floral influence adds interest to the nose. Smooth, well-balanced palate with good, lively, ripe berry fruit and nice length in the finish.
Kidneys with mustard; cold chicken on a picnic

AC Fleurie Joseph Drouhin 97

Gilbeys ©

Medium-bodied red

Intense and attractive fruit of the forest aromas with lovely balance between ripe summer fruit, soft ripe tannins and crisp acidity. Smooth and velvety in the mouth with an elegant finish.

Good with charcuterie or rabbit pie

AC Fleurie *Paul Sapin* 97
Febvre   ®

Light fruity red

Cherries and redcurrants on the nose following to the palate which is lovely and ripe with satisfying concentration and refreshing acidity. A bit short in the finish.

ChInese food such as Peking duck or smoked sausages or chicken casserole

AC Fleurie 'Dom. de Poncereau' *Louis Jadot* 96
Grants   ®

Light fruity red

Rich concentrated fruit aromas—stylish Fleurie with smooth, ripe fruit flavours and lingering quite floral finish.

Great with a saddle of rabbit or chicken with red wine and mushrooms

AC Juliénas Ch. d'Envaux *P. Ferraud et Fils* 96
Febvre   ®

Light fruity red

Quite light fruit aromas, red berries with a touch of cherry. Very light and fresh on the palate with racy red fruit flavours. Good with food, but expensive for the style.

Salami or pizza with olives, also good with marinaded chicken

AC Moulin à Vent Ch. des Jacques *Louis Jadot* 96
Grants   ©

Medium-bodied red

Brambly fruit aromas, and good weight of ripe blackberries and plums on the palate. Succulent and quite rich with nice dry finish.

Carpaccio of beef or a roast fillet

Red £12 - £15

AC Fleurie *Edouard Delaunay et ses Fils* 96
Brangan   ®

Light fruity red

Tantalising, concentrated aromas of blackberry and charcoal! Lively and fresh with cherry and blackberry fruit and enough tannin to hold it all together.

Charcuterie or mushroom pie; Chinese-style duck

Fine wines,
individually selected,
direct to you

Wines Direct

'*Paddy Keogh, a wine merchant*
whose very name is a guarantee of quality
and something slightly off the well-trodden path.'
Tom Doorley, The Sunday Tribune magazine.

48 hour nationwide delivery service guaranteed.
Ring today on freephone 1800 579 579 for our brochure.

Discover more about Wines Direct on our website at:
http://www.wines-direct.com/

Taserra Wine Merchants Ltd

Shippers of Fine Wines and Spirits
Hogan House, Grand Canal St., Dublin 2.
Tel: 01-6613022,4900537.   Fax: 01-4904052.

Bordeaux

The top wines of Bordeaux are fast becoming commodities for investment rather than enjoyment. However, these wines make up only a tiny percentage of the overall output of the largest, quality wine-producing region in France. Cru bourgeois and many petits chateaux have benefited from price rises at the top and from improvements in wine-making. Outside the top five first growths, many wines challenge their place in the classification of 1855. Crus bourgeois such as Chateaux d'Angludet, Poujeaux and La Lagune, outclass many classified wines vintage after vintage.

St Emilion and Pomerol are similarly expensive areas which are relatively small and always in demand. The top St Emilions, Ausone, Figeac, Cheval Blanc and the fashionable Pomerols Petrus and Le Pin, continue to rise in price. The wines of Se Emilion and Pomerol have a plummy, fleshy character which is wonderfully appealing and allows them to be drunk much younger than any of the Médoc.

Good lesser wines from this area of Bordeaux are harder to find; with a number of individual exceptions, they are expensive yet ordinary.

The lesser appellations and generic Bordeaux do produce some good wines with classic claret style at a very affordable price. The Côtes de Francs, Fronsac and the Côtes de Castillon are areas to look for value and quality.

Vintage is always important in Bordeaux. After the string of great years at the end of the eighties the nineties started really badly and improved only slowly. 1991 and most of 1992 are long past their best if they ever had a best; some 1993 is still attractive in a light way, 1994 is sturdier and the best wines still need a little time. 1995 is excellent on the whole, the top wines have a long future and the Crus Bourgeois should drink well in the early years of the next century. 1996 is less uniform than 1995, but classic in style and generally sound. 1997 is much less good and reliable in spite of high prices and en primeur marketing.

White Bordeaux has made great strides in recent years. Simple Entre-deux-Mers and AC Bordeaux are fresh, lively, usually Sauvignon-led and good accompaniments to seafood.

A few wines labelled AC Bordeaux are made in a very Graves-like fashion with oak ageing.

Graves itself, and Pessac-Léognan especially, is producing some excellent white wines with ripe fruit, well-judged oak and an ability to age and gain complexity.

White £5 - £6

Calvet Sauvignon AC Bordeaux 96

Grants ®

Aromatic white

Good intensity of gooseberry-type fruit, sharp and lively with crisp acidity. Good example of a well-made white Bordeaux.

Simple shellfish—mussels, cockles—and seafood salads

Ch. Fleur Grandchamps AC Entre-Deux-Mers 97

Quinnsworth ®

Aromatic white

Fresh grassy aromas, slightly catty tones. Lots of gooseberry fruit on the nose with grapefruit acidity and clean finish.

Seafood such as mussels in a stew or gratin

White £6 - £8

Baron Philippe de Rothschild Mouton Cadet AC Bordeaux Sec 96

Findlater ®

Aromatic white

Very ripe fruit aromas and a creamy rich taste with well-balanced acidity and spicy, lengthy finish.

Brill, sole etc served with buttery sauces

Barton & Guestier Fondation 1725 AC Bordeaux 96

Dillon ®

Aromatic white

Subtle green fruit aromas which develop into quite a grassy, lean and green palate. Balanced with a good finish.

Seafood and cheese salads

Calvet Réserve AC Bordeaux 96

Grants ®

Aromatic white

Rather attractive aromas of ripe gooseberries and creamy, ripe flavours with mouthwatering acidity.

Simply cooked fish or warm salads, especially containing cheese

Ch. Boisset 'La Chapelle' AC Entre-Deux-Mers 96

Febvre ®

Aromatic white

Melon and gooseberry with a touch of peardrops on the nose. Good weight of green fruits with mouthwatering acidity. A touch soft in the finish.

Mixed fish and shellfish salad

Ch. Lamothe de Haux AC Bordeaux 97

Findlater ®

Aromatic white

Very pleasant style with fairly subtle fruit flavours of tart apples, lemon zest and goose-berries. Well- balanced with some length.

First courses—warm salad, light fish etc

Ch. Tour de Mirambeau AC Bordeaux 97

Wines Direct ®

Aromatic white

Fresh, easy style with opulent ripe fruit and balanced acidity
Refreshing with highly flavoured food, even Thai-style spices

Michel Lynch AC Bordeaux 97

Barry & Fitzwilliam ®

Aromatic white

Aromas of blackcurrant leaves and gooseberry and plenty of ripe fruit flavours. Quite an exuberant style.
Cheesey ravioli, fillets of trout or even smoked trout

White £8 - £10

Ch. Bonnet AC Entre-Deux-Mers 97

Febvre ®

Aromatic white

Nice grassy aromas with hints of elderflowers. Weight of fruit on the palate—ripe apple, gooseberry and greengae. Crisp acidity and long finish.
Mussels or oysters and most seafoods

Ch. Thieuley AC Bordeaux 95

TDL ®

Aromatic white

Fresh, clean, slightly floral aromas and similar palate with some gooseberry fruit flavours, a bit of weight and a nice finish.
Escalopes of chicken or turkey; salmon cutlets

White £10 - £12

Ch. Thieuley Cuvée 'Francis Courselle' AC Bordeaux 95

Wines Direct/TDL ®

Aromatic white

Well-rounded with quite a good weight of rather honeyed fruit; slightly oily with medium length in the finish.
Sauced fish or pork and mustard

White £12 - £15

Ch. Olivier AC Pessac-Léognan 94 Grand Cru

Brangan ®

Full-bodied white

Lots of tropical fruit with a touch of vanilla on the nose. Ripe attack with broad, oaky, fruit flavours and balancing acidity. Crisp, spicy finish.
Mussels in a curry cream or spicy fish; chicken with mustard

White £15 - £20

Ch. Bouscaut AC Pessac-Léognan 94 Grand Cru

Febvre ☆

Full-bodied white

Complex nose of apricots and tropical fruit. Beautifully balanced with ripe fruit, oak and fresh acidity. Rich butter-scotch flavours develop. Long finish.
Salmon en croûte with a rich sauce or chicken in saffron

White £25 - £30

Ch. Carbonnieux AC Pessac-Léognan 96 Grand Cru

Mitchell ☆ ☆

Full-bodied white

Quite subtle on the nose with

complex mix of good berry fruit and spicy oak. Quite young on the palate yet complex layers of flavour in a tight structure. Excellent weight of ripe fruit. Delicious, expensive wine.

Roast veal or glazed quail, or chicken with cream and mush-rooms

Red £6 - £8

Baron Philippe de Rothschild Cadet Claret AC Bordeaux 96

Findlater ©

Medium-bodied red

An accessible Bordeaux with a touch of complexity and balanced structure. Great for a Sunday lunch and good value.

A roast or some cold beef

Baron Philippe de Rothschild Mouton Cadet AC Bordeaux 95

Findlater ®

Medium-bodied red

Pleasant, fruity nose. Dry, with soft, blackberry fruit and short finish.

Meat pies, hard cheeses, shepherd's pie

Barton & Guestier AC St-Julien 95

Dillon ©

Medium to full-bodied red, classic, tannic

Lovely cedar and blackcurrant aromas—typical claret. Rich fruit and firm tannin; very well-balanced with a good finish.

Good dinner party wine especially with lamb or guineafowl

Calvet Réserve AC Bordeaux 94

Grants ®

Medium-bodied red

Fairly obvious, fruity nose, plenty of raspberry fruit flavours with slightly smoky tones and soft tannin. Easy-drinking.

Lighter meat dishes, ploughman's lunch or meat sandwiches

Ch la Coudraie AC Bordeaux 96

Quinnsworth ®

Medium-bodied red

Quite rich and plummy style with a touch of chocolate on the nose. Ripe up-front blackcurrant fruit with a soft but balanced structure. Easy-drinking and well made.

Roast meat, cutlets or minute steak

Ch. Bertinierie AC 1ères Côtes de Blaye 96

Wines Direct ££

Medium-bodied red

Lovely warm tobacco character on the nose; in fact, colour, fruit and style—it has them all and will be even better in a year's time. The price charms, too.

Irish stew

Ch. de Rabouchet AC Bordeaux Supérieur 95

Jenkinson ®

Medium-bodied red

Classic autumnal nose and good overall fruit, balance and character. A little short but pleasant, easy drinking.

Works well with meat pie or mixed grill

Ch. La Croix de Millorit AC Côte de Bourg 96

Quinnsworth ®

Medium-bodied red, tannic

Deep brambly, plummy aromas.

Ripe juicy attack with firm tannin following. Quite a chewy mid-palate. Chunky—slightly rustic but pleasant.

Mixed grill or chops; lentil and pulse dishes

Ch. le Grand Verdus AC Bordeaux Supérieur 96

Quinnsworth ©

Medium-bodied red, tannic

Quite spicy, stalky nose with ripe blackcurrant aromas. Lively fruit with balanced acidity and tannin. Develops quite rich chocolatey fruit with a bite of pepper in the finish. Plenty of interest for the price.

Cold beef or a navarin of lamb

Ch. le Menaudat AC Premières Côtes de Blaye 95

Searson ££

Medium-bodied red

A great rustic farmyard nose with plenty of fruit and good weight. For the price it's a winner.

Cold beef or mild to medium hard cheeses

Les Douelles AC Bordeaux 96

Allied Drinks ®

Medium-bodied red

Ripe fruit aromas, soft easy palate with ripe flavours. Well-balanced.

Light meat dishes, pies etc; good with lunchtime food

Michel Lynch AC Bordeaux 95

Barry & Fitzwilliam ®

Medium-bodied red

Well-made with good ripe fruit on the nose and palate. Approachable and true to style at a friendly price.

Medallions of lamb or a stuffed shoulder of lamb

MITCHELL AND SON

Claret 1995

BORDEAUX SUPÉRIEUR
APPELLATION BORDEAUX SUPÉRIEUR CONTRÔLÉE

12% alc./vol. 75cl.
PRODUCE OF FRANCE

Mis en bouteille pour Mitchell and Son, Dublin, par P. A. Sichel, à F 33270, Bordeaux, France

Mitchell and Son Claret AC Bordeaux Supérieur 95

Mitchell ®

Medium-bodied red, tannic

Ripe, soft fruit aromas with similar berry fruit flavours. Soft tannin and nice finish.

Cold roast meat, pies and grills

Premier de Lichine Claret AC Bordeaux Supérieur 96

Greenhills ®

Medium-bodied red

Ribena-type aromas with a touch of spice. Blackberry and blackcurrant fruit flavours. Pleasant, slightly short finish.

Lighter meat dishes, ham, even mild spices

Tesco's Medoc AC Médoc nv

Quinnsworth ®

Medium-bodied red, tannic

Typical stalky claret nose with ripe fruit aromas. Ripe blackcurrant and plums with nicely balanced acidity and tannin. Clean dry finish.

Roast meat—a real Sunday lunch wine

Red £8 - £10

Baron Philippe de Rothschild AC St-Émilion 96

Findlater ℞

Full-bodied red

Ripe berry fruit aromas with stalky savoury tones. Rich and fleshy, very forward style with redcurrrant jelly and plum flavours. Soft but well-balanced. Well-made with nice easy style.

Roast turkey or roast beef; chicken and wine casserole

Barton & Guestier AC St-Émilion 95

Dillon ℞

Medium-bodied red

Slightly slow nose—mainly stalky, savoury red fruit aromas. Quite plummy, satisfying mouthful with balancing tannins.

Chicken casserole or Christmas turkey

Ch. Moulin Haut Villar AC Fronsac 94

Quinnsworth ℞

Medium-bodied red

Earthy and quite developed on the nose. Slightly under-ripe character to the fruit, earthy and quite typical of Fronsac. Balanced and quite interesting.

Lamb boulanger or casseroled or pot roast guineafowl

Ch. Boisset 'La Chapelle' AC Bordeaux 96

Febvre ℞

Medium-bodied red

Fruit to the fore for an easy, soft, juicy-style Bordeaux with no great depth but a nice wine.

Grilled lamb chops or a plate of cold meats

Ch. Cadillac Lesgourgues AC Bordeaux Supérieur 95

Mitchell ☆☆

Medium to full-bodied red, classic

Lovely, typical claret nose: ripe fruit with a touch of wood. Rich and full on the palate with deep spicy fruit and good length.

Classically cooked meat such as beef Wellington or rack of lamb

Ch. Charron AC Premières Côtes de Blaye 94

Febvre ℞

Medium-bodied red

Smoky, vegetal nose, perhaps not everyone's favourite but plenty of character, Well-made and rounded on the palate with warm plummy fruit and some length.

Beef and mushrooms or a lamb casserole

Ch. Côte Montepezat AC Côtes de Castillon 96

Quinnsworth ℞

Medium-bodied red, tannic

Quite attractive nose with savoury fruit character and spicy, plummy fruit. Ripe and easy-drinking with direct soft fruit flavour and nice bite of tannin. Slightly lean and stalky in the finish.

Casserole, spaghetti bolognese, shepherd's pie and other mixed meat dishes

Ch. Faizeau AC Montagne St-Émilion 94

Wines Direct ©

Medium-bodied red, tannic

Lovely jammy fruits on the nose; rich and rounded with

notable smokiness in the background. Soft, ripe tannins. Very good for the vintage and good value.

Fillet of beef with a herb crust or a roast guineafowl

Ch. Haut Bertinerie AC Premières Côtes de Blaye 95

Wines Direct ®

Medium-bodied red

Wonderful nose of sultry black fruit and mocha coffee. Good structure and weight with tarry fruit at the back of the mouth and a long finish; only the price disappoints.

Magret of duck or a casserole of guineafowl; also pheasant with black cherries

Ch. La Prade AC Bordeaux Côtes de Francs 95

Wines Direct ☆

Medium-bodied red, tannic

Inviting nose with plums and spice and a definite hint of chocolate. Plummy, velvety palate with nicely developed fruit and ripe balanced tannins. Well-rounded wine with lots of character.

Fillet steaks with a mushroom or brandy sauce; pheasant and richly cooked poultry

Ch. Méaume AC Bordeaux Supérieur 95

Findlater ®

Medium to full-bodied red, classic, tannic

Berry fruit aromas; ripe soft fruit on the palate with firm tannin and well-balanced structure.

Casseroles or sauced meat dishes

Ch. Rocher Lideyre AC Côtes de Castillon 94

Gilbeys ®

Medium-bodied red

Rich aromas of spicy cedarwood. Still a bit closed on the palate but promises well.

Steaks served with wine or cream sauce or with beef strogonoff

Ch. Thieuley AC Bordeaux 96

TDL ®

Medium-bodied red

Stylish, easy-drinking, no great complexity. Nicely balanced fruit and soft tannin. Good for a party.

Enough fruit for a not-too-spicy stir-fry or a creative, meat-based pasta; good party wine

Chai de Bordes AC Bordeaux 96

Brangan ®

Medium-bodied red

Ripe fruity nose; dry with a soft bite of tannin, medium body and quite subtle fruit. Balanced and quite long.

Roast meats, meat pies and similar savoury foods

Red £10 - £12

Ch. de Gironville AC Haut-Médoc 95

Findlater ®

Medium-bodied red, classic, tannic

Some complexity shows on the nose. Silky smooth with lovely ripe fruit and friendly tannins. A nice wine, though one taster thought it overpriced.

Magret of duck with a fruit-based sauce—apple or blackcurrant.

Ch. de Terrefort-Quancard AC Bordeaux Supérieur 95

Brangan ®

Medium-bodied red, tannic

Deep, ripe fruit aromas, spicy and inviting. Lots of berries and spicy flavours on the nose, good bite of tannin and long, spicy finish.

Casserole of beef or lamb or grilled meat

Ch. du Vieux Moulin AC Montagne St-Émilion 96

Brangan ®

Medium-bodied red

Ripe and plummy. Slightly stalky fruit character with a spicy edge. Fruit flavour carries through nicely to the end.

Roast meats, turkey etc; chicken casserole or monkfish in red wine

Ch. L'Annonciation AC St-Émilion 97

Brangan ®

Medium-bodied red

Mellow autumn fruit aromas with hints of violets and fruitcake richness. Dry and nicely balanced with reasonable concentration and length.

Chicken and mushrooms; medallions of beef

Ch. La Fleur St Georges AC Lalande de Pomerol 96

Wines Direct ®

Full-bodied red, tannic

Really delivers on the palate though the nose needs a bit of coaxing. Plenty of deep fruit flavours, well-rounded and balanced by ripe but firm tannin. Beginning to show a rich chocolatey side. Good weight of flavour which lasts through a long finish.

Pork with prunes or lamb chops or steaks; also côte de boeuf

Ch. Magnol AC Haut-Médoc 95 Cru Bourgeois

Dillon ®

Full-bodied red, classic, tannic

Red and blackcurrant fruit with vegetal aromas on the nose. Rather hard palate at the moment with youthful tannins dominating the fruit.

A good casserole or even confit of duck would soften the tannins

Ch. Peychaud AC Côtes de Bourg 95

Febvre ®

Medium-bodied red

Especially attractive on the nose with damson fruit and cedarwood aromas. Similar marriage of ripe fruit and wood makes a big, rather delicious mouthful.

Butterfly leg of lamb, roasted or barbecued with herbs and garlic

Red £12 - £15

Ch. Duplessis AC Moulis-en-Médoc 94 Cru Bourgeois

Febvre ©

Full-bodied red, tannic

Quite spicy cigar box aromas with ripe blackcurrant and blackberry fruit underneath. Ripe, mouthfilling fruit with attractive spicy overtones. The tannins are quite firm and the finish is long and dry. A good '94.

Roast leg of pork with its own jus; lamb fillet in a garlic crust; guineafowl

Ch. Tour du Haut-Moulin AC Haut-Médoc 93 Cru Bourgeois

Wines Direct ®

Full-bodied red, classic

Attractive ripe blackcurrant nose, well balanced fruit, refreshing acidity and good finish.

Hot pot or stew or cold meats

Frank Phélan AC St-Éstephe 93

Barry & Fitzwilliam ©

Full-bodied red, classic

Restrained rather blackberry fruit on the nose and tightly-knit palate of blackberry fruit and spicy pepper. Needs to be opened ahead of drinking and should develop further over a year or so. Good value for quite a classic style.

Meat, especially lamb with mushrooms

Red £15 - £20

Ch. de France AC Pessac-Léognan 95

Jenkinson ®

Full-bodied red, classic

Intriguingly complex on the nose with deep, rather gamey fruit. The palate needs more time—two to three years—for the generous fruit to show through.

Steak and kidney pie

Ch. Franc Pipeau AC St-Émilion Grand Cru 95

Brangan ®

Full-bodied red

Ripe and plummy with a spicy edge of tobacco. Mouthwatering spicy, slightly earthy fruit

with undertones of vanilla. Complexity of flavour lasts right through the finish.

Guineafowl or roast pheasant; fillet of beef

Ch. Ségur de Cabanac AC St-Estèphe cru bourgeois 93

Brangan ☆ ☆

Full-bodied red, tannic

Lovely nose of blackcurrant fruit and wild herbs—very appealing. Loads of plummy, blackcurrant fruit with elegant spice and smoky tones. Firm but ripe tannins add the perfect frame. Beautifully balanced and long with that magical something extra.

Roast or rack of lamb; venison

Red £20 - £25

Ch. Roc de Cambes AC Côtes de Bourg 94

Wines Direct ®

Medium-bodied red, classic

Fruit aromas with a touch of toffee Lovely rich ripe flavours of mint and black cherry. Soft yet well-balanced with a good finish.

Lean, simply cooked meat, especially lamb.

Red £25 - £30

Ch. Carbonnieux AC Pessac-Léognan 95 Grand Cru

Mitchell ☆

Full-bodied red, classic

A heady melange of aromas and similar complexity on the palate with subtle fruit and elegant silky smooth structure. Should develop further over three to four years.

Roast pheasant or leg of lamb

Ch. Lascombes AC Margaux 94 Grand Cru Classé

Greenhills ☆ ☆

Full-bodied red, tannic

Lovely fragrant Margaux nose with cedar, cigar and spice mingling with ripe fruit. Delicious attack of ripe forward fruit in good weight with plenty of intensity. Tannins are already balanced. Drinking now but should hold well in the short term.

Magret of duck with a wine or shallot sauce; also good with rack or saddle of lamb or noisettes with herbs

Ch. Malescot St Exupery AC Margaux 93 Grand Cru Classé

Febvre ©

Full-bodied red, tannic

Nose shows some development of spicy, even slightly earthy character. Ripe blackcurrant and berry fruit on the palate with very firm tannin at present dominating. Beginning to develop but with a long way to go. Potentially very good.

To drink now try the slightly softening effects of rare beef or goose

➡ *For details of what the symbols ® and ©, etc., mean, see pages 34-5*

➡ *wines styles are explained on pages 8–9*

La Réserve du General AC Margaux 95

Mitchell ®

Full-bodied red, tannic

Quite ripe, scented nose with a touch of cigar and spice. Very full, rich, fruit attack, spicy plums and ripe blackcurrants. Really firm tannin at present dominates but lots to come. A good keeper.

Roast duck or goose or leg of lamb

Red £30 - £35

Ch. Tertre Rôteboeuf AC St-Émilion Grand Cru Classé 94

Wines Direct ☆ ☆ ☆

Full-bodied red, tannic

Very rich, chocolatey nose with meaty aromas beginning to show. Lovely plumminess comes through with layers of spice and chocolate. The weight of fruit balances the structure of ripe tannin and acidity. A real beauty to drink now and onwards.

Pheasant cooked with mushrooms or perfectly roasted beef; or simply a fine Camembert

Rosé £6 - £8

Ch. Thieuley AC Bordeaux Clairet 97

TDL/Wines Direct ®

Slightly stalky nose, red fruits with a touch of spice. Dry, with good weight of berry fruit. Balanced and refreshing.

Nice with a chunky terrine or cured meats in general

Burgundy

Burgundy extends from Chablis in the north, along the Côte d'Or and finally into Mâcon. It is unique in having both red and white wine of equal importance. Compared with Bordeaux as it invariably is, the area is small, but the only common factor is a high price.

Burgundy is a frustrating maze of good and bad. White wines are a marginally easier proposition than red. Chablis has changed in style in recent years and really steely, bone-dry examples are hard to find. Less expensive Chablis can be quite soft with ripe fruit and balancing acidity.

At their best the white wines of the Côte de Beaune are gloriously full, layered and complex with subtle variations from the different villages. Further south in the Côte Chalonnaise and ultimately in Mâcon the wines become softer and rounded, with warmer fruit and less power. The use of oak has improved in Côte Chalonnaise wines, and the villages of Mâcon–Viré, Clessé etc. provide whatever value there is in Burgundy from the best producers.

Red Burgundy is an even trickier matter. The Pinot Noir grape, added to the Burgundian appellation system, in which different wines can effectively share one name, leads to very erratic quality. There is plenty of adequate, pretty well-made Bourgogne around, the problem is that it is too expensive for what it offers.

Red Burgundy at its best is matchless in intensity of flavour and elegance of structure. At this level it is good value set against the cost of a similar wine in Bordeaux. A few of the wines tasted for the guide did come up to this level and proved the point that the lower rungs of Burgundy, the broad ACs and most of the Village wines, are simply expensive bad value.

White £5-£6

AC Bourgogne Blanc Tesco's Burgundy nv
Quinnsworth ®
Full-bodied white
Lemon and wet wool on the nose. Dry with apple and pear flavours, some buttery overtones with fresh tingling finish.
Omelette or seafood chowder

White £6-£8

AC Mâcon Lugny *Victor Bérard* 96
Greenhills   ®

Full-bodied white

Quite complex, nutty aromas. Full and well-rounded with ripe dessert apple fruit and a touch of pepper.
Fish in a relatively rich sauce—cream, cheese—especially hake, brill and haddock

AC Mâcon Blanc Villages 'Les Jumelles' *F. Chauvenet* 97
United Beverages   ®

Full-bodied white

Attractive peach and apricot aromas signal a well-made, balanced Mâcon with a good weight of ripe fruit. Good value too.
Ceamy pasta or chicken dishes

AC Rully *Charles Viénot* 96
Superquinn   ®

Full-bodied white

Ripe, slightly oily fruit with subtle fennel and spring flower overtones. Buttery melon-type fruit of reasonable intensity. Well-balanced with some length.
Chicken pie or a rich fish soufflé; ray and black butter

White £8-£10

AC Bourgogne Aligoté Bouzeron *Bouchard Père et Fils Ancien Domaine Carnot* 96
Findlater   ®

Medium-bodied white

Light bouquet. Dry with juicy grapefruit flavour and nicely balanced acidity. Well made.
Light fish and chicken dishes

AC Chablis *Pierre Ponnelle* 96
Dunnes Stores   ®

Medium-bodied white

Good fruit, body and finish. Quite a depth of fruit with youthful freshness. Well made.
Shellfish

AC Chablis *Dom. Grand Roche* 96
Wines Direct   ©

Full-bodied white

Floral and mineral aromas with crisp palate of earthy fruit flavours and a dash of lemon and lime. Young with quite a long finish.
Especially good with deep-fried fish and vegetables

AC Chablis *F. Chauvenet* 96
United Beverages   ®

Full-bodied white

Subdued aromas of damp wool and Granny Smith apples. Dry, with a broad band of minerally fruit and crisp acidity. Well balanced with a good finish.
Seafood, especially oysters; crisp, elegant fishcakes or a chunky fish terrine

AC Chablis *Charles Viénot* 97
Superquinn   ®

Light dry white

Floral aromatic nose. Dry, even steely, with green fruit flavour and zesty acidity. Good example, quite typical.
Shellfish, especially mussels

AC Mâcon Lugny 'St Pierre' *Bouchard Père et Fils* 96
Findlater   ®

Medium-bodied white

Fresh, rather herbal aromas with a lean taste. Slightly

unusual style but correct and well-balanced.
Lighter fish and fish salads

AC Mâcon-Villages *Laroche* 96
Allied Drinks ££
Medium to full-bodied white
Subtle, buttery nose; nicely balanced in taste with fresh acidity and apple-type fruit. Very good for this price range.
Fish in cream sauce or baked or grilled chicken, also savoury pastries

AC Mâcon-Villages *Edouard Delaunay et ses Fils* 96
Brangan ®
Full-bodied white
Appealing aromas of melon, even a touch of peach. Fresh but rounded with a slightly creamy mouthfeel and decent weight of green apple fruit.
Creamy dishes such as fricassé or veal or chicken hash

AC Mâcon-Villages Dom. de la Condemine Mâcon-Péronne *Veronique et Pierre Janny* 97
Wines Direct ☆
Full-bodied white
Apple blossom and scented melon aromas lead into a palate of honeyed melon and peach fruit with balanced acidity and a twist of spice in the finish.
Chicken or fish kebabs, or monkfish with a ginger and mango sauce

AC Montagny 1er Cru 'La Grande Roche' *Louis Latour* 96
Gilbeys ®
Full-bodied white
A straightforward wine with clean mineral and fruit aromas, dry minerally fruit and good finish.
Fish en croûte or a creamy pasta

AC Pouilly-Fuissé *Pierre Ponnelle* 96
Dunnes Stores ®
Medium-bodied white
Buttery, quite aromatic nose. Plenty of rather loose-knit fruit, balanced acidity and body.
Fish, soufflés, and lighter chicken dishes

AC St-Véran *Dom. Saumaize-Michelin* 96
Wines Direct ©
Full-bodied white
Ripe fruit aromas with a palate of apple and pear, even peach, fruit. Dry in the finish with good length.
Mildly spiced food such as chicken with cumin and walnuts or fish with ginger

AC St-Véran *Joseph Drouhin* 95
Gilbeys ®
Full-bodied white
Rather muted on the nose with well-balanced palate of appley fruit. Dry, clean finish.
First course of fish with herbs or a seafood pasta

AC St-Véran *Domaine (Gilles) Corsin* 96
Burgundy Direct ®
Full-bodied white
Delicate nose, floral aromas of Galia melon. Easy, refreshing style with ripe green fruit and good weight, Rather lactic, yoghurty finish.
Fish in pastry or a creamy gratin or pie

VDQS Sauvignon *William Fèvre* 97

Febvre ®

Aromatic white

Fruity, aromatic nose, a touch grassy. Dry and light with zesty acidity and green fruit flavour. Relatively short.

Seafood salad or deep-fried fish

VDQS Sauvignon de St Bris *Dom. Grand Roche* 96

Wines Direct ©

Aromatic white

Nettles and asparagus on the nose with sherbety background. Lots of fruit flavour develops in the mouth with a long, spicy finish. Impressive.

Goat's cheese or brill and herbs

White £10–£12

AC Chablis *Louis Latour* 95

Gilbeys ©

Full-bodied white

Intense aromas of damp wool and mineral on the nose. Good weight of green apple fruit, well-balanced with a lingering finish.

Seafood or a sharp, densely textured cheese

AC Chablis *Roland Thévenin* 96

Leinster Merchant Wines ®

Full-bodied white, ageing potential

All steel, gunflint and wet wool on the nose not really followed through by a palate of stark grapefruit-type fruit. Rather one-dimensional but still young.

Mussel stew or oysters

AC Chablis Chablis St Martin *Laroche* 96

Allied Drinks ®

Medium-bodied white

Fresh, clean bouquet with good weight of fruit and nice balance. Good finish and with some length.

Shellfish especially

AC Chablis 1er Cru 'Beauregards' *Dom. Grand Roche* 96

Wines Direct ®

Full-bodied white

Meadow flowers dominate the nose. Dry, with balanced acidity and a stoney, mineral character to the fruit. A touch of alcohol in the finish.

Oysters or dishes of mixed fish and seafoods

AC Chablis 1er Cru Côte de Lechet *Pierre Ponnelle* 96

Dunnes Stores ®

Full-bodied white, classic

Generous aromas of buttery, slightly floral fruit. Nice balance of acidity and fruit in the taste. Green apple flavours and creamy texture. Well-rounded with a good finish.

Chicken or simply cooked lobster or turbot

AC Givry *Dom. Joblot* 96

Burgundy Direct ☆

Full-bodied white

Quite complex aromas with oak showing. Ripe fruit with balancing citrus acidity and full mouthfeel. Good, well-sustained finish.

Lobster mayonnaise or baked salmon; roast poussin

AC Marsannay Chardonnay-Musque 'Les Favières' *Dom. Bart* **96**

Wines Direct ®

Full-bodied white

Quite vigorous, floral aromas with lemony fruit. Full, well-rounded palate with balancing citrus fruit acidity. Nice touch of white pepper in the finsih. Good in a rustic style.

Roast chicken or brill in a cream sauce

AC Rully *Joseph Drouhin* **96**

Gilbeys ®

Full-bodied white

Leafy, asparagus aromas. Dry and full-bodied with crisp acidity and refreshing fruit with a touch of honeysuckle.

Asparagus in a rich hollandaise sauce with a few mushrooms

White £12-£15

AC Chablis *Edouard Delaunay et ses Fils* **96**

Brangan ®

Full-bodied white

Very minerally fruit on the nose with light citrus aromas. Quite steely with good, ripe apple fruit and marked acidity giving a clean, classic Chablis finish.

Shellfish such as mussels and oysters

AC Chablis 'Champs Royaux' **William Fèvre 96**

Febvre ®

Full-bodied white

Quite ripe aromas with a hint of meadow blossoms; dry but quite rounded for a Chablis with the typical steely, chalky character just discernible. Crisp acidity with some length.

Well-textured fish like turbot and brill with butter and herb sauces

AC Mâcon Viré *Dom. Emilian Gillet* **95**

Wines Direct ®

Full-bodied white

Complex, mature aromas of dried flowers. Intense flavours of apple and honeydew melon; silky-textured with a honeyed finish. Mature and very drinkable.

Chicken in a wine or Madeira sauce or good old roast chicken

AC Montagny 1er Cru 'Les Burnins' *Ch. de Cary Potet* **96**

Febvre ®

Full-bodied white

Intriguing nose with aromas of baked biscuits. Melon, pear and apple fruit flavour with a streak of zesty lime acidity.

Chicken with cream and courgettes or a rich creamy chicken pie

AC Pouilly-Fuissé *Carbillet de Bellecherre* **96**

Brangan ®

Full-bodied white

Quite lactic, damp wool aromas, slightly nutty too. Good weight of melon-type fruit in a creamy, mouthfilling texture. Dry with a spicy finish of white pepper.

Pasta with Parma ham and mushrooms; grilled fish steaks or baked chicken

AC Pouilly-Fuissé 'Clos de la Roche' *Domaine Sumaize-Michelin* **96**

Wines Direct ®

Full-bodied white

Aromatic nose with lots of green fruit aroma. Well-structured with plenty of ripe fruit with floral shades. Finishes well.

Chicken cooked with white wine, herbs, etc; John Dory

AC St-Romain 'Mon Village'
Roland Thévenin et fils **96**
Leinster Merchant Wines ©
Full-bodied white
Citrus tones with a good dash of
vanilla. Dry and well-structured
with ripe apple fruit and spicy
flavours which linger well in the
finish.
*Classically cooked scallops, John
Dory with a saffron or other cream
sauce or cold salmon*

White £15-£20

**AC Chablis 1er Cru 'Les
Vaillons'**
Allied Drinks ®
Full-bodied white, classic
Restrained, elegant, yet quite
aromatic nose. Nicely balanced
palate. Good structure, honeyed
fruit and crisp acidity.
Shellfish and mixed fish dishes

**AC Chablis 1er Cru 'Monts de
Milieu'** *Dom. de la Meulière* **97**
Febvre ®
Full-bodied white
Restrained aromas with
suggestions of chalk, apple and
lemon peel. Rather shy at first
but nice honeysuckle and apple
fruit flavours slowly emerge. A
touch of almonds in the finish.
Should get better.
*Grilled Dover sole or a plate of
fashionably warm oysters*

**AC Chablis 1er Cru Chablis-
Vaillons** *Ropiteau* **96**
TDL ®
Full-bodied white
Muted on the nose and quite
lean on the palate but with good
concentration in the background. Crisp but not aggressive acidity. Everything in order

for the future.
*A creamy sauce on bream or hake,
especially of a shellfish origin,
would soften the edges of youth*

AC Meursault *Ropiteau* **94**
TDL ®
Full-bodied white
Evolving aromas of buttermilk
and nuts. Full, with a youthful
palate of hazelnuts, brioche,
apple and citrus fruits which
linger on the palate. Should
develop nicely.
*Firm- textured white fish such as
brill or turbot cooked with a butter
sauce, or with lobster; also good
with Brie.*

AC Meursault *Ropiteau* **93**
TDL ©
Medium-bodied red classic
Great ripeness on the nose with
a touch of spice. The palate has
a weight of intensely fruity
flavour, berries, cherries, with
earthy tones just beginning to
show. Quite a stylish wine.
*Poultry, game, fillet of beef and
some offal, cooked with classic
sauces and flavours; try kidneys
and mushrooms or beef with
tarragon*

White £20-£25

AC Meursault *Antonin Rodet* **94**
Febvre ®
Full-bodied white
Still a bit closed on the nose
with dominant aroma of
lemongrass. Dry and crisp with
good concentration of flavours
still sleeping but suggesting
nutty, minerally complexity to
come. One to hold.
*Richly cooked monkfish or chicken
and truffles*

White £25-£30

AC Chablis Grand Cru Ch. Grenouille *Pierre Ponnelle* 92

Dunnes Stores ®

Full-bodied white

Quite mature hazelnut and citrus character on the nose. The palate lives up to the nose with an impressive concentration of mature flavours. Well-balanced with a lingering spicy finish. Drinks well now but will hold a bit more.

Turbot or sole with a rich shellfish sauce

AC Meursault *Edouard Delaunay et ses Fils* 95

Brangan ®

Full-bodied white

Buttery, warm lemon aromas. Similarly broad, buttery palate with dessert apple and lemon fruit flavours. Nice balance of ripeness, butter and refreshing acidity and good length of flavour.

Classic seafood dishes like Coquille St Jacques or turbot with hollandaise sauce; ripe Brie

White £30-£35

AC Puligny-Montrachet 1er Cru Monopole 'Clos de la Mouchère' *Jean Boillot et Fils* 94

Findlater ®

Full-bodied white

Oaky, buttery aromas mingle with apple and melon fruit to give nice complexity. Full, weighty palate with toasty, buttery fruit which is round and mouthfilling. Flavours develop well in the mouth and last through a long, complex finish.

Well-textured fish like monkfish with a cream sauce; roast chicken

Red £5-£6

AC Coteaux du Tricastin 'Lestoulas' *Reine Pedauque* 95

Barry & Fitzwilliam ®

Light fruity red

Slightly stewed fruit on the nose and a touch of damp leaves. Warm, peppery alcohol and nice fruity flavour extending into the finish. Good for a winter party.

Real 'garbage' pizza or robust pasta

Red £6-£8

AC Bourgogne Tesco's Red Burgundy *Louis Josse* 95

Quinnsworth ®

Light fruity red, tannic

Berry fruits on the nose and similar soft fruit flavours; fresh with light tannin and clean fruity finish.

Mushroom pastries or gougère or a fondue

AC Côte de Nuits-Villages *Pierre Ponnelle* 96

Dunnes Stores ®

Medium-bodied red, classic

Open, ripe berrry fruit on the nose; soft and rich fruit palate with balanced acidity. Attractive wine.

Lighter meats and dishes, some fish and mild spices; red mullet and rosemary or chicken dijonnaise

AC Côtes de Beaune Bourgogne *Pierre Ponnelle* 96

Dunnes Stores ☆

Medium-bodied red, classic, tannic

Very appealing summer fruit on the nose with a bit of spice underneath. Beautifully balanced wine with lots of sweet, ripe fruit and savoury earth tones. Refreshing acidity

and silky tannins. Great value.
Poultry, game and beef—pheasant casserole or medallions of beef with mushrooms

Red £8-10

AC Bourgogne Pinot Noir *Louis Latour* 96

Gilbeys ®

Medium-bodied red, classic

Good rich strawberry fruit on the nose; well-balanced: elegant ripe fruit mix with earthy flavours on the palate.
Good strong savoury flavours such as cheese pastries or mushroom pasta

AC Bourgogne Taste-Vinage *Roland Thévenin* 95

Leinster Merchant Wines ®

Medium-bodied red, classic

Nice scented nose of plums and violets. Straightforward Burgundy with good weight of ripe fruit—cherry and red berry flavours in reasonable intensity.
Chicken in a mushroom sauce or a splendid pastry of wood mushrooms

AC Givry *Pierre Ducret* 96

Wines Direct ®

Medium-bodied red, classic

Summer fruit aromas with hints of chocolate. Quite rich fruit nicely balanced by acidity and dryness with a touch of spice in the finish. Good example for the price.
Poultry and game, especially pheasant pie

AC Pommard *Dom. Jacques Thevenot-Machal* 96

Wines Direct ®

Medium-bodied red, classic, tannic

Spicy, smoky aromas mingle with red fruit on the nose. Quite a depth of flavour on the palate with mild tannin and balanced acidity. Good finish.
Sauté of kidneys with brandy or mustard; wild duck or roast ribs of beef

AC Savigny-lès-Beaune 1er Cru Les Lavières *Charles Viénot* 95

Superquinn ®

Medium-bodied red, classic

Really earthy aromas balanced by rich cherry fruit, Dry with reasonable fruit intensity and balance. Some spice in the finish.
Chicken or even a veal chop or red mullet and olives

Red £12-15

AC Chassagne-Montrachet Dom. *Marc Colin et Fils* 96

Burgundy Direct ®

Medium-bodied red, classic

Spicy, slightly vegetal aromas. Rich fruit, well-balanced acidity and smooth tannins. Quite spicy flavours and good dry finish.
Quail, even cooked with Oriental spices, or duck in a fruity sauce

AC Chorey-lès-Beaune *Tollot-Beaut et Fils* 95

Findlater ☆

Medium-bodied red, classic, tannic

Good concentrated, ripe red berry fruit. Firm tannin and

mouthwatering redcurrant fruit flavour. A good wine with lots of potential to age wonderfully well. Excellent value.

Magret of duck or confit of goose

AC Côte de Beaune-Villages *Edouard Delaunay et ses Fils* 95

Brangan

Medium-bodied red, classic

Red berry fruit aromas with a hint of farmyard. Soft and supple with ripe, velvety fruit and balanced acidity. Should gain richness with a few years' ageing.

Poultry in creamy mushroom sauce; chicken Dijonnaise

AC Fixin *Dom. Bart* 95

Wines Direct ®

Medium-bodied red, classic

Very attractive nose of strawberries and plums. Dry with rich dark cherry fruits, fruit compote flavours. Soft with balancing acidity. The taste does not quite live up to the nose but nice for the price.

Duck breast served with wine or shallot sauce; roast turkey

AC Gevrey-Chambertin *Pierre Ponnelle* 94

Dunnes Stores ®

Medium-bodied red, classic

Brambly fruit with vegetal, slightly gamey, overtones. Well-balanced with good weight of ripe fruit with spicy, gamey complexity of flavour. Rather good for the price.

Venison fillet with redcurrant jelly sauce

AC Nuits-St-Georges 1er Cru Les Damodes *Pierre Ponnelle* 95

Dunnes Stores ©

Medium-bodied red, classic

Lovely sweet ripe nose with strawberry and cherry aromas really satin-like palate with layers of fruit and a long lingering finish.

Quite strong flavours in poultry and game dishes; try pheasant pie, chicken with wild mushrooms

Red £15-£20

AC Aloxe-Corton *Dom. Louis Latour* 96

GIlbeys ☆

Medium-bodied red ,classic

Nice complexity on the nose with good rich fruit and savoury, earthy spice. Layered flavours of ripe fruit, earthy complex influences and long elegant finish.

Game: wild duck with wine sauce, grouse with brambles

AC Aloxe-Corton Taste Vinage *Roland Thévenin et Fils* 95

Leinster Merchant Wines ®

Medium-bodied red, classic

A little closed on the nose, spicy red fruits just coming through. Good weight of ripe fruit on the palate, round and quite velvety in spite of its youth.

Milder game like pheasant; fillets of beef with mustard or truffle sauce

AC Mercurey 1er Cru 'Clos L'Evêque' *Edouard Delaunay et ses Fils* **95**

Brangan ®

Medium-bodied red, classic, tannic

Perfumed raspberry and strawberry fruit aromas. Smooth and velvety though with noticeable tannin well-balanced by ripe berry fruit. Opening up nicely with some time to go.

Classically cooked ris de veau; rich mushroom pasta

Red £20-£25

AC Beaune 1er Cru *Edouard Delaunay et ses Fils* **95**

Brangan ®

Medium-bodied red, classic, tannic

Hints of liquorice and bramble on a rather dumb, evolving nose. Firm tannins with raspberry and redcurrant fruit behind. Needs time to show its true colours.

Pheasant or quail with dark winey sauces

AC Beaune 1er Cru 'Les Teurons' *Albert Morot* **93**

Brangan ®

Medium-bodied red, classic

Seductive, ripe raspberry aromas. Powerful, well-integrated attack of raspberry fruit and developing earthy flavours. Nice balancing acidity. Smooth, silky texture and plenty of length. Should gain complexity with age.

Mushroom-stuffed chicken; duck with wine and fruit sauce

AC Beaune 1er Cru 'Clos de la Féguine' *Dom. Jacques Prieur* **94**

Febvre ®

Medium-bodied red, classic

Vegetal, earthy nose with ripe strawberry fruit. Good fruit with quite high acidity and mature spicy character.

Beef en croûte; sauté of beef or even roasted salmon

AC Chambolle-Musigny 'Clos du Village' *Antonin Guyon* **94**

Febvre ©

Medium-bodied red, classic, tannic

Elegant nose with strawberries and spices. Concentrated fruit balances quite obvious youthful tannin. Quite rich, smooth palate with a long spicy finish. Should improve in bottle.

Rich beef casserole especially the traditional boeuf bourgignonne

AC Corton 'Clos du Roi' Grand Cru *Pierre Ponnelle* **93**

Dunnes Stores ☆

Medium-bodied red, classic

complex aromas of spice and fruit with mocha tones. Ripe tannins and a great weight of rich, dark fruit flavour lingering through a long delicious finish.

Game or richer dishes of poultry— wild duck with port, stuffed quail

AC Nuits-St-Georges 1er Cru *Roland Thévenin et Fils* **93**

Leinster Merchant Wines ®

Medium-bodied red, classic

Lovely rich red fruit aromas mingled with spice and gamey tones. Dry with fair weight of ripe fruit developing meaty, rich flavours mid-palate and

finishing with spice. Nice complexity here.
Casseroled guineafowl or pheasant or even richly cooked chicken

Red £25-£30

AC Chambolle-Musigny *Dom. Comte Georges de Vogue* 92
Brangan
Medium-bodied red, classic
Earthy woodland aromas. Silky, supple fruit. Very harmonious and balanced with a long lingering finish.
Truffle-flavoured dishes; poultry and game

AC Gevrey-Chambertin *Edouard Delaunay et ses Fils* 95
Brangan
Medium-bodied red, classic
Raspberry and hazelnut skins on the nose. Quite firm palate with raspberry and strawberry fruit. May improve with time.
Wine-enriched casserole, coq au vin or boeuf bourguignonne

AC Gevrey-Chambertin 1er Cru 'Clos Prieur' *Dom. Rossignol Trapet* 93
Febvre
Medium-bodied red, classic
Real Burgundian nose with earthy vegetal character and rich, sweet fruit. Layers of taste in a velvety texture with a very long, complex finish.
Game, preferably wild duck with a dark, rich sauce

AC Pommard 1er Cru 'Les Epenots' *Antonin Rodet* 94
Febvre
Medium-bodied red, classic
Sweet, gamey, quite developed aromas with hints of violet and black cherry. Rich, slightly chocolatey strawberry fruit with well-balanced structure and nice spice in the finish.
Roast goose or a sirloin of beef

AC Volnay 1er Cru 'Les Fremiets' *Jean Boillot et Fils* 93
Findlater ☆
Medium-bodied red, classic
Lovely nose of ripe strawberries, plums and raspberries with a touch of earthiness. Good concentration on the palate also with underlying savoury edge and elegantly balanced structure. Very long and impressive finish.
Lighter meats, veal, poultry, duck breast and savoury, classic flavours: veal cutlets with mushrooms, quail with mushrooms

Red £30-£35

AC Vosne-Romanée 1er Cru 'Les Beaux-Monts' *Dom. Daniel Rion* et Fils 92
Brangan ☆ ☆
Medium-bodied red, classic
Pronounced bouquet of old wood, brambles and coffee beans. Really harmonious blend of ripe redcurrants and raspberries with a lovely elegant balanced structure. A perfect Burgundy.
Venison and game in general, especially wild duck

Red £35-£40

AC Clos de Vougeot Grand Cru
Roland Thévenin et Fils 95
Leinster Merchant Wines Ⓡ
Medium-bodied red, classic
Very young and rather dumb on
the nose but definite hints of the
quality to come. Very concentrated dark brambly fruit with
other flavours just beginning to
show. Long finish. Drinks well
now but will improve.
*Fillet of beef served rare, medal-
lions of venison or a beef or game
casserole*

Rosé £8-£10

AC Marsannay *Roland
Thévenin 95*
Leinster Merchant Wines Ⓡ
Rosé
Ripe berries on the nose and
lovely strawberry fruit character on the palate. Very dry style
with subtle fruit and clean dry
finish. Well-balanced but
expensive.
*Grilled or cold salmon; spiced
kebabs*

The Loire

A visit to the Loire convinces that the region is full of quality and variety in wine. Back home it is a different story. The Loire is represented by frequently boring Muscadet, and over-priced Sancerre and Pouilly Fumé. Unfortunately, the wines tasted for this year's guide showed much the same problem. There are now some terrific wines being made around Anjou-Saumur, and in lesser appellations. But these seem to be ignored in favour of the well-known names.

On a positive side, however, the quality of Muscadet has certainly improved. There are more true 'sur lie' wines with that essential mix of fruit and yeast and body. Extract and aroma have also improved and wines are really fresh and appetising.

Red Loires are also better represented than in previous years. These are subtle, cool wines with classic, lean stalky fruit, the perfect antidote to the super-rich reds which dominate today's market.

White £5 or less

Le Fontillet AC Muscadet de Sèvre-et-Maine 97
Quinnsworth ℝ

Light dry white

Fresh and clean on the nose with a touch of boiled sweets. Zippy and fresh on the palate. Not a typical Muscadet but a nice glass at the price.
Good party wine or with a light first course salad

Maurice Brunet Chenin VdP du Jardin de la France nv
Barry & Fitzwilliam ℝ

Light dry white

Typical Chenin with good fruit and body. Balanced and fresh in the finish.
Sauced dishes or a fish mousse or pâté

White £5 - £6

Les Saules AC Vouvray 96
Superquinn ℝ

Light fruity white, off dry

Damp wool on the nose, relatively sweet and honeyed with fresh lemony character to balance.
Tangy cheeses or scallops in a rich tomato sauce

Goulaine Chardonnay VdP du Jardin de la France 96
Gilbeys ℝ

Light fruity white

Hints of Chardonnay character on the nose. Nicely balanced fruit and acidity. Fresh, clean and good at the price.
Good at a summer buffet to complement light, cold foods and vegetable and salad flavours

Goulaine Sauvignon VdP du Jardin de la France 96

Gilbeys   ®

Aromatic white

Fresh, aromatic nose with clean, fresh fruit palate, balanced acidity and clean finish. Simple but nice.

Light salads or cheese, vegetables etc or simple fish

White £6 - £8

Dom. du Salvard AC Cheverny 97

Brangan   ®

Aromatic white

Really intense aromas of garden herbs. Very dry and fresh with green apple and lime flavours.

Greek salad or pan-fried fish

Ch. de la Cassemichère AC Muscadet de Sèvre-et-Maine sur lie 96

Grants   ☆

Light dry white

Lovely nose with fruit showing through; nice weight in the mouth with balanced acidity and fruit flavours and good length. A good example of a 'sur lie'.

Enough weight for pasta with clams or mussels, seafood pastries etc

Domain du Ch. de l'Hyvernière AC Muscadet de Sèvre-et-Maine sur lie 96

Allied Drinks   ®

Light dry white

Some fruit aromas. Fresh and clean flavours with light fruit character and crisp acidity.

Seafood in general, fish and seafood salads

La Chatellenie (Joseph Mellot) AC Sancerre 96

Allied Drinks   ®

Aromatic white, classic

Fresh, slightly herbal nose, plenty of green fruit on the palate with fresh acidity. Not a classic but good value Sancerre.

Mixed salade of goat's or feta cheese or simply-cooked river fish

White £8 - £10

Ch. de la Gravelle AC Muscadet de Sèvre-et-Maine sur lie 97

Febvre   ®

Light dry white

Fresh, clean nose with clean, dry palate and crisp acidity. Simple but correct.

Seafood, especially mussels

Dom. Masson-Blondelet Thauvenay AC Sancerre 97

Wines Direct   ©

Aromatic white, classic

Typical gooseberry dominated nose and similar fruit on the palate with nice balance and generous weight of fruit.

Salmon, trout, brill, sole etc; works well with flavoursome saffron or mustard sauces and with stronger cheeses

White £10 - £12

Dom. de Chatenoy AC Menetou-Salon 97

Febvre   ®

Aromatic white, classic

Pronounced gooseberry and grassy aromas; lively palate with a weight of green fruit and balanced acidity.

Fish in cream and herb sauce or goat's cheese croûtons

Dom. Henry Pellé Morogues AC Menetou-Salon 97
Findlater ££

Aromatic white, classic

Clean fresh aromas of green fruit. Lively palate with a lovely depth of flavour and balancing acidity. Long minerally finish.
Well-flavoured fish, especially fish and shellfish mixtures; strong tangy cheeses

Chatelain AC Pouilly-Fumé 96
Findlater ®

Aromatic white, classic

Rather subtle fruit on the nose. Full on the palate with aromatic green fruit really showing through with crisp acidity and quite a long finish.
Rich mousse of salmon; smoked trout

Dom. des Berthiers AC Pouilly-Fumé 96
Allied Drinks ©

Aromatic white, classic

Quite intense aromas of gooseberry fruit . Nice balance of fruit and acidity on the palate—very much as a Pouilly Fume should be and at a reasonable price.
Salmon in pastry or a warm fish mousse or soufflé

Dom. Masson-Blondelet Villa Paulus AC Pouilly-Fumé 97
Wines Direct ®

Aromatic white, classic

Lovely, fresh grassy nose. Quite full on the palate with nice balance of fruit and acidity though one taster found it a bit one-dimensional.
A nice choice for a summer day with baked hake or trout and sorrel, salmon and basil or other fish and herb creations

Clos du Roy AC Sancerre 97
Febvre ®

Aromatic white, classic

Ripe gooseberry and elderflower nose. Very well-balanced and full with lots of green fruit, mouthwatering acidity and long finish.
Grilled goat's cheese, simply cooked river fishes or salmon

Cuvée C.M., Jean Max Roger AC Sancerre 96
Findlater ©

Aromatic white, classic

Subtle, stylish nose and good weight of fresh, appetising fruit. Full, ripe fruit, zippy acidity, creamy and long.
Well-textured fish and rich sauces; cheese soufflé

Dom. du Colombier AC Sancerre 96
Brangan ®

Aromatic white

Lovely aromas of sappy green vegetation and creamy richness. Lime and kiwi flavours dominate the palate, finishing fresh with a slight mineral character.
Goat's cheese; simply cooked river fish

White £15 - £20

Ch. de Tracy AC Pouilly-Fumé 97
Febvre ©

Aromatic white, classic

Punchy Sauvignon aromas

A small excerpt from our cellars,
stocked with the benefit of years
of experience in satisfying
the discerning Irish palate.

Febvre & Company Limited
15-17 Maple Avenue,
Stillorgan Industrial Park,
Stillorgan, Co. Dublin
Tel: (01) 295 9030 Fax: (01) 295 9036

followed by a well-balanced palate with green fruit flavour, crisp acidity and decent, weighty mouthfeel. A nice glass of wine at a price.
Grilled goat's cheese salad and other strong flavours such as spicy scallops or mustard-crusted brill

Prestige du Colombier AC Sancerre 96

Brangan ®

Aromatic white

Slightly earthy asparagus aromas. Lime-fruit acidity lifts with whole palate to a long, lingering gooseberry finish. Expensive but a classic.
Goat's cheese, marinated fish salad or smoked trout

Le Haut Lieu (Sec) AC Vouvray 94

Brangan ®

Aromatic white

Definte lanolin and wet wool aromas. Waxy fruit with lively acidity. Full-bodied and quite austere but very correct.
Rich salmon mousse or river fish in cream sauce

Red £5 or less

Tesco's Gamay AC Touraine nv

Quinnsworth ®

Light fruity red, tannic

Ripe, jammy fruit on the nose; ripe, jammy and soft on the palate, too, with little tannin.
Mushroom pastries or cold meats

Red £8 - £10

Charles Joguet 'Cuvée Terroir' AC Chinon 97

Brangan ©

Light fruity red, tannic

Quite earthy on the nose— raspberries and autumn leaves. Good weight of soft, supple fruit well balanced by acidity and light tannins. Quite long and spicy in the finish.
Charcuterie or mushroom risotto

Dom. Filliatreau AC Saumur-Champigny 96

Searson ☆

Light fruity red

Very enticing nose of deep, ripe, concentrated fruit. Good concentration of spicy dark fruit on the palate, too; violet and floral nuances with slightly earthy touch. Beautiful length of fruit flavour and very lively.
Rack of very young lamb, with herb-flavour souvlaki or chicken with mustard; also good with richer salmon dishes

Justin Monmousseau AC St-Nicholas-de-Bourgueil 95

Febvre ®

Light fruity red

Immediate ripe and intense red berry fruit. Light friendly style with lean fruit—redcurrants, berries—and refreshing lively acidity.
Country pâté or goat's cheese

Red £10 - £12

Charles Joguet Jeunes Vignes AC Chinon 96

Brangan ©

Light fruity red, tannic

Quite pronounced aromas of plum and strawberry with pencil shavings. Good weight of ripe fruit with a savoury, slightly meaty edge balanced with light stalky tannin and

fresh acidity. Long and appetising finish.
Roasted salmon or other firm-textured fish especially with rich flavoursome sauces

Rosé £10 - £12

Charles Joguet Jeunes Vignes AC Chinon 97
Brangan   ®
Rosé

Lively raspberry fruit aromas, slightly stalky. Very fresh with good weight of ripe berry fruit and dry backdrop. Long dry finish—a good rose.
Ratatouille or a chunky terrine

Rosé £21 - £15

Dom. Vacheron AC Sancerre 97
Febvre   ®
Rosé

Racy vegetal aromas—Pinot Noir jumps out. Quite complex with good dry structure and subtle fruit character. Expensive.
Brandade or aïoli, or a carpaccio salad

Party Wines

Wines for party drinking, chosen with an eye on budget. They suit a variety of tastes and work with or without food, and with different flavours.

White
Peter Lehmann Barossa Valley Chenin Blanc 97 (Australia)
Hardys Nottage Hill Riesling 95 (Australia)
Berres Hahnher Bereich Bernkastel 97 (Germany)
Simonsig Adelblanc 98 (South Africa)
San Pedro Chardonnay 97 (Chile)
Ruffino Libaio Chardonnay e Pinot Grigio 96 IGT (Italy)
Red
Cape Indaba Merlot 96 (South Africa)
Concha y Toro Cabernet Sauvignon/Merlot 97 (Chile)
Badia Frasca DOC Montepulciano d'Abruzzo 96 (Italy)
Alto Mesa VR Estramadura 97 (Portugal)
Tsantalis Nemea 94 (Greece)
Agramont Tempranillo DO Navarra 96 (Spain)

The Rhône

The Rhône is really two regions: the north with its great, long-lived Syrah-based reds and rare and exotic white wines of Condrieu, and the more varied South with a mix of grape varieties and spread of red, white, rosé and sweet wines.

In the North, Hermitage, Côte Rotie and Cornas are all longlived potentially great wines; the best are single vineyard versions, from Guigal and Jaboulet in particular, which command a premium.

The best-known wine is Côtes du Rhône which comes from the South and falls into two styles. Basic, cheap Côtes du Rhone is simple and fruity, often made by maceration carbonique to drink young. Other wines are more structured, meaty and full-bodied and generally more expensive. These are traditionally vinified and come from producers such as the Perrin brothers of Beaucastel. The most famous of the Southern Rhône Villages, Châteauneuf-du-Pape, makes rich, full-bodied wines with a character typical of a really hot environment. Recently the style seems to have altered with many producers' wines becoming richer, less structured and certainly less complex.

Other villages, Gigondas, Vacqueras, Rasteau, often produce wines as good as or better than an average Châteauneuf and at a lesser price.

Rhône North

Red £6 - £8

Labouré Roi AC Crozes-Hermitage 96

Quinnsworth ®

Full-bodied red, tannic
Clean fruity nose, ripe fruit on the palate with balanced acidity and soft easy tannins. Some spice in the finish. A pleasant wine.
Meatloaf or pot roast; game pie

Cave de Tain l'Hermitage Les Nobles Rives AC St-Joseph 94

Dunnes Stores ®

Full-bodied red
Quite an earthy, mature nose. Decent weight of fruit in a rather firm structure with fresh acidity and good length.
A wine for winter: warming stews and cassoulet or a home-made meat pie

Red £8 - £10

Roland Thévenin et Fils AC Crozes-Hermitage 95

Leinster Merchant Wines ®

Full-bodied red, tannic

Quite earthy, gamey nose with truffles and smoky bacon aromas adding to the enjoyment. Rich dark fruit with balanced tannin and acidity make for a well-rounded style with nice spicy backdrop and long finish.

Game pie or cold pheasant or guineafowl; also raised pie or beef in wine; sounds like a wine for after a shoot!

Jaboulet 'Les Jalets' AC Crozes-Hermitage 96

Gilbeys ®

Full-bodied red, tannic

Quite a rich nose with ripe fruit, raspberry and forest fruit aromas, touch of meatiness also. Well-balanced palate with quite easy tannins and a good weight of ripe berry fruit. Well made if not profound.

Steak and mushrooms or chunky home-made hamburgers

Red £10 - £12

Les Nobles Rives AC Cornas 93

Dunnes Stores ££

Full-bodied red, tannic

Understated aromas of black cherry and violet; ripe, tarry fruit overshadowed by the tannins which should soften out in time to reveal a lot more. But is there enough fruit ? The price is good so give it time.

For drinking now venison steaks or rare roast beef would be good for the tannins or try smoky roasted aubergines

Les Launes AC Crozes-Hermitage 94

Febvre ☆

Full-bodied red, tannic

Warm, quite plummy, fruit aromas mixed with smoky, truffley scents. A good weight of currant fruit balances the firm but ripe tannins and mouthwatering acidty. Finishes with a long spicy aftertaste.

A big wine needs hearty food such as game, especially braised pheasant or beef casserole

Red £12 - £15

J. Vidal-Fleury AC Crozes-Hermitage 94

Fitzgerald ®

Full-bodied red, tannic

Youthful blackcurrant and bramble aromas. Lean but well-concentrated fruit on the palate with very firm young tannins and marked acidity. Potentially very good but pricey and you will have to wait.

At present needs robust food to tame the tannins: rare meat or a hearty casserole should do the trick

Dom. de Thalabert AC Crozes-Hermitage 92

Gilbeys ®

Full-bodied red

Attractive quite complex nose with blackberries and currants mixed with earthier tones. Very firm palate but with plenty of dark berry and blackcurrant fruit, full body and a long finish. A good if expensive Crozes.

Winter dinner party of pheasant or venison casserole

Les Noble Rives AC Hermitage 92

Dunnes Stores ®

Full-bodied red, tannic

Blackberry aromas and slightly gamey nuances starting to show. Well-concentrated dark fruits with firm tannins give quite a chewy, young wine which is big and flavoursome with a long finish. Needs time.

Warming winter fare especially venison casserole

Red £15 - 20

Chante-Perdrix AC Cornas 92

Febvre ®

Full-bodied red, tannic

Pronounced leathery, cigar box aromas with plenty of dark, inky fruit beneath. Quite intense, rich and spicy on the palate with firm tannin well supported by fruit. A very good wine from '92 which is still young and should develop further.

Roast saddle of venison or pheasant with wine; great with old-fashioned game dishes

Rhône South

White £6-£8

Belleruche AC Côtes du Rhône 97

Grants ®

Full-bodied white

Rather floral aromas; well-balanced, rounded fruit sustained by acidity and alcohol and quite a long finish.

Nice to drink on its own or with delicate fish like salmon or trout or with creamy chicken

Dom. du Vieux Chêne VdP de Vaucluse 97

Brangan ®

Full-bodied white

Slightly nutty, minerally fruit aromas. Dry and fresh—almost herbal and nutty in the finish.

On its own or with salads and light chicken dishes

White £8-£10

Guigal AC Côtes du Rhône 97

United Beverages ©

Full-bodied white

Ripe, aromatic nose: floral, apricot aromas of the Viognier grape. Lovely weight of ripe peach fruit with balanced acidity and a long, lingering finish. Quality shows.

Raw salmon or sushi, or crab

Perrin Réserve AC Côtes du Rhône 96

Allied Drinks ®

Full-bodied white

Quite rich nose with ripe fruit and floral tones. Full-bodied and dry with balanced aromatic

fruit and a twist of pepper in the finish.
Fish stew or scallops in cream

Red £5-£6

Honoré Lavigne Les Capucines AC Côtes du Rhône 97

Greenhills ®

Light fruity red

Bramble fruit on the nose with a touch of black pepper. Nice fruit if somewhat simple. Unpretentious wine, well made and with a good finish.
Sausages, shepherd's pie or lentil lasagne

Red £6-£8

J. Vidal-Fleury AC Côtes du Rhône 95

Fitzgerald ®

Medium-bodied red

Lots of red berry and bramble aromas. Very ripe, pleasing fruit with a nice touch of pepper. Easy-drinking and a good example of the style.
Moussaka or kebabs or a vegetable casserole

Carte Blanche AC Côtes du Rhône 96

Peter Dalton ®

Light fruity red, tannic
Stewed fruit and black pepper on the nose. Dry with quite lively acidity and relatively soft tannin. Ripe brambly fruit with slight vegetal touches. Dry and quite short to finish.
Salami or a spicy bacon, tomato and pepper pasta

Carte Or AC Côtes du Rhône 95

Allied Drinks ®

Medium-bodied red

Ripe, slightly jammy fruit on the nose, firmer on the palate but still the fruity, easy-drinking side of Côtes du Rhône. Generous, if lacking a bit of character.
Meat and tomato casserole or lasagne

Carte Réserve Cave de Rasteau AC Côtes du Rhône 96

Peter Dalton ®

Light fruity red, tannic
Aromas of plums and ripe brambles. Ripe fruit and nicely balanced tannin and acidity. Pleasant fruit flavour carries through the finish.
Chunky terrines or meat loaf and moussaka or stuffed vegetables

Dom. des Trois Oratoires AC Côtes du Rhône 96

Brangan ®

Medium-bodied red

Intriguing smokiness on the nose. Weighty berry fruit with cinnamon and clove; firm structure with a dry, spicy finish.
Cassoulet or casserole; robust meaty foods

Dom. la Tour Saint Remy AC Coteaux du Tricastin 97

Brangan ®

Light fruity red

Spicy, red berry fruit aromas, red cherries with a touch of liquorice on the nose. Young—should open more in six months
Sausages or robust but not spicy pasta or hard cheeses

Dom. Richaud Cairanne AC Côtes du Rhône-Villages 97

Wines Direct ®

Medium-bodied red

Ripe jammy fruit on the nose in

good concentration. Great ripeness on the palate—almost sweet. Relatively soft structure but enough extract to hold it together.

Chicken and pepper casserole or pigeon stuffed with olives

Baron de Beaufis AC Gigondas 95

Superquinn ®

Full-bodied red

Meaty, savoury nose with blackberry fruit and sappy, stalky overtones. Ripe, if slightly vegetal fruit and mellow flavour. Good value food wine.

Rich beef or lamb casserole or venison stew

Red £8-£10

Guigal AC Côtes du Rhône 95

United Beverages ®

Medium-bodied red, tannic

Red berry, redcurrant jelly aromas and fair intensity of fruit on the palate with quite firm tannin and spicy finish.

Beef or lamb steaks, chunky sausages or aubergine gratin

Dom. du Vieux Chêne AC Côtes du Rhône-Villages 96

Brangan ®

Medium-bodied red, tannic

Plums and blackberries with a touch of cloves on the nose. Good concentration of dark cherry fruit offset by firm tannin.

Rabbit stew or sauté pigeon and hearty casseroles in general

Réserve des Voconces Cairanne AC Côtes du Rhône-Villages 95

Molloy's ®

Medium-bodied red, tannic

Spicy, peppery fruit, really warm aromas. Sturdy wine with noticeable tannin and quite marked alcohol. Long, warm finish with the fruit flavour carring through.

Pigeon, casseroles and minced meat dishes

J. Vidal-Fleury AC Vacqueyras 95

Fitzgerald ®

Medium-bodied red, tannic

Quite subtle aromas of black-currant and brambles with an earthy touch. Deep, inky fruit and warming alcohol, firm not aggressive tannin and a pep-pery finish.

Meat casseroles, marinated grill lamb steaks or shepherd's pie

Red £10-£12

Victor Bérard AC Châteauneuf-du-Pape 97

Greenhills ®

Full-bodied red

Brambles and redcurrants dominate the nose with smoky hints and a touch of jam. Easy-drinking style with good fruit flavours, a touch of spice and nice balance.

Lamb and beans or a wine-rich rabbit stew

Labouré Roi AC Châteauneuf-du-Pape 96

Quinnsworth ®

Full-bodied red

Perfumed, slightly gamey nose. Soft fruit flavours and peppery spice; quite intense and well-balanced.

Goose, sausages with lentils or a rich casserole

Coudelet de Beaucastel AC Côtes du Rhône 95

Allied Drinks ®

Medium-bodied red, tannic

Deep, earthy fruit aromas of baked plums and damsons. Generous blackberry and redcurrant-type fruit with firm tannin and spicy flavours underneath emerging in a long finish.

Flavoursome meat casserole or pigeon

Red £12-£15

Ch. St André AC Châteauneuf-du-Pape 96

Febvre ☆

Full-bodied red, tannic

Aromatic dark fruit with a touch of leather and smoke on the nose. Nice balance of ripe fruit and quite firm, though ripe tannins with a kick of alcohol and a spicy backdrop. A nice wine, quite elegant for this far south.

Pheasant or venison casserole

Dom. de Nalys AC Châteauneuf-du-Pape 95

TDL ®

Full-bodied red

Dusky, spicy cigar and tobacco aromas with a touch of white pepper. Plenty of ripe berry fruit in the taste supported by good structure in a well-balanced wine with a long, pleasant finish.

Game pie or casserole of lentils and sausages

Dom. Ste Anne Syrah AC Côtes du Rhône 93

Brangan ☆

Medium-bodied red; tannic

Dense aromas of mulberry and polished wood. Delicious blackberry fruit with ripe, easy tannins. Very vigorous and young for its age—can only get better

Game or steak

Red £15-£20

J. Vidal-Fleury AC Châteauneuf-du-Pape 92

Fitzgerald ®

Full-bodied red

Rich, dried fruit aromas. Concentrated, structured palate with brambly fruit and spicy, slightly gamey flavours coming through.

Game such as pheasant or venison cooked in a casserole or braised

Dom. Duclaux AC Châteauneuf-du-Pape 94

Febvre ☆ ☆

Full-bodied red

Gamey, leathery nose, rich and deep. A big, weighty mouthful with lots of flavour of dark, almost baked, fruits and balancing alcohol and acidity. Long, mellow finish with hints of chocolate.

Venison pie or casserole or pheasant with lentils

Dom. de Montpertuis AC Châteauneuf-du-Pâpe 95

United Beverages ®

Full-bodied red, tannic

Ripe fruit on the nose with herbaceous undertones. Good concentration of ripe fruit and peppery spice, soft ripe tannins and balanced acidity. Long, intense and fruity finish.

Game and goose especially pies and casseroles

The South of France

The South of France, especially the Languedoc-Roussillon area, has been a focus of much improvement and innovation. One of the most significant developments was of the vin de pays wines. This classification, introduced in the 70s to encourage better quality and reduced quantity production, not only raised standards, it gave winemakers more freedom to experiment with grape varieties and consumer-friendly labelling. Skilled young wine-makers were attracted by land prices and the freedom from restrictive AC laws. This brought a wave of new winemaking and serious investment which culminated in the state-of-the-art wineries like Skalli's Fortant and joint French Australian ventures such as Chais Baumière.

The ACs of the Languedoc such as Corbières, Fitou, Faugères are the best sub-zones with individual character and winemaking tradition. They are becoming increasingly important as the quality of wine improves and consciously reflects the area, the terroir from which it comes. They combine the fruit and easy-drinking style of the South with typicité, structure and complexity and are currently great bargains.

While the Languedoc is now well established, the South-West vineyards are just beginning to become popular. This area extends from Bordeaux almost to the Spanish border. Regions such as Bergerac and Montravel are similar in style and grape variety to the wines of Bordeaux. Further south, the wines become more distinctive. There is Cahors made from Malbec and Merlot grapes in different proportions, dark, brambly and full-bodied with a dense structure and earthy character. Madiran is quite tough and austere; made from the Tannat grape it needs a few years in bottle to soften out but is then very rewarding. Jurançon, made near the town of Pau, is made in both dry and sweet versions. The dry wine is round, rich and spicy distinctive and very attractive; the sweet version is luscious and Sauternes-like but with refreshing spice and acidity.

Provence is the remaining South wine region which continues to make better and better red wines almost with each vintage. Bandol has long produced full-bodied, complex and long lived reds, but other areas of the Côte de Provence and the

Coteaux d'Aix have followed and standards are high. Rosé
continues to be made in quantity and greatly for local consumption along the Côte d'Azur. The best are dry and quite
full and blend well with strong food flavours.

Languedoc-Roussillon

White £5-£6

**Alexis L Chardonnay VdP d'Oc
97**

Greenhills   ®

Light fruity white

Ripe fruit flavours, lively acidity
and good weight in the mouth.
*Light dishes, perhaps cold foods
and salads, enough acidity for
mayonnaise*

**Fortant de France Chardonnay
VdP d'Oc 96**

Fitzgerald   ®

Light fruity white

Full-flavoured with ripe melon
and peach-type fruit; quite
honeyed with a touch of white
pepper and refreshing acidity.
*Good for a buffet as this works well
with mixed dishes and lightly
spiced food*

**Hugh Ryman Chardonnay VdP
d'Oc nv**

Quinnsworth   ®

Light fruity white

Rich nose of ripe fruit character.
Apricot and lemon flavours in a
soft, smooth texture. Crisp
finish.
*Chicken and fruit salad or stir-fried
chicken and asparagus*

White £6-£8

**Ch. Viranel AC Coteaux du
Languedoc 97**

Wines Direct   ®

Full-bodied white

Attractive aromas of lime
cordial and sherbet. Warm
alcohol enfolds ripe peach fruit
with a floral touch of rosewater.
Good finish with some length.
Cheese fondue

**DLC Original Chardonnay
VdP d'Oc 95**

Allied Drinks   ®

Full-bodied white

Buttery aromas with lemon,
peach and honey. Dry, with nice
rounded fruit and buttered toast
flavours. Well-balanced and
good value.
Baked or roast cod or an omelette

**DLC Original Sauvignon VdP
d'Oc 96**

Allied Drinks   ®

Aromatic white

Floral and minerally aromas
with a hint of lime. Good
weight with tropical fruit
flavours offset by mouthwatering acidity and long finish.
*Versatile with enough weight for
chicken and meatier fish cooked
with herbs, peppers and other
strong flavours*

Dom. de l'Hortus VdP Val de Montferrand 97

Wines Direct   ®

Aromatic white

Nice balance between crisp acidity and ripe, scented fruit with a rounded, waxy character and fruity finish.
Quite a gentle wine and a good partner for grilled or baked salmon or trout with dill

Dom. Piquemal Muscat Sec VdP Côtes Catalanes 97

Wines Direct   ☆

Aromatic white

Floral nose with rose petals, herbs and lychees. Lots of exciting fruit flavours with cinnamon and white pepper. Complex and interesting.
Oriental dishes and rich pâtés

James Herrick Chardonnay VdP d'Oc 96

Wines Direct   ®

Light fruity white

Rich, soft flavours of ripe tropical fruit balanced by crisp acidity. Plenty of well-sustained flavour.
Brill, hake etc with cream sauce; lighter chicken dishes

La Baume Chardonnay VdP d'Oc 96

Quinnsworth   ®

Light fruity white

Some peach and citrus aromas; lively lemony fruit on the palate with a clean crisp finish.
Spicy satay kebabs or curried seafood

Sauvignon de l'Arjolle VdP des Côtes de Thongue 96

Brangan   ®

Aromatic white

A hint of honey and beeswax with minerally fruit aromas. Lively and crisp with an unusually broad, nutty palate.
Fish and saffron stew or vegetable salads

White £8-£10

Cuvée des Lilas Muscat VdP d'Oc 96

Brangan

Aromatic white

Heady perfume of honeyed fruits and boiled sweets. Dry with lemondrop flavour and honeyed finish. Quite full-bodied.
Chicken and asparagus or pasta with sun-dried tomatoes

White £10-£12

Dom. de l'Arjolle 'Equinoxe' VdP des Côtes de Thongue 96

Brangan

Full-bodied white

Honeyed citrus fruit with spice in the background. Dry and full-bodied with spicy flavours and ripe melon fruit. Quite marked alcohol but balanced by fruit and spice.
Brandade or smoked fish pâté; fish casserole

Red £5 or less

Dom. Bosquet-Canet Cabernet Sauvignon VdP De Sables du Golfe du Lion 96

Superquinn   ££

Medium-bodied red

Good, rather jammy fruit

aromas with slightly herbal twist. Good weight of dark blackcurrant fruit and firm structure. Excellent for the price.
Hamburgers, chops or shepherd's pie

Dom. de Belvize VdP d'Oc nv

Jenkinson ®

Medium-bodied red

Cherry fruit on the nose. Soft, rounded fruit flavours: ripe berries dominate with a slightly spicy finish.
Sausages or a meat pie, or vegetables

J. L. Quinson Cabernet Sauvignon VdP d'Oc nv

Barry & Fitzwilliam ®

Medium-bodied red, fruit-driven

Ripe, dark fruit and boiled sweet aromas with plenty of similar fruit on the palate. Soft and easy-drinking and good for the price.
Hamburgers with mustard or a good club sandwich

Tesco's Cabernet Sauvignon Reserve VdP d'Oc nv

Quinnsworth ®

Medium-bodied red

Ripe juicy berries—raspberry tart aroma. Soft but quite well-balanced with loads of ripe blackcurrant fruit flavour and dry clean finish.
Beef and broccoli stir-fry or spiced kebabs

Tesco's Cahors AC Cahors nv

Quinnsworth ©

Full-bodied red

Earthy nose with beetroot and coughdrop aromas. Quite a complex palate, very typical of the region—dark fruits with gamey nuances. Very long finish. Lots of character and unbelievable value.
Nothing beats cassoulet or confit of duck, but try also a good beef pie

Red £5–£6

Baron Philippe de Rothschild Cabernet Sauvignon VdP d'Oc 96

Findlater ®

Medium-bodied red

Light aromas of blackcurrant leaves and fruit. Simple and well-balanced with lively acidity and nice blackcurrant fruit.
Simply cooked red meats especially lamb

Baron Philippe de Rothschild Merlot VdP d'Oc 96

Findlater ®

Light fruity red

Youthful aromas of ripe plums. Easy-drinking style with nice fruit and good dry balance.
Spicy chicken wings or pizza; good party wine

Ch. la Grave Expression AC Minervois 95

Searson ☆

Medium-bodied red, tannic

Stalky, fresh blackcurrant aromas. Lean but concentrated fruit, plenty of acidity and balanced tannins. Quite chewy and appetising dry finish. Very good value if you like a wine with bite.
Handles the richest of casseroles and robust flavoursome country fare like duck with lentils or chunky sausages

Ch Milhau-Lacugue AC St-Chinian 95

Quinnsworth   ®

Medium-bodied red

Brambles, mint and chocolate—a really southern nose. A weight of rounded, exciting fruit—blackcurrant and plums. Well made and highly drinkable.
Turkey or a casserole of chicken with wine, mushrooms etc

Cuvée Antoine de Montpezad AC Coteaux du Languedoc 95

Dunnes Stores   ®

Light to medium-bodied fruity red

Rich, ripe berries and baked plums on the nose; juicy berry flavours follow. Soft, easy-drinking—good at the price.
Hard and semi-hard cheeses, dry sausages and light casseroles

Dom. Coste Rouge AC Coteaux du Languedoc 95

Dunnes Stores   ®

Light to medium-bodied fruity red

Nice intensity of berry-type fruit with a touch of spice and chocolate. Well-balanced palate, medium weight with refreshing lively fruit. Easy-drinking pleasure.
Casseroles, hard and semi-hard cheeses and sauced poultry

Dom. des Rebouls AC Fitou 95

Dunnes Stores   ®

Light to medium-bodied fruity red, tannic

A rich nose with aromas of plums, cherries and a touch of chocolate. Ripe fruit flavours in an easy-drinking style with balanced acidity and soft tannin. Nice dry finish.
Good savoury wine with meat casseroles, stews and grain-based dishes

Dom. de la Masette VdP de l'Hérault 96

Brangan   ££

Medium-bodied red

Warm, slight tarry, aromas of bramble fruit. Ripe and sweet fruit flavours with firm finish. Easy-drinking.
Casseroles and meat-based pastas; milder spices also work

Dom. Ste Nathalie AC Faugères 95

Dunnes Stores   ®

Light to medium-bodied fruity red

Ripe berry and dark cherry aromas. Soft, with good weight of rather warm fruit.
Kebabs, aubergine dishes and meaty pasta

Fortant de France Cabernet Sauvignon VdP d'Oc 96

Fitzgerald   ®

Medium-bodied red, fruit-driven

Aromatic with cherries and blackcurrant tones. Soft and generous palate with balancing acidity and smooth finish.
Cold meat platters, meat pastries or lamb chops

Fortant de France Merlot VdP d'Oc 96

Fitzgerald   ££

Light fruity red

Attractive raspberry and strawberry fruit with good weight and lively acidity. Well made and good value.

Spicy food such as marinated chicken wings or kebabs

Fox Mountain Syrah/Merlot VdP d'Oc 96

Wines Direct ®

Medium-bodied red

Intense blackberry and plum fruit on the nose with a touch of leather aroma. Fresh and fruity with a direct attack of ripe fruit similar to the nose. Simple, straightforward wine, well-priced.
Liver and bacon or light meat stews

Goûts et Couleurs Cabernet Sauvignon VdP d'Oc 96

Supervalu/Centra ££

Medium-bodied red

The nose is light with just a hint of blackcurrant but this wine delivers on the palate with plenty of stalky blackcurrant fruit and a spicy edge. Appetising stuff with lots of taste at the price!
Red meats in general but especially stews, casseroles and lamb cutlets or medallions with a sauce

Goûts et Couleurs Syrah/ Mourvèdre VdP d'Oc 97

Supervalu/Centra ££

Medium-bodied red

Stalky fruit aromas with earthy, spicy overtones. Lots of peppery fruit on the palate with a firm, well-balanced structure and lovely ripe fruit ending. Plenty of character and very good value.
Meat casserole; sausage and lentils; robust pastas

Hugh Ryman Cabernet Sauvignon VdP d'Oc 96

Quinnsworth ®

Medium-bodied red, tannin

Lots of ripe blackcurrant aromas mix with earthy, even rubbery, tones. Dry with ripe tannin and supple mouthfeel. Rich substantial fruit. A flavoursome wine.
Lasagne or a meat pie or casserole

Hugh Ryman Merlot VdP d'Oc 96

Quinnsworth ®

Medium-bodied red, tannic

Plummy, spicy aromas with hints of dried fruit also. Quite obvious tannin but nicely balanced by weighty fruit and lively acidity. Well made and keenly priced.
Goes especially well with liver and bacon

Hugh Ryman Syrah VdP d'Oc 96

Quinnsworth ®

Medium-bodied red

Ripe fruit and spice on the nose. Dark cherry fruit on the palate with a bite of sharper damson. Dry and spicy in the finish.
Stir-fried duck with peppers; hard, moderately strong cheese

Red £6-£8

Arnaud de Villeneuve AC Côtes du Roussillon 96

Allied Drinks ®

Light to medium-bodied fruity red, tannic

Ripe berry fruit flavours with slightly stalky notes. Rich, soft fruit flavours with soft tannin

and lively acidity. Light, easy-drinking—could be served slightly cool.
Excellent picnic wine with mixed cold meats, cheeses etc

Cabernet/Syrah VdP d'Oc 97

Molloy's   ®

Medium-bodied red, tannic

Lots of ripe, jammy fruit aromas. Lovely ripe fruit with a spicy, peppery edge and an appetising bite of tannin.
Pan-fried liver with mushroom or mustard sauce; also beef salad or a meat pie

Ch. Belvize AC Minervois 94

Jenkinson   ®

Medium-bodied red, tannic

Rather stalky bramble-type fruit on the nose; balanced palate with ripe tannin and lively acidity, quite firm with a dry finish.
Good for chunky food, sausages with beans or lentils, salami or aubergine casserole

Ch. des Estanilles AC Faugères 96

Wines Direct   ©

Full-bodied red, tannic

Ripe brambles and plums on the nose with a real touch of warm earth. Full-bodied with ripe tannins and well-rounded fruit flavours with a medicinal, liquorice touch in the finish.
Lamb and haricot beans or a robust gratin of aubergines

Ch. Etang des Colombes Bicentenaire AC Corbières 95

Quinnsworth   ®

Medium-bodied red

Fruit-driven aromas of cherry

and blackcurrant. Similar ripe fruits on the palate with lots of spicy flavours interwoven. A lot of taste and good value.
Spicy casseroles such as lamb with cumin or a tagine

Ch. la Baronne Montagne d'Alaric AC Corbières 96

Wines Direct   ®

Medium-bodied red, fruit-driven

Soft red fruit aromas of a super-ripe, youthful style. Balanced in an easy-drinking, round soft style.
Salami or pizza

Ch. Lasfons AC Côtes du Roussillon 96

Molloy's   ®

Medium-bodied red, tannic

Sunripened fruit, berries and brambles on the nose. Raspberry fruit dominates the palate with soft tannin and nice refreshing acidity. Good ending, too.
Ratatouille-type vegetable dishes or a robust vegetable pasta

Ch. Roubaud AC Costières de Nîmes nv

Peter Dalton   ®

Light fruity red

Simple, clean, fruit flavours, ripe cherries with a touch of spice. A bit one-dimensional but well-made and enjoyable.
Great picnic wine with mixed meats, sandwiches etc

Ch. Roubaud Cuvée Prestige AC Costières de Nîmes 96

Peter Dalton   ®

Light fruity red

Lots of red fruits and peppercorns on the nose—concentrated, a touch stalky. Ripe, juicy fruit easily quaffable. Exemplary simple wine and good value.

Moussaka or a vegetable-based casserole perhaps with lentils or beans; also ratatouille

Ch. Viranel AC St-Chinian 96
Wines Direct ®

Medium-bodied red, tannic

Very aromatic nose with hints of herbs and orange peel. Soft and mellow yet with nice concentration of fruit balanced by moderate tannin and acidity. Long and dry in the finish.

Quite a stylish partner to lamb with herbs and garlic, spatchcocked quail or guineafowl

Chevalière Réserve Syrah VdP d'Oc 96
Allied Drinks ®

Medium-bodied red

Raspberry aromas with a hint of white pepper. Dry, but very soft and accessible with cherry and red berry fruit. Easy-drinking style.

Platter of mixed salamis and sausages or with bacon

DLC Original Cabernet Sauvignon VdP d'Oc 96
Allied Drinks ®

Medium-bodied red, fruit-driven

Blackcurrant leaves and a touch of smokiness show on the nose with lots of ripe fruit and balancing acidity in the taste.

Simple meat dishes, barbecues and robust pastas

Dom. des Chênes 'Les Grands-Mères' AC Côtes du Roussillon-Villages 95
Wines Direct ©

Medium-bodied red, fruit-driven, tannic

Ripe, quite mature aromas with lots of jammy fruit of the forest flavours and balancing tannin and acidity. Lovely fruit comes through all the way.

Casseroles and mixed dishes, pastas etc

Dom. de l'Hortus AC Coteaux du Languedoc 96
Wines Direct ®

Medium-bodied red, tannic

Earthy and plummy on the nose; up-front fruit dominates the palate with balancing tannin and acidity. Lively, peppery finish.

The peppery flavours complement beef—steaks or roast or a rich lasagne

Dom. du Grand Crès AC Corbières 95
Wines Direct ®

Medium-bodied red, tannic

Soft, mellow nose with very rich, ripe fruit aromas. Ripe tannins balance the weight of similar fruit on the palate. Long, mellow finish.

A good casserole wine especially for lamb and apricots or pork and prunes

Dom. de Limbardie VdP des Coteaux de Murviel 96
Brangan ®

Medium-bodied red

Plums, cloves and a touch of leather give quite an interesting

nose. Firm palate with plummy, blackberry fruit. Should develop a bit more over the next two years.
Stews and warm, aromatic Middle Eastern spices

Dom. de Terre Megere Cabernet VdP d'Oc 96
Brangan ©

Medium-bodied red, tannic

Inviting aromas of autumn brambles with rather earthy character, too. Delicious juicy fruit, loganberries and blackcurrants with a nice bite of tannin. Rich cassis-like finish.
Garlicky dishes of grilled or barbecued meats—lamb steaks, kebabs etc

Dom. de Terre Megere Merlot VdP d'Oc 96
Brangan ©

Medium-bodied red, tannic

Rich, spicy nose with plummy fruit and herbal notes. Plum-type fruit flavours also with spice and green pepper. Quite intense with softening tannins.
Lamb and beans; grilled meats and kebabs; baked aubergine pasta

Edouard Delaunay et ses Fils Syrah VdP d'Oc 96
Brangan ®

Medium-bodied red, tannic

Blackberries and boiled sweets on the nose. Good weight of ripe fruit with dry, slightly tannic finish.
Casseroles or grills

Foxwood Old Bush Vine Syrah VdP d'Oc 96
Wines Direct ®

Medium-bodied red, fruit-driven, tannic

Brambly fruit nose with a palate of soft, ripe fruit, soft tannins and acidity. Rich, yet with a nice twist of pepper to give a refreshing finish.
Pasta with a rich tomato sauce or pizza

Vanel Pinot Noir Spécial Réserve VdP de l'Aude nv
Molloy's ®

Light fruity red

Rather floral violet edge to the fruit on the nose. Nicely balanced with good ripe fruit and a long smooth finish.
Cajun chicken or duck with plum sauce

Red £8-£10

Ch. Étang des Colombes Bicentenaire AC Corbières 94
Febvre ®

Medium-bodied red

Ripe, dark fruits on the nose; soft with good weight of fruit and balancing acidity. Nice but pricey.
Rich tomato and olive pasta or bean casserole

Dom. de Terre Megere 'Les Dolomies' AC Coteaux du Languedoc 95
Brangan ®

Medium-bodied red

Mature, dried fruit aromas with gamey, leathery tones. Earthy, brambly fruit with a mineral edge. A distinctive wine of character.
Steak; game casserole

Red £10-£12

Ch. de Flaugergues La Méjanelle AC Coteaux du Languedoc 96

Dunnes Stores ©

Medium-bodied red, tannic

Deep brambly, summer pudding aromas with a touch of woodland earthiness. Good weight of fruit compote flavours with a spicy background. Ripe tannins and balanced acidity and long finish. Well made with typicité and a touch of complexity.

Casseroles, couscous and Middle Eastern spices in general; chunky sausages

Ch. Haut Gléon AC Corbières 94

Jenkinson ®

Medium-bodied red

Mature aromas show through on the nose—earthy, vegetal scents with fruit behind. Soft and mellow with good weight.

Couscous, lamb stew or robust pasta dishes

Red £12-£15

Prieuré de St Jean de Bébian AC Coteaux du Languedoc 93

Wines Direct ®

Medium-bodied red

Aromas of rich fruit—redcurrants, dried fruit—mingle with earthy tones to give quite a complex nose. Follows through to the palate which has concentrated subtle fruit and a long, chocolatey finish.

Lamb and milder game; dark, winey rabbit stew

Cabernet de l'Arjolle VdP des Côtes de Thongue 94

Brangan ©

Full-bodied red, tannic

Heady perfumes of blackcurrant, cedar and sandalwood. Firm but ripe tannins frame a concentration of dark fruit with cigar box spice beginning to show. Great potential.

Red meats, especially lamb; guineafowl or quail; carefully cooked turkey

Rosé £5-£6

Fortant de France Rosé Syrah VdP d'Oc 96

Fitzgerald ®

Rosé

Soft strawberry fruits on the nose; dry but with lots of ripe, juicy red berry flavours. Simple but attractive and refreshing with a nice touch of peppery spice in the end.

Canapés, ratatouille and garlicky dips

Rosé £6-£8

DLC Chevalière Réserve Cuvée Rosé VdP d'Oc 97

Allied Drinks ®

Rosé

Slightly stalky berry fruit on the nose. Well made in an easy-drinking style with reasonable weight of berry fruit flavour and balancing acidity.

Antipasti salad or a garlicky dip

Provence

Red £12-£15

Ch. Romanin AC Les Baux-de-Provence 95

Findlater ©

Full-bodied red, tannic

Really inky, deep aromas of tightly packed fruit—brambles and plums. Young—tannin shows above the fruit but good intensity of concentrated dark fruit flavours underneath. Needs a year or so but should be worth the waiting.

As it is now, the wine need rare meat or a good robust casserole to tame the tannins

Red £15-£20

Dom. Tempier AC Bandol 94

Brangan ☆ ☆

Full-bodied red, tannic

Intoxicating cigar box aroma with earthy, leathery fruit. Very complex. Black, tarry fruit flavours with herbal notes well balanced by ripe tannin and beautifully integrated flavours which linger right through the long finish.

Braised pheasant or beef simmered in wine with herbs: côte de boeuf with grilled vegetables

Dom. Tempier Cuvée Speciale La Migoua AC Bandol 94

Brangan ©

Full-bodied red, tannic

Slightly muted nose—earthy, farmyard impressions dominate. Ripe, dark fruits with firm frame of tannin and a touch of spice. A developing wine with a big future.

A robust casserole or chargrilled steak would suit the weight of the wine

Red £30-£35

Clos d'Ière Cuvée 1 AC Côtes de Provence 90

Brangan ®

Full-bodied red, tannic

Tarry, inky, herbal bouquet. Lots of flavour from ripe blackcurrant fruit through to black pepper spice. Firm but ripe tannins with a lingering vanilla scent mingling with the fruit. Lots of quality at a price.

A daube de Provence is an obvious and successful partner

South-West

White £5-£6

Honoré de Berticot Sauvignon AC Côtes de Duras 97
Searson ££

Aromatic white

Gooseberry and new-mown hay dominate the nose. Lively and fresh with green fruit flavours and zippy acidity. Good weight in the mouth. Very stylish for the price.
Goat's cheese soufflé or salad; herb-baked fish

Dom. de Joy VdP Côtes de Gascogne 96
TDL ®

Light fruity white

Light, slightly floral nose, lemon and pear aromas. Broad floral fruit, a hint of boiled sweets. Crisp finish. Easy-drinking—a good party wine.
Mixed foods at a buffet party or on its own

White £6-£8

Ch. de la Colline AC Bergerac Sec 96
Findlater ®

Aromatic white

Green fruits on the nose with some boiled sweet aromas. Ripe citrus and apple flavours with balancing acidity. Simple and quite fresh.
Simply grilled trout or escalopes of chicken

Ch. Jolys AC Jurançon Sec 95
Wines Direct ®

Aromatic white

Slightly honeyed apricot with pink grapefruit freshness on the nose. Full in the mouth with rich fruit. Balanced but lively fresh acidity and a long, white pepper finish.
Chicken and mustard or a warm salad of grilled vegetables

Dom. du Tariquet Ugni Blanc Colombard VdP des Côtes de Gascogne 97
Brangan ®

Light fruity white

Lovely floral, lemon peel aromas. Bone-dry with refreshing, minerally fruit finishing with lively lemon zest.
Fish salad or mousse

Red £5 or less

Maurice Brunet VdP du Gard nv
Barry & Fitzwilliam ®

Light fruity red

Light attractive bramble fruit aromas with similar fruit on the palate. Soft and easy-drinking.
Croque-monsieur type sandwiches or picnic food

Red £6-£8

Ch. de la Colline AC Bergerac 96
Findlater ®

Medium-bodied red, tannic

Ripe blackcurrrant with a whiff of peppermint on the nose. Dry with quite firm tannin and ripe fruit with the same twist of peppermint and vanilla as the nose. Quite long finish.
Grilled lamb steaks or pork roasted with fennel

Ch. Pique Sègue AC Bergerac 94

United Beverages ®

Medium-bodied red, tannic

Slightly baked fruit on the nose. Dry, with plenty of berry fruit and quite firm tannin. Blackberry and redcurrant flavours dominate with a dry finish.
Roast chicken and sausages or a meat or poultry pie

Dom. Fleury Laplace AC Madiran 96

Molloy's ©

Full-bodied red

Ripe, spicy, slightly stalky brambles on the nose. Dry with plenty of structure but good ripe fruit and peppery spice. Long fruity finish and surprisingly smooth. Good now—even better in six months.
Cassoulet or duck legs cooked with herbs and garlic; also robust casseroles

Red £8-£10

Les Hauts de Montauriol AC Côtes du Frontonnais 95

Brangan ®

Full-bodied red, tannic

Very earthy farmyard aromas. Brambly fruit, slightly medicinal with balanced tannin and acidity. Finishes dry and typically hard. Lots of character in a particular style.
Regional food—cassoulet, duck with lentils etc.

Germany

For some time now it has been hard to write about German wines. The country produces some of the world's greatest wines, but wines we never saw. Too many poor quality wines lined the shelves and gave the whole industry a bad image. Now everything is changing; in this year's listing there are more wines and a lot more stars which is a much truer reflection of German wine than ever before.

The introduction of Trocken and Halbtrocken wines was intended to rid the consumer of the assumption that all German wines were sweet. The trend to slightly higher alcohol levels, 10 and 11 per cent rather than 8 or 9 per cent, has greatly improved the dry wines, giving the balance needed for the naturally high acidity. Sweetness was originally intended to balance the acidity and allow the fruit to show, not to make a boring wine simply sweet which was what happened in many cases.

Labels on the whole have become easier to read and understand; beware, however, of the over-trendy designer versions which may or may not contain a quality wine!

German Riesling is perhaps the perfect wine for today. It is light, fresh and bracing, and very versatile with lighter contemporary foods.

When buying German wine it is advisable to go to a specialist supplier, a merchant or wine store. The wines still have a limited market and the big shops, supermarkets etc tend to stock only the inexpensive brands of poor quality and thankfully diminishing following.

The difference in price between a medium sweet brand and a delicious fresh, varietal from a quality-driven co-op is usually in favour of the co-op. In quality it is streets ahead. At the higher end of the market Kabinett, Spätlese and Auslese wines from the Mosel Rheingau etc offer some of the best value in fine wines on today's market.

White £5 or less

Berres Hahner Bereich Bernkastel Q 97
Supervalu/Centra ®

Light fruity white, off-dry

Herb garden aromas. Off-dry with apple and pear fruit flavour. Light and fresh easy-drinking party wine.
On its own or with light spicy or sweet-sour foods; good party wine

White £5 - £6

Frank Kaltenthaler Huxelrebe spätlese QmP 96
Octavius ®

Light fruity white, off-dry

Grassy hedgerow aromas. Off-dry with honeyed pear fruit and a touch of mint. Nice acidity and long finish.
Good on its own or with spring rolls or wontons

Frank Kaltenthaler Kerner Hernsheimer Schloss Spätlese QmP 96
Octavius ®

Light fruity white, off-dry

Herby, fruity aromas. Medium-dry with pear-type fruit. Light with refreshing acidity.
Light and spicy stir-fry or chicken or fish

White £6 - £8

Kallstadter saumagen Riesling spätlese halbtrocken 97
Octavius ®

Aromatic white, off-dry

Quite aromatic on the nose—full of citrus and apple fruit aromas. Off-dry with plenty of appley fruit.

Chinese squid or fishy noodles; also spring rolls and wontons as well as chicken and fruit salad

Ungsteiner Herrenberg Riesling Spätlese trocken QmP 94
Octavius ☆

Aromatic white

Developed nose with petrol and kerosene aromas showing through tropical fruit scents. Nicely balanced fruit and acidity; clean and refreshing.
Smoked eel or river fish in a creamy sauce

Ungsteiner Nussriegel Riesling Kabinett trocken QmP 96

Octavius ®

Aromatic white

A bit neutral on the nose with slightly citrusy notes. Delightfully fresh palate with plenty of ripe apple fruit and crisp lemon acidity. Long finish.
Mixed smoked fish salad

Ungsteiner Unico Gewürztraminer & Muscat QmP 97
Octavius ®

Light fruity white, off-dry

Fruity spearmint aromas, just off-dry with lovely pear and greengage fruit. Fresh, light and balanced.
Spicy Oriental food, especially Dim Sum and light Chinese dishes

Ungsteiner Weilberg Riesling Spätlese halbtrocken 94
Octavius ©

Aromatic white, off-dry

Golden maturity in appearance, honey, cooked apples and

apricot jam on the nose. Off-dry with refreshing balance of crisp acidity and honeyed fruit. A lovely wine.
Good on its own but also with spicy Oriental food especially Chinese dishes and Dim Sum

Weingut C. Schumacher Herxheimer Himmelreich Riesling Kabinett trocken QmP 97

Mitchell ©

Aromatic white

Fruit pastilles on the nose. Plenty of ripe green fruits with balancing acidity. Clean and refreshing, a true Riesling and good value for money.
Smoked trout or smoked fish and avocado salad or a mixed seafood pastry

White £8 - £10

Dr F. Weins-Prüm Graacher Himmelreich Riesling Q 95

Karwig ®

Light fruity white, off-dry

Floral spearmint aromas. Elegant off-dry style with pear and mint flavours. Delicate with some length.
With spicy food or as an unusual accompaniment to scallops

Weingut Klaus Hilz Dirmsteiner Herrgottsacker Gewürztraminer Spätlese trocken QmP 96

Octavius ®

Aromatic white

Aromatic mix of rose petals, lychees and Turkish Delight. Similar flavours on the palate, fresh and fruity with a good finish. Easy-drinking.

Good choice in an Oriental restaurant—works well with spicy foods in general

Weingut Schneider Jesuiten Hof Kirchheimer Geisskopf Weisser Burgunder trocken spätlese QmP 96

Octavius ®

Light fruity white

Lactic hint in the aroma, very fresh and quite dry with green and lemon fruit character.
Good aperitif or with a gentle first course such as scallop salad

Herrenberg Honigsackel Ungsteiner Weillberg Riesling Auslese QmP 92

Octavius ☆

Aromatic white, off-dry

Very pronounced nose of honey, beeswax and ripe fruit. Sweet but not cloying, the luscious fruit flavours balanced by crisp acidity. An excellent classic.
Good on its own or at the end of a meal; also with apple tart or strudel

White £10 - £12

Palmberg Gerolsheimer Lerchenspiel Kerner spätlese trocken QmP

Octavius ®

Light fruity white

Mature, honeyed, oily nose. Dry palate, some tropical fruit with prevailing butterscotch and toffee flavours and crisp acidity.
Warm salad of chicken or quail; poached trout

**Weingut C. Schumacher
Herxheimer Himmelreich
Riesling Spatlëse QmP 97**
Mitchell ®

Aromatic white, off-dry

Lemon and limes on the nose;
spritzy with nice sugar/acid
balance and long finish. Still
young, should improve.
*Rich savoury food such as black
pudding with apples or a pâté*

**Weingut C. Schumacher
Herxheimer Himmelreich
Riesling Spatlëse trocken
QmP 97**
Mitchell ®

Aromatic white

Fragrant though youthful nose,
green apple aromas dominate.
Crisp green apple fruit, dry
with balanced acidity. Light
and refreshing.
*Duck or goose salad; papillotes of
trout or deep-fried fish and
vegetables*

Red £6 - £8

**Herringberg Honigsackel
Ungsteiner Kobnert
Dornfelder trocken QbA 96**
Octavius ®

Light fruity red

Quite mature nose with some
red berry fruit showing
through. Good concentration of
ripe strawberry and cherry fruit
flavours; firm with balanced
acidity.
*Really good with black pudding or
with pork and peppers*

From our *Himmelreich** (*Paradise) in Germany

WEINGUT SCHUMACHER
HERXHEIM AM BERG

1997
Herxheimer Himmelreich

Riesling Spätlese
trocken

GUTSABFÜLLUNG
12,0 % vol PFALZ 750 ml
Qualitätswein mit Prädikat • A.P.Nr. 5 122 087 004 98
Weingut Schumacher • D-67273 Herxheim am Berg/Deutsche Weinstraße

Estate bottled

Red £10 - £12

**Herrenberg Honigsàckel
spätburgunder spätlese
trocken QmP 96**
Octavius ®

Light fruity red

Interesting nose with stewed
fruit and woodland aromas.
Dry, with sappy vegetal flavour
and dry, quite hard, finish.
Chunky country pâtés and terrines

**Palmberg Schwarzerde
Dirmsteiner Dornfelder
Rotwein trocken QbA 96**
Octavius ®

Light fruity red

Lovely nose of ripe blackcurrant fruit. Delicious mouthwatering fruit on the palate—
blackcurrant, brambles. Light
and easy with a fresh finish.
Expensive for the style.
Salami or sausages, or a casserole

Greece

The country which began cultivation of the vine in Mediterranean lands, is extremely confusing for visitors. Red wines tend to be sweetish, white Retsina tastes more like furniture polish than any other wine they have ever encountered. Retsina is certainly an acquired taste and probably better not acquired, but modern Greek wine goes way beyond its holiday resort image. Government investment in technology and expertise has improved winemaking , especially through the introduction of temperature control in a hot country. An increasingly quality conscious home market has also stimulated the production of better made wines.

A country such as Greece has all the raw materials in its grape varieties and has an established tradition of wine cultivation. Add the benefits of modern vinification and there is great potential. At present Greek wine production is made up of a number of very large companies such as Tsantalis and Boutari, and a number of dedicated individuals such as Domaine Carras. The simple, fruity, flavoursome reds at low prices show the improvement in the craft of making wine. Whites are also improving and higher, cooler locations are being found to grow the grapes. This is only the beginning for Greek wine. Time and money, and a lot of hard work should develop a fine industry for the next century.

Red £5 or less

Tsantalis Dry Red Wine 92
Dunnes Stores ££
Medium-bodied red, tannic

Quite complex spice and red berry aromas. A little rustic with gripping tannins, beetroot and blackcurrant flavours.
Casseroles of meat or pulses

Tsantalis Nemea 94
Dunnes Stores ©
Medium-bodied red, tannic

Rather floral raspberry and blackberry fruit, with an earthy twist. Dry and rather chewy with softening tannins and attractive fruit. Good value.
Moussaka or tomato-based casseroles

Hungary

Hungary was arguably the most stable of the former Eastern bloc countries and so was relatively successful in attracting the much needed investment in the post-communist period. The famous name of Tokay in particular created excitement and investors from many different parts of Europe sought to revitalise this fine sweet wine of long and noble pedigree.

Tokay is unique and its wines potentially rival the greatest sweet wines of Sauternes or the Rhine. They are made by a special process of blending botrytised grapes with fresh must in different proportions to attain different levels of sweetness. The regions grape varieties, mainly Furmint and Harslevelu, are now vinified dry and Furmint, in particular, produces clean light fruity wines.

Foreign wine companies such as the German giant Henkell, and Antinori from Italy, have also invested in Hungary and are producing good quality wines from international grape varieties.

Flying winemaker Hugh Ryman developed the Gyongys Estate, while Kim Milne worked at Chapel Hill and such influences have brought a decidedly New World style to the country's wine-making. Most recently there has been a swing towards indigenous grape varieties. The white Irsai Oliver makes aromatic, rather Muscat-like wines, and the red Kekfrankos makes juicy rather spicy reds.

White £5 - £6

Chapel Hill Balatonboglár Oaked Chardonnay 96
Barry & Fitzwilliam   ®
Full-bodied white, oak

Quite mellow aromas of light, orchard fruit character. Green apple fruit, quite rounded with a touch of buttery oak. Crisp finish.
Fish and light meats in creamy sauces, fish gratin, chicken fricassé etc.

Chapel Hill Irsai Oliver 97
Barry & Fitzwilliam   ®
Light fruity white

Quite aromatic with ripe apple and pear aromas; fresh and fruity, very ripe flavours, easy-drinking with good crisp finish.
Good aperitif or for drinking on its own, also good with light food: vegetable pastries, rice or noodle dishes

White £6 - £8

Mandulás Tokaji Furmint 97
Mitchell ®
Light fruity white
Fresh fruity aromas with a
touch of honey; clean, light fruit
with a nice zesty, citrus flavour
and clean, dry finish.
*Good aperitif or with light first
courses: vegetable mousse, seafood
salad*

Red £5 or less

Tesco's Reka Valley Merlot nv
Quinnsworth ©
Medium-bodied red, tannic
Blackberries and plums with a
touch of spice on the nose.
Gentle tannins and slightly
green currant fruit flavours. A
bargain which can only get
better.
Stew or liver and apples

Red £5 - £6

**Chapel Hill Balatonboglár
Cabernet Sauvignon 95**
Barry & Fitzwilliam ®
Medium-bodied red
Rather attractive brambly nose
with soft, ripe blackcurrant and
bramble flavours. Soft and
easy-drinking.
*Sausages, shepherd's pie and
meaty pastas*

**Chapel Hill Balatonboglár
Merlot 96**
Barry & Fitzwilliam ®
Light fruity red
Quite rich and jammy on the
nose with lots of juicy fruit
taste. Nicely balanced and easy-
drinking style.
*Mild meat dishes and many
vegetarian foods; good with nut
roast and savoury minced meat*

Best-value Bordeaux

Claret is now an expensive commodity, but its classic
style is irreplaceable. These six wines pick out the many
shades of red Bordeaux at affordable prices.

Baron Phillipe de Rothschild Cadet Claret AC Bordeaux
   96
Barton & Guestier AC St Julien 95
Ch. Bertiniere AC 1ères Côtes de Blaye 95
Ch. Faizeau AC Montagne St Emilion 94
Ch. La Prade AC Bordeaux Côtes de Francs 95
Ch. La Fleur St Georges AC Lalande de Pomerol 96

Italy

Beyond the old reliable Valpolicella, Soave and Chianti, Italian wine is often relegated to specialist territory. It is true that the sheer quantity and variety of wine produced all over the country from the Alps to the Mediterranean, are daunting to say the least. It is also a treasure-trove.

During the 1980s Italy went through a time of intense innovation and advance in winemaking. Legislation could not keep pace with the result that some of the country's greatest wines—Tignanello, Sassacaia—shared a classification with the most basic: vino da tavola. It was not a happy situation for either producer or consumer; but it was better than the bad old days of industrial Soave and Chianti flasks. For those prepared to seek it out, there was great wine in Italy.

Given that the country produces around 60 million hl of wine a year from co-ops, state-of-the-art modern wineries and dedicated artisans, consistency is unlikely. There is some pretty nasty stuff around, much of which seems to end up on restaurant wine lists, but there is also some wonderful wine, the product of passion and commitment. I thought my expectations of Italian wine were accurate, but they were bowled over by the quality and variety which emerged in this year's tastings. Here it will only be possible to pick out a few of the most outstanding points.

Chianti, after much change, development and discussion has really emerged triumphant. Many Riservas, from Classico and Rufino in particular, are stunning wines with concentration, complexity and length. There is still some inconsistency, and the best is expensive but in quality rivals a good Bordeaux or, perhaps more accurately, a fine Burgundy. It is no surprise that one of the few Three Star grades awarded by the guide this year comes from Chianti.

The South of Italy is perhaps most exciting of all. The success of Salice Salentino, a rich fruity red from Puglia, is by now almost a legend. This area is almost too hot for winemaking, yet a combination of modern skill and traditional craft is producing some stunning results and not only in reds. The achievement in the South of Italy is that while many hot regions seek to over-ride their climate through technology, producers in Southern Italy have harnessed that heat to produce wines which are distinctive and true to their origins.

One thing to remember about all Italian wines is the Italian way of life. Wine is as much a part of a meal as a loaf of bread, but it is a part of a meal. Few Italian wines are good without food and even without a particular kind of food. They lack the immediate fruit and up-front aromas so beloved by modern wine makers. White wines are often criticised as neutral and lacking fruit. In fact their role is to cleanse the palate, to accompany the vibrant mixed flavours of antipasti or to cut the richness of shellfish or a risotto. A really aromatic wine would be quite inappropriate.

White £5 or less

Tesco DOC Frascati Superiore 97

Quinnsworth ®

Light dry white

Zesty, citrusy aromas; light, tangy fruit flavour with citrus acidity. Clean fresh finish.
Omelette or light, first-course pasta

White £5 - £6

Folonari DOC Soave nv

Dillon ®

Light dry white

Light nose—floral and slightly nutty. Crisp and refreshing with apple and citrus zest and clean, dry finish. Well made—lovely summer drinking.
Simple seafood, deep-fried fish and vegetables or tempura

Fontana Candida DOC Frascati Superiore 97

Dillon ££

Light dry white

Delightfully fresh aromas. Excellent weight of ripe fruit— apples and pears—with crisp acidity, creamy texture and decent length. A very good Frascati.
Chinese food, scampi and seafood salad

Lamberti DOC Bianco di Custoza 96

Gilbeys ®

Light, dry white

Delicate nose of lime and dessert apples. Fresh, with plenty of apple and pear fruit and crisp finish. Good value.
Lovely with spinach ravioli

Mediterraneum Chardonnay IGT Salento nv

Gilbeys ®

Light fruity white

Peardrops and lime on the nose. Dry with apple-type fruit and balanced acidity. Simple but pleasant.
Mixed vegetable antipasti, even works with artichokes or asparagus

MezzaCorona Pinot Grigio Atesino IGT Atesino 97

Mitchell ®

Light dry white

Very fresh aromas of pears and melon, quite grapey. A simple wine yet with good balance of

ripe fruit, zippy acidity and lightness and a crisp finish.
Vegetable fritters, goujons and Greek salad

Ricasoli DOC Orvieto Classico 96

Fitzgerald ®

Light fruity white, off-dry

Hazelnut and floral aromas. Smooth and round with broad fruit flavours. Off-dry, nicely balanced with good length.
Good party wine or to drink with spicy foods

White £6 - £8

Alasia Muscaté Sec VdT 96

Findlater ®

Aromatic white

Nettle and herb aromas. Nice balance between ripe fruit and acidity; plenty of flavour of spicy, nutty apples. Sharp, clean finish.
Risotto of sun-dried tomatoes or avocado, tomato and mozzarrella salad

Antinori Campogrande DOC Orvieto Classico 96

Grants ®

Light dry white

Clean, fresh aromas of citrusy fruit. Apple and gooseberry-type fruit flavours with crisp acidity. Light and clean.
Fried fish and fritters and salads

Bigi Torricella DOC Orvieto Classico Secco 96

Findlater ®

Light dry white

Nutty, minerally aromas. Quite unusual palate of almonds and pistachio nut flavours with the

same mineral quality as the nose. Very fresh with a crisp dry finish.
Fried fish, especially fishcakes; Chinese spring rolls and sesame toasts

Cantina Tollo Colle Secco DOC Trebbiano d'Abruzzo 97

Febvre ®

Light dry white

Dry, with nice appley fruit and lively citrus acidity. Quite long and refreshing.
Spinach ravioli or canneloni or deep-fried chicken

Grigio Luna Pinot Grigio DOC Valdadige 97

TDL ®

Light dry white

Slightly muted nose with peardrops and citrus aromas just coming through. Fresh, with green apple fruit and clean crisp finish.
Cheesey pasta

Masi DOC Soave Classico Superiore 96

Grants ®

Light dry white

Lightly aromatic with crisp green apple fruit flavours and refreshing acidity. Clean, dry finish.
Shellfish and deep-fried foods

MezzaCorona Pinot Grigio DOC Trentino 97

Mitchell ®

Light dry white

Fresh, citrusy aromas, slightly floral. Clean, fresh green fruit flavours with citrusy tones. Refreshing acidity, dry and well made.

Good aperitif wine with crostini or antipasti especially

Ruffino Libaio Chardonnay e Pinot Grigio VdT IGT 96
Dillon ££

Light dry white

Floral and citrus aromas and good weight of ripe apple, melon and pear-type fruit with refreshing acidity and length of finish. Delicious and great value.
Simply cooked fish—especially plaice and hake

Santi Sortesele Pinot Grigio DOC Trentino 97
Findlater ®

Light dry white

Delicate nose with light aromas of peach and toasted almond, a touch floral. Citrus and apple fruit flavours and lively acidity with well-balanced finish.
Light seafood pasta or a cream sauce

Sella & Mosca DOC Vermentino di Sardegna 96
Grants ®

Light aromatic white

Lightly aromatic with plenty of fruit on the palate: citrus, pear, melon and apple flavours. Very fresh with clean, dry finish.
Pasta with oilive oil and herbs; tuna salad; simply-cooked fish

White £8 - £10

Alois Lageder Benefizium Porer Pinot Grigio DOC Alto Adige 95
Febvre ©

Aromatic white

Quite complex honey and melon on the nose with under-lying nuttiness. Broad and impressive style of Pinot Grigio with lovely weight of honeyed tropical fruits lingering in a complex finish.
Mushroom ravioli or grilled bass or brill

Eisacktaler della Valle Isarco Gewürtztraminer Qba Südtirol DOC Alto Adige 96
Select Wines from Italy ®

Aromatic white

Fresh apples and spices on the nose; richly flavoured with broad spicy fruit and balancing acidity. Long and lingering.
Salad of red peppers or bruschettas, also with hummus

Eisacktaler della Valle Isarco Sylvaner Qba Südtirol DOC Alto Adige 96
Select Wines from Italy ®

Light dry white

Fresh, vinous nose. Slightly spritzy on the palate with lemon and peach kernel flavours and good balancing acidity. Slightly too sharp in the finish, otherwise well made.
Shellfish

Eisacktaler della Valle Isarco Veltliner Qba Südtirol DOC Alto Adige 96
Select Wines from Italy ®

Light dry white

Light fruit on the nose. Ripe fruit with a green tinge and slightly spritzy. Nice floral influence and clean finish.
Spaghetti carbonara or simply cooked lemon sole, plaice and other light fishes

Eisacktaler della Valle Isarco Muller Thurgau Qba Südtirol DOC Alto Adige 96

Select Wines from Italy ®

Light dry white

Aromatic nose; dry with broad ripe fruit, good weight and crisp acidity. Attractive fresh citrus finish. Pricey for the grape

Courgette or cauliflower fritters or prawn toasts

Fazi-Battaglia DOC Verdicchio dei Castelli di Jesi 97

Select Wines from Italy ®

Light dry white

Citrusy aromas with hints of peardrop and apple; dry with medium weight of citrus fruit flavour and crisp, clean finish.

Seafood salad or goujons of sole

Ghiaiolo Sauvignon IGT 96

Findlater ☆

Aromatic white

Aromatic nose of apples, gooseberries and cut grass. Quite exuberant palate with blackcurrant leaf, gooseberry and greengage flavours. Good weight with nice balance and a long finish.

Salmon cooked with basil or sorrel; grilled monkfish; pasta tossed with feta, sundried tomatoes and olives

I Frati Lugana Cà dei Frati DOC Lugana 96

Findlater ☆

Light dry white

Peaches and almonds dominate on the nose followed by flavours of ripe fruit and nuts with a creamy texture. Good supporting alcohol and crisp acidity. Quite elegant, long

finish.

Chinese food or fresh prawns

Il Vignale Santa Sofia DOC Bianco di Custoza 97

Select Wines from Italy ®

Medium-bodied red

Peardrops and melon dominate the nose. Dry, with grassy, citrus fruit and relatively mild acidity. Balanced and well made.

Light fish; baked cod or plaice or a delicate fish soup

Kettmeir Tridentum Pinot Grigio DOC Trentino 96

Select Wines from Italy ®

Aromatic white

Restrained on the nose, apple and melon fruit with a touch of mineral aromas. Dry and refreshing with a good weight of green apple fruit and same minerally influence as the nose. Good value.

Grilled mussels or a shellfish stew

Le Rime Pinot Grigio/Chardonnay IGT Toscana 97

Gilbeys ©

Light dry white

Quite a floral nose with orange blossom and tangerine aromas. Dry and fresh with lots of mandarin orange and peach fruit flavours.

Spiced dishes like prawn stir-fry

Musaragno Chardonnay DOC Lison-Pramaggiore 96

Select Wines from Italy ®

Light fruity white

Delicate, floral nose also showing honey and vanilla; dry and fresh with good weight of peachy fruit and crisp finish.

Vegetable quiche or tart or avocado salad.

Musaragno Pinot Bianco DOC Lison-Pramaggiore 96

Select Wines from Italy ®

Light dry white

Pronounced aromas of pear and honey, slightly oily. Very dry with crisp acidity and good weight of pear and apple fruit.

Works quite well with omelettes and simple, lightly sauced pasta

Ocone Vin Giocondo VdT del Sannio Beneventano nv

Peter Dalton ®

Light dry white

Quite nutty on the nose. Mellow flavours with crisp acidity and green apple fruit. Quite sharp in the finish.

Deep-fried fish including calamary

Podium Garofoli DOC Verdicchio dei Castello de Jesi Classico Superiore 96

Febvre ☆

Light dry white

Ripe and quite developed nose with hints of honey and toasted almond. Dry with good weight of honeyed tropical fruit and hazelnut with a lingering finish.

Seafood pasta with mussels or prawns

White £10 - £12

Cormòns Pietra Verde Isonzo DOC Friuli 97

Select Wines from Italy ®

Light dry white

Difficult to identify the fruit on the nose; the palate, too, is quite light with balanced green fruits and acidity. Nicely balanced, though.

Salad or antipasti or simple seafood

Croara Santa Sofia Barrique VdT Veronese 97

Select Wines from Italy ®

Aromatic white

A touch of yeast and lanolin on the nose along with ripe lemons; good body and delicate lingering fruit flavours. Well made and a good aperitif but expensive.

Small bruschetta or deep-fried calamary, fish and vegetables

Fazi-Battaglia "San Sisto" DOC Verdicchio dei Castelli di Jesi Classico 94

Select Wines from Italy ☆

Light dry white

Lovely nose with honey, vanilla and tropical fruit beautifully entwined. Dry, with balanced acidity and lots of creamy vanilla and stewed apple flavours—elegant stuff.

Pasta and clams, prawns with herbs or elegant fish'n chips

Kettmeir Pinot Grigio Rulander DOC Alto Adige 96

Select Wines from Italy ☆

Aromatic white

Pronounced nose with pineapple, peach and citrus-type fruit aromas. Dry and balanced with ripe fruits and a steely core. Nice, elegant wine.

Mixed seafood salad or shrimp pastries

Leone de Castris "Donna Lisa" DOC Salice Salentino 96

Select Wines from Italy ®

Full-bodied white

Delightful and complex nose with vanilla, butter and ripe tropical fruit aromas. Dry and

lively with melon and pineapple flavours and smooth, warm finish.
Stuffed squid with herbs and olives, or mullet

Mastroberardino DOC Lacryma Christi del Vesuvio 96
Select Wines from Italy ®

Full-bodied white

Rather slow on the nose but palate opens out into flavours of peach and bitter almond. A lovely if idiosyncratic wine for which one would expect to pay!
Seafood soup or mixed fish salad

Pieropan Vigneto Calvarino DOC Soave Classico Superiore 96
Superquinn ®

Light dry white

Interesting nose, stewed apple and citrus tones—'Mediterranean hillside' to one taster. Dry, with mineral and nutty tones, mixed with ripe apple and pear fruit. Very good, long finish.
Works well with a herby pasta or with fried prawns

Planeta Chardonnay VdT di Sicilia 95
Superquinn ®

Full-bodied white

Lots of toasty caramel and ripe fruit on the nose; concentrated palate with hidden complexity of tropical fruit and honey flavours with a nutty finish.
Gruyère soufflé or leek and mushroom tart; also fish gratin

Puiatti Pinot Grigio DOC Collio 96
Superquinn ®

Aromatic white

Restrained nose with biscuit and toast elements mixing with citrus fruit. Dry and balanced with lots of peaches and pears in the flavour. Warm and rounded in the finish.
Escalopes of chicken with basil or tarragon; also baked hake or cod

Puiatti Sauvignon DOC Collio 96
Superquinn ®

Aromatic white

Interesting nose of yeast and damp wool with elderflower nuances. Refreshing wine with green apple and gooseberry fruit flavours.
Tomato and mozzarella salad

White £12 - £15

Castello di Brolio Torricella VdT Toscana 95
Fitzgerald ☆

Full-bodied white

Lovely developed nose of honeyed tropical fruits. Slightly oily. Dry with crisp acidity and rich, ripe fruit—peaches and melons with a hint of smoke adding to the complexity. Goes on and on.
Stuffed chicken breasts with a light sauce or escalopes of veal in cream

Marchesi di Barolo DOC Gavi di Gavi 97
Select Wines from Italy ®

Light dry white

Apples and pears on the nose follow through to the palate with lemony, nutty flavours also. Very clean and fresh but rather short.
Good first course wine with prawns or sardines; pasta with broccoli

An Italian Tour

This year the range of Italian wines is bigger and brighter than ever, from a country of endless variety. This is a small sample of the major styles it produces.

Sella & Mosca DOC Vermentino di Sardegna 96

I Frati Lugana Cà Dei Frati DOC Lugana 96

Pieropan Vigneto Calvarino DOC Soave Classico Superiore 96

Eisacktaler della Valle Isarco Gewürztraminer Qba Südtirol DOC Alto Adige 96

Alois Lageder Benefizium Porer Pinot Grigio DOC Alto Adige 95

Ceppi Storici oak-aged Barbera DOC Barbera d'Asti 95

Serègo Alighieri (single vineyard) DOC Valpolicella Classico 95

Liburnio Orlandi Contucci Ponno VdT Colli Aprutini 92

Ruffino Ducale DOCG Chianti Classico Riserva 94

Leone de Castris DOC Salice Salentino Riserva 94

Musaragno Refosco dal Pedunculo Rosso DOC Lison-Parmaggiore 96

Mezzacorona Teroldego Rotaliano DOC Trentino 9

Mastroberardino DOC Fiano di Avellino 95

Select Wines from Italy ®

Full-bodied white

Aromas of honey, almond and stewed apple give quite a complex nose. Dry, with soft acidity and a slightly salty, mineral quality. Needs food.
Brandade or a rich fish stew or soup

Red £5 - £6

Badia Frasca DOC Montepulciano d'Abruzzo 96

Greenhills ®

Medium-bodied red

Ripe fruit aromas of bramble, cherries and raspberries. Juicy, chewy mouthful with plenty of bite. Simple, enjoyable wine with satisfying fruit and flavour and surprising elegance.
Robust pasta with tomatoes, peppers and the like

Cecchi IGT Sangiovese di Toscana 96

Quinnsworth ®

Medium-bodied red

Quite peppery aromas and similar influence on the palate with cherries, liquorice and soft berry fruit. Refreshing and attractive for easy-drinking with food.
Robust pizza or pasta dish

Contado di Molisi Moli' DOC Biferno Rosso 97

Burgundy Direct ®

Medium-bodied, tannic

Rich, baked aromas of blackberries and cherries. Direct fruit

flavours with firm tannin and rather low acidity.
Rabbit and peppers or spaghetti

La Tripi DOCG Chianti 96

Greenhills ®

Light to medium-bodied fruity red

Typical slightly plummy spice on the nose, high acidity and red fruit flavours. Balanced structure—an honest example of Chianti normale.
Meat antipasti, pizza and lighter pastas

Melini Isassi DOCG Chianti Classico 96

Gilbeys ®

Medium-bodied red, tannic

Dark cherries and slightly herbal aromas come through on the nose. Dark fruit flavours and very firm tannin with a bitter twist in the finish.
Grilled lamb chops or roast pork

Red £6 - £8

Antinori Santa Cristina IGT Toscana 96

Grants ®

Medium-bodied red, tannic

Not especially pronounced aromas of dark damson and plum fruit; chunky, robust wine with cherry and sharp plum flavours and balanced tannins. Dry finish.
Robust meaty pastas or liver with polenta

Badia a Passignani DOCG Chianti Classico 96

Grants ☆

Medium-bodied red, tannic

Intense aromas of blackberries, plums and vanilla following

through to the taste which is lively with appetising tannin. Very good length in the finish.
Beef or lighter game such as pheasant or pigeon

Barone Ricasoli DOCG Chianti Classico 94

Fitzgerald ®

Full-bodied red, tannic

Ripe soft fruit aromas. Chunky palate of ripe fruit, hard tannins and acidity. Quite long in the finish—give it a year or so to mellow.
Rare steak or aubergine pizza

Barone Ricasoli San Ripolo DOCG Chianti Classico 95

Fitzgerald ©

Medium-bodied red, tannic

Rather rich plum and cherry aromas. Simple fruit on the palate but well-balanced with quite mild tannin, slightly short finish.
Meat-based pasta or beef or lamb kebabs (not spiced)

Candido DOC Salice Salentino Riserva 93

Findlater ☆ ☆

Full-bodied red

Very attractive nose of ripe fruits with a touch of white pepper and a hint of truffle. Generous palate, similar to the nose and nicely balanced. Very good value.
Aubergines; stuffed peppers; pasta with black olives; rabbit stew and rich olive-oil based sauces

Ceppi Storici oak-aged Barbera DOC Barbera d'Asti 95

Findlater ☆

Full-bodied red

Subdued aromas of cherry and

bitter chocolate. Very intense fruit flavours—deep and rich with a subtle bitter twist and bracing acidity. Long, bitter chocolate finish.
Lasagne or lamb and mushroom casserole with sage; liver cooked with sage and mushrooms

Di Majo Norante Ramitello Riserva DOC Biferno Rosso 94

Burgundy Direct ®

Full-bodied red, tannic

Heady nose of black cherry and sandalwood. Mouthwatering and unusual fruit, like blackcurrant coughdrops! A dry edge of tannin, spicy flavour and slightly short finish.
Casserole of poultry or game with strong garlic and herb flavours or marinated lamb

Fattoria La Parrina DOC Parrina 93

Superquinn ®

Medium-bodied red, tannic

Earthy dark fruit aromas; rather angular wine with gripping tannins and acidity which demand food..
Lasagne or robust meat casserole

Fazi-Battaglia Marche Sangiovese IGT 96

Select Wines from Italy ®

Medium-bodied red

Chocolate and cold tea come through on the nose. Quite austere but with plenty of cherry and damson fruit flavours and refreshing acidity.
Pizza or meaty pasta

Leone de Castris Copertino DOC Salice Salentino 96

Select Wines from Italy ☆

Full-bodied red, tannic

Spicy, woodland aromas. On the palate, fruit of the forest flavours mingle with spice and herbal tones. Good weight of alcohol and firm tannins—a winter-warmer!

Vegetable and olive oil-dominated dishes such as stuffed aubergines or baked peppers

Marchesi de Frescobaldi Rèmole DOCG Chianti 97

Allied Drinks ®

Medium-bodied red, tannic

Redcurrants and cherries on the nose. Light and fresh with rather bitter fruit and firm tannins.

Cold, rare meat or grilled chops

Masi DOC Valpolicella Classico Superiore 95

Grants ®

Light fruity red

Lots of cherry fruit on the nose and lively flavours of ripe cherries and berries with fresh acidity and clean, slightly bitter, finish.

Meat-based antipasti and Bresaola

MezzaCorona Cabernet Sauvignon Trentino DOC 96

Mitchell ®

Medium-bodied red

Attractive aromas of juicy berry fruit though slightly green in character followed by lean blackcurrant fruit on the palate. Rather one-dimensional but attractive.

Cold meats and pasta with meat

sauces; also sausages if not highly spiced.

MezzaCorona Teroldego Rotaliano DOC Trentino 95

Mitchell ©

Medium-bodied red, tannic

Smoky autumn fruits with a touch of liquorice; chunky, savoury flavour with quite marked acidity and firm tannin. Slightly dusty fruit. Dry and appetising.

Casseroles of meat, robust pastas and really chunky pizza

Musaragno Refosco dal Pedunculo Rosso DOC Lison-Pramaggiore 96

Select Wines from Italy ®

Light fruity red

Pepper and blackberries on the nose with a touch of bitter cherry. Light and slightly stalky with redcurrant and raspberry flavours.

Pizza or a light smoky bacon pasta

Santa Sofia DOC Valpolicella Classico 97

Select Wines from Italy ®

Light fruity red

Vibrant aromas of red cherries; weighty palate with a savoury bitter twist to quite a long finish. Well priced and certainly not boring!

Grilled tuna, or tuna and bean salad or sausages

Tesco DOCG Chianti Classico Riserva 94

Quinnsworth ®

Full-bodied red, tannic

Quite pronounced aromas of leather and tea. Dry, with balanced tannin and acidity and

reasonable weight of cherry fruit. Nice dry bite in the finish. Well made and good value.
Roast pigeon and this wine make a great bargain dinner party

Vigna Flaminio DOC Brindisi 94
Karwig   ®

Medium-bodied red, tannic

Dark ripe fruit with scents of cold tea and tobacco on the nose. Dry, with relatively soft tannins. Flavours of prune juice, dark fruit and black pepper.
Casseroles of meat and vegetables; aubergine and pepper bake or bean stew

Red £8 - £10

Badia a Coltibuono DOCG Chianti Classico 96
Findlater   ®

Medium-bodied red, dry

Some red fruit on the nose. Quite a structured wine with good balance of fruit and acidity. Very pleasant with some length in the finish.
Rare meat and more robust, meat-based pastas

Barbaglio VdT Rosso del Salento 93
Findlater   ®

Medium to full-bodied red

Ripe fruit aromas from a rather gentle nose. Well-balanced, smooth and rounded with nice fruit. Very pleasant drinking.
Olive oil-based dishes and rich Mediterranean vegetable pasta and couscous

Brusco dei Barbi Toscana IGT 96
Select Wines from Italy   ®

Medium-bodied red, tannic

Spicy, wholesome wine with brambly fruit and smooth mouthfeel, well-cloaked tannins. Nice bitter twist in the finish.
Lamb chops or a mixed grill or kebabs

Carignano del Sulcis VQPRD DOC 94
Superquinn   ®

Medium-bodied red

Earthy and very ripe fruit aromas. Smooth and rounded with flavours of dark fruit and bitter chocolate in the finish. Slightly rustic but attractive.
Pasta and peppers and other spicy pasta sauces

Cormòns Isonzo Merlot DOC Friuli 96
Select Wines from Italy   ®

Light fruity red

Blackberry and light spicy aromas. Dry, with simple fruit flavours of cherry and strawberry. Lively acidity and quite long in the finish but expensive for the style.
Meat-based antipasti or tuna

Fassati Le Gaggiole DOCG Chianti 96
Select Wines from Italy   ®

Medium-bodied red, tannic

More generous on the nose than the palate which is quite firm with dark fruit and bitter chocolate flavours. A good finish.
Steaks or chops or roast pork

Giacosa Fratelli DOCG Barolo 94

Quinnsworth ®

Full-bodied red, tannic

Muted aromas of tarry, black-skinned fruit. Dry with gripping tannins and rather vegetal fruit. Gamey flavours are beginning to emerge mid-palate and the finish is good. Needs time.
Long-simmered beef cooked in the same wine

Laborel DOCG Chianti Classico Riserva 93

Gilbeys ®

Full-bodied red, tannic

Redcurrants with a whiff of cold tea on the nose. Very coating tannins and rather loose-knit fruit with macha and spice flavours in the background. Satisfying and chunky rather than elegant. Needs a bit of time.
Rare rib steaks, grilled duck or leg of lamb

Leone de Castris La Rena Primitivo IGT Salento 96

Select Wines from Italy ®

Full-bodied red

Baked, dried fruit aromas of the south. Lively red berry fruit and some length in the bittersweet finish.
Anchovy and olive pasta or turkey with a fruity stuffing and sauce

Leone de Castris DOC Salice Salentino Riserva 94

Select Wines from Italy ☆

Full-bodied red

Highly complex heady mixture of black plums and cherries, chocolate and spice on the nose.

Smooth, well-integrated palate with dark berry flavours and chocolatey richness. Slightly bitter in the finish.
Venison casserole

Lungarotti Rubesco DOC Rosso di Torgiano 95

Findlater ©

Medium-bodied red, tannic

Earthy ripe fruit on the nose; deep fruit flavours, damsons, plums with a real chocolatey richness. Nicely balanced tannin and acidity and long finish.
Kidneys or grilled meats

Marchesi di Barolo 'Ruvei' DOC Barbera d'Alba 95

Select Wines from Italy ®

Medium-bodied red, tannic

Subtle nose—plummy, fragrant. Quite complex flavour of sweet-sour fruit, bitter cherries, ripe plums. Chewy mouthfeel with pronounced acidty. A bracing food wine.
Pasta with Bolognese or rich tomato sauce; fried liver or kidneys with pancetta

Musaragno Merlot DOC Lison-Pramaggiore 96

Select Wines from Italy ®

Light fruity red

Dark plums and blackberries on the nose. Youthful and very dry at present, yet ripe fruit flavours. Light, with refreshing acidity.
Pasta with olive oil-based sauce; salami

Ocone Vin Giocondo VdT di Sannio di Benneventano nv

Peter Dalton ®

Medium-bodied red

Cherry and warm earth on the nose. Ripe, easy style with light cherry fruit and pleasant spiking of white pepper.
Sausages, Bresaola or a tuna fish bake

Serègo Alighieri (Masi) DOC Valpollicella Classico Superiore 95
Grants ©

Medium-bodied red

Lovely ripe cherries and a hint of tar on the nose; full, rounded palate with a nice weight of cherry and plum fruit. Well-structured wine with more weight than most Valpolicella and ripe fruit flavours. Sharp, dry and flavoursome finish.
Duck breast or chicken with ham and peppers

Vigneto Antica Chiusina DOCG Vino Nobile de Montepulciano 93
Febvre ®

Full-bodied red, tannic

Restrained on the nose with aromas of black cherry and wax polish. Firm tannins and bracing acidity with ripe cherry fruit which lasts through a concentrated tarry finish.
Game casserole or roasted pheasant especially with mushroom flavours

Villa Cerna DOCG Chianti Classico Riserva 93
Quinnsworth ®

Full-bodied red

Ripe fruit, polished leather and tea aromas. Good ripe fruit and spice flavours of peppery damsons, cherries and cigars. Dry finish. Good classic style.
Steaks, especially with mushrooms

or rare roast beef; also beef casseroles

Red £10 - £12

Castello di Brolio DOCG Chianti Classico Riserva 93
Fitzgerald ©

Full-bodied red, tannic l

Black cherries and a touch of vanilla on the nose. Quite a depth of complex cherry and plum fruit with ripe but very firm tannins and balancing acidity. The archetypal Tuscan—making a virtue of austerity.
Rare grilled beef, preferably a good T-bone

Castello di Nipozzano DOCG Chianti Rúfina Riserva 94
Allied Drinks ®

Medium-bodied red

Herbal tones mixed with redcurrant and cherry-type fruit, Quite good, intense fruit with rather light structure—elegant enough even so.
Rack of lamb or roast beef

Lamole di Lamole DOCG Chianti Classico 96
Select Wines from Italy ☆ ☆ ☆

Medium-bodied red, tannic

Smoky, rich dark fruit aromas, fruitcakey effect; smooth silky palate with rich black cherry and chocolate flavours perfectly balanced by ripe tannin, weight and great length. A real beauty!
Pheasant or guineafowl or classically cooked quail

Lamole di Lamole barrique aged DOCG Chianti Classico 95

Select Wines from Italy ®

Medium-bodied red, very tannic

Quite a complex nose with red fruits, spice and a hint of something herbal. Red fruits come through very firm tannin. Needs time to mellow but the finish is spicy and long.
Duck or roast rib of beef

Liburnio Orlandi Contucci Ponno VdT Colli Aprutini 92

Findlater ®

Full-bodied red, tannic

Pleasant aromas of plums and black cherries with hints of vanilla. Nice balance between firm tannin, fleshy fruit and plentiful alcohol. Long finish to a very satisfying wine.
Magret of duck or goose with chestnuts; roast leg of port

Mastroberardino DOCG Lacryma Christi del Vesuvio 97

Select Wines from Italy ®

Full-bodied red, very tannic

Inky, tarry concentration on the nose with brambly fruit. Firm tannins almost cover the blackcurrant and blackberry fruits. Young, needs about two years to show its colours.
Hard cheeses or a game casserole

Pasiteo Fassati DOCG Vino Nobile di Montepulciano 94

Select Wines from Italy ®

Full-bodied red, tannic

Rather tarry nose with hints of plum-type fruit. Flavours of plums and dark cherries with hard tannins and a touch of bitter chocolate in the finish. Rustic style.
Steak or casserole of beef

Rocca Rubia Riserva DOC Carignano del Sulcis 92

Superquinn ☆

Full-bodied red, tannic

Rich cherry fruit mixed with herbal, hedgerow aromas. Full-bodied with well-cloaked tannins, dense dark fruit flavour and warming alcohol.
Vegetable and meat stews such as aubergine and lamb casserole

Ruffino Ducale DOCG Chianti Classico Riserva 94

Dillon ☆ ☆

Full-bodied red, tannic

Great complexity of ripe fruit aromas and leathery overtones. Round and mouthfilling with good weight and elegant tannins. Long finish. Well worth its price.
Beef fillet and game such as pheasant

Santo Stefano Boscaini VdT Veronese 94

Febvre ®

Full-bodied red, tannic

Spicy, cherry fruit on the nose with toffee and chocolate nuances. Ripe red fruit flavours, firm tannins and a bittersweet finish.
Duck or a typically Italian sauté of lamb with sage and mushrooms

Vigneto Assolo Vistarenni DOCG Chianti Classico 96

Select Wines from Italy ®

Medium-bodied red, very tannic

Bitter cherries on the nose with a dash of mint; rather hard palate with very firm tannins and high acidity with fruit beneath—needs food.
Steak or a slightly rare leg of lamb

Red £21 - £15

Kettmeir Cabernet Sauvignon DOC Alto Adige 93

Select Wines from Italy ®

Medium-bodied red, tannic

Blackcurrant and bitter cherry aromas. Ripe lively fruit, plenty of acidity and well-cloaked tannins. Good grip and length—holding well for a '93.
Grilled meat—works well with ostrich steaks

La Grola (Allegrini) DOC Valpolicella Classico Superiore 93

Superquinn ®

Medium-bodied red, tannic

Concentrated nose of bitter cherry and dark brambly fruits. Well-flavoured dark fruit and sweet pepper with chewy tannins and a long satisfying finish.
Pigeon or calves' liver, traditionally cooked

Lamole di Lamole DOCG Chianti Classico Riserva 94

Select Wines from Italy ☆

Full-bodied red, very tannic

Rather warm nose of ripe plums with hints of dark chocolate and something quite gamey. Tannins still very much to the fore ahead of the fruit but a long, satisfying finish promises more in a year or so.
Rare meat will soften the tannins—try farmed venison

Leone de Castris Donna Lisa DOC Salice Salentino Riserva 92

Select Wines from Italy ®

Full-bodied red, tannic

Lovely aromas of ripe juicy blackberries. Opulent fruit balances the tannins, with rich chocolatey tones and warming alcohol.
Especially good with game either a casserole or pie

Petri del Castello Vicchiomaggio DOCG Chianti Classico Riserva 94

Febvre ®

Full-bodied red, tannic

Rather earthy cherry fruit on the nose. Rich, ripe cherry fruit with vanilla undertones. Firm but ripe tannin—generally well-integrated and harmonious.
Roast pork, especially flavoured with truffles; pasta and wild mushrooms

Red £15 - £20

Bolla DOC Amarone Valpolicella Classico 89

Dillon ®

Full-bodied red

Layers of complex, intense fruit on the nose. Big, rich and complex with lots of mature fruit flavours, spice and dried fruit nuances. Warm finish of alcohol and spice. A wine to sip and savour.
On its own with shavings of Parmesan to nibble

Brigante dei Barbi VdT Toscana 94

Select Wines from Italy ℝ

Full-bodied red

Plums and chocolate on the nose; plenty of dark fruit flavours and a firm structure laced with chocolate richness especially in the finish.
Turkey or pheasant or a casserole of pigeon or game

Castello di Brolio Casalferro VdT Toscana 94

Fitzgerald ℝ

Full-bodied red

Open, fruity nose—forest fruits, cherries. Good weight and nice savoury fruit; lacks a bit of excitement at the price but enjoyable nevertheless.
Roast leg of pork or a casserole

Lamole di Lamole Campolungo DOCG Chianti Classico Riserva 93

Select Wines from Italy ☆ ☆

Full-bodied red, very tannic

Elegant, spicy nose of fruit and well-integrated oak. Ripe, red fruit flavours with deliciously savoury nuances of complex elegance with a chocolatey finish. A big wine that will last.
Perfect choice with game such as pheasant or wild duck

Mastroberardino Radici DOCG Taurasi 94

Select Wines from Italy ℝ

Full-bodied red, tannic

Ripe berry and cinnamon aromas. Tannins still quite assertive but will soften in time. Plenty of spicy complex fruit and supporting alcohol. Needs

time and is relatively expensive.
Rich rabbit or guineafowl stew with wine, herbs etc; also hard cheeses

Salarco Fassati DOCG Vino Nobile di Montepulciano Riserva 93

Select Wines from Italy ☆

Full-bodied red, very tannic

Rather scented cherries on the nose, quite complex, unusual aromas; nicely integrated oak on a very spicy palate which should soften to something potentially very fine.
Casserole of meat or game with a dark, wine-rich sauce

Santa Sofia DOC Amarone della Valpolicella Classico 90

Select Wines from Italy ℝ

Full-bodied red, tannic

Banoffi nose! Tangerines, almonds, toffee. Big and beautiful with loads of fruit and alcohol but not without elegance.
Not a food wine as such; try it with shaved Parmesan at the end of a meal

Red £20 - £25

Barbi DOCG Brunello di Montalcino 93

Select Wines from Italy ☆

Full-bodied red, very tannic,

Rather understated nose, redcurrants, cherries and a whiff of tobacco. Piquant acidity sets off intense and delicious fruit and ripe tannins. Long, lingering finish and lovely balance—should hold well.
Venison or spit-roasted pigeons

'The Cork Wine Merchants'

- Over 500 quality wines
- Quality staff on hand for advice
- 8 shops to choose from
- Full party/function service
- Wine consultancy service available
- Corporate and private tastings arranged
- Direct wine deliveries nationwide arranged
- Wholesale price-list for on-trade available on request
- Wine list available on request
- Wine Club—

'Douglas and Bishopstown Wine Club'

Main Office
Unit 27, St Patrick's Mall, Douglas, Cork
Phone: (021) 895 227/746
Fax: (021) 893 391
Wine consultant: Gary O'Donovan 087 263 2211

Branches
Douglas (021) 363 650 Bishopstown (021) 343 416
Blackpool (021) 398 177 Summerhill (021) 505 444
Oliver Plunkett St. (021) 277 626 Shandon St. (021) 399 121
Midleton (021) 613 001

'We have all the wine in the world'

Marchesi di Barolo DOCG Barbaresco Riserva 91

Select Wines from Italy ®

Full-bodied red, very tannic

Tobacco and plums on the nose, Dustily dry with high acidity and good extract but rather scarce fruit. Promises well with food. Good but not great of the style.
Dark, winey casserole

Red £25 - £30

Antinori Tignanello VdT Toscana 94

Grants ☆ ☆

Full-bodied red, tannic

Deep, complex aromas of tarry fruit, spice, blackcurrants and damsons. Full and intriguingly complex on the palate with layers of fruit and spice, developed smoky flavours and long savoury finish. Beautifully balanced with firm but ripe tannins.
Roast pigeon stuffed with olives and herbs, pheasant casserole, beef fillet or saddle of venison

Red 35 - £40

Marchesi di Barolo Cannubi DOCG Barolo Classico 90
Select Wines from Italy ©

Full-bodied red, very tannic

Bitter herbs, tar and strawberries all come through on the nose, along with tobacco and truffle. Big, full and smooth, high acidity and lashings of fruit though tannins also huge. A beautiful, Barolo still in the cradle—give it seven or eight years !
If you must drink it now, try with beef cooked in Barolo

Rosé £8 - £10

Kettmeir Lagrein Rosato DOC Alto Adige 96

Select Wines from Italy ®

Rosé

Fruity aromas of strawberry and cherries followed by attack of ripe, sharp red fruit. Plenty of flavour and good mouthfeel with some length in the finish. Very tasty but pricey.
Anchovies, tapenade or black olives

Lebanon

There is a long history of wine and winemaking in Lebanon which is especially significant when you realise that it includes the area which was the ancient land of Canaan. Now most winemaking is confined to the area around the Bekaa Valley. There is a strong French influence as in North Africa especially in the grapes. Château Musar is the most important name. In fact for most of the export market, it *is* Lebanese wine. Musar is full bodied with classic depth and character but a style all of its own. It has a high percentage of Cabernet Sauvignon which gives structure and the wine ages well. Its origin, and the charm of its producer Serge Hochar, combine to make Musar almost a cult wine and older vintages change hands at high prices.

Red £10 - £12

Ch. Musar (Gaston Hochar) 91
Grants ☆

Full-bodied red

Complex farmyard aromas with ripe jammy fruit. Baked strawberry fruit balanced by firm tannin. Warmth of alcohol in the finish. Lovely mature wine with great character.
Game and long-simmered casseroles; roast lamb

For a detailed explanation of wine styles, see pages 7–9

New Zealand

New Zealand's modern wine industry stormed on to the world stage with the mind-blowing aromatics of Marlborough Sauvignon Blanc and the Cloudy Bay phenomenon but since then seems to have retreated in consumer imagination.

It is a young industry, and its much hyped cool climate means considerable vintage variation not normally associated with the New World. It is also a small-scale industry with high running costs and cannot compete on price with its neighbour. However, put another way it is a creative, innovative producer, which makes fashionably cool wines, unique in the southern hemisphere, with an element of exclusivity.

New Zealand's strength is in the variety of styles it produces which are all marked by a subtlety and elegance much harder to achieve in the heat of Australia. Apart from Sauvignon Blanc, which can be quite over the top, it makes some fine Chardonnay, carefully oaked and balanced. New Zealand Riesling, both dry and late harvested, can be stunning. It has all the racy finesse of the grape combined with deliciously aromatic lime-scented fruit. New Zealand also succeeds with the fickle Pinot Noir to capture the intense flavour in a delicate shell which makes the wine great.

As a footnote, 1998 was an extraordinary year for New Zealand wineries, in which El Nino's antics with the weather caused a near drought, great confusion and possibly the vintage of the century.

White £5 - £6

Cooks Gisborne Chardonnay 96

Fitzgerald ®

Full-bodied white

Smoky minerally aromas with a touch of toffee apple. Reserved palate with buttery apple flavours enlivened with citrus fruit. Well-balanced with a long creamy finish.

Smoked foods including pasta with smoked bacon; avocado and chicken salad or pork and apple

White £6 - £8

Montana Marlborough Chardonnay 96

Grants ®

Full-bodied white

Inviting nose with rich honeyed and buttery aromas and a refreshing touch of lemon. Full-bodied with ripe fruit and balancing acidity. Very good value.

Textured fishes like bass and mullet especially when cooked with stronger flavours; also chicken in cream sauce and mild to medium-hot spiced foods

Montana Marlborough Sauvignon Blanc 97

Grants ®

Aromatic white, fruit-driven

Exuberant exotic fruit aromas with a twist of lime. Crisp, refreshing palate with plenty of fruit. Well-balanced for the style and highly drinkable.
Thai-style dishes; smoked fish chowder; asparagus

Stoneleigh Vineyard Marlborough Sauvignon Blanc 96

Fitzgerald ®

Aromatic white, fruit-driven

Fresh youthful aromas of green fruits, nettles and limes. Dry and fresh with green fruit and nettles coming through. Drink before summer '99.
Stir-fried prawns with lemongrasss, coriander and ginger or squid with tomatoes and spices

The Sounds Marlborough Sauvignon Blanc 97

Dunnes Stores ®

Aromatic white, fruit-driven

Pungent aromas of pea-pods and grass. Good weight of minerally citrus flavours balance grapefruit-like acidity. Good length.
Zesty seafood mayonnaise with spicy herb flavours

White £8 - £10

Esk Valley Hawkes Bay Sauvignon Blanc 96

Findlater ®

Aromatic white, fruit-driven

Typical Sauvignon aromas followed by punchy attack of crisp green apple fruit with a touch of green pepper. A lovely refreshing wine, fruit-driven but not without elegance.
Needs strong flavours and works well with chicken or fish kebabs, feta cheese baked with peppers and many warm salads

Fall Harvest Chardonnay (unoaked) 96

Barry & Fitzwilliam ®

Full-bodied white, oak

Very buttery on the nose with ripe peach and melon fruit. Definite oaky tones and clean dry finish.
Creamy pasta, baked or roasted chicken especially with fruity stuffing

Montana Reserve Marlborough Sauvignon Blanc 97

Grants ©

Aromatic white

Elderflowers and acid drops on the nose followed by an equally up-front palate with plenty of varietal character; crisp acidity, mouthwatering, mouthfilling fruit. A positive statement but balanced nevertheless.
Goat's cheese; smoked trout with avocado; Dim Sum

Montana Reserve Marlborough Barrique-Fermented Chardonnay 97

Grants ☆

Full-bodied white, oak

Attractive aromas of honey, toast and rather floral fruit. A gorgeous, ripe, fruity wine with a smooth, slightly oily texture of well used new oak with balanced acidity and length.

Well-flavoured, creamy chicken dishes, fish, chicken barbecue and turkey

Morton Estate Hawkes Bay Chardonnay 96

Dillon

Full-bodied white

Lovely ripe fruit aromas with ripe tropical and citrus fruit on the palate backed by balanced acidity and alcohol. Long finish. A big wine at a small price.

Chicken in cream sauce; smoked fish pie

Morton Estate Hawkes Bay Sauvignon Blanc 96

Dillon ®

Aromatic white, fruit-driven

Green apples and gooseberries on the nose. Broad and mouthfilling with green fruits and a touch of lime and balanced acidity. Well-made, straightforward varietal.

Rich tomato sauces, stir-fried chicken and chunky fish such as snapper cooked with peppers

Sauvignon Blanc Premier Selection 98

Karwig ®

Aromatic white, fruit-driven

Green fruit and lemongrass aromas. Quite elegant, crisp green fruits and good clean refreshing finish.

Highly flavoured and spicy food, seafood with mayonnaise, spicy prawns with tomato

Shingle Peak Marlborough Pinot Gris 96

Mitchell ☆

Aromatic white, fruit-driven

Intriguing aromas of smoky, earthy fruit with floral overtones. Dry but creamy, peaches mixed with kiwi and starfruit. Long, lingering flavours with real complexity.

Fillet of pork with cream and warm spices—cumin, coriander, juniper; also spicy chicken or a vegetable flan

Shingle Peak Marlborough Riesling 97

Mitchell ☆

Aromatic white, fruit-driven

Very intense aromas of citrus fruit, honeysuckly and a definite oily hint. Full but racy with lots of floral fruit flavour and a very long finish. Lovely now and can only get better.

Fish and vegetable dishes, with spices and strong flavours: crab salad with ginger, Thai spiced fishcakes, chicken with coriander

Villa Maria Private Bin Chardonnay 97

Allied Drinks ☆

Full-bodied white

Assertive aromas of ripe exotic fruits—pineapples, melons. Dry, but with mouth-watering luscious ripe pear and banana spiked with pepper. Long finish with a touch of butterscotch. Good value.

Richly sauced lobster or monkfish with vegetables and cream. Also chicken breast with a rich creamy sauce.

Villa Maria Private Bin Sauvignon Blanc 97

Allied Drinks ☆

Aromatic white, fruit-driven

Aromas of ripe gooseberry mixed with cut grass and nettles. Dry, with tart green fruit and lively citrus acidity. Good long finish. Enjoy its youth and drink before the end of '99.

Red peppers baked with feta or goat's cheese; or scallops and coriander

White £10 - £12

Hunter's Chardonnay 95

Gilbeys ☆ ☆

Full-bodied white, oak

Quite Burgundian aromas. A wine with lovely balance between elegant complexity and ripe, buttery fruit in a lean classic style.

Roast farm chicken or turbot or snapper with cream sauce

Hunter's Sauvignon Blanc 97

Gilbeys ®

Aromatic white, fruit-driven

Nettles, herbs and fresh green asparagus on the nose, Dry with quite mouthfilling texture and tight green fruit which should open nicely in the coming months.

Asparagus and hollandaise sauce; smoked fish soup

Lawson's Dry Hills Gewurztraminer 97

Febvre ®

Aromatic white

Rose petals and marmalade meet on the nose. Dry but with intense fruit flavours of Turkish Delight and orange peel. Balanced acidity cleanses the palate. Good length, too.

Spicy Indian pastries or stir-fried noodles, generally good with Oriental spices

Lawson's Dry Hills Riesling 97

Febvre ®

Aromatic white, fruit-driven

Attractive floral, lime aromas. Dry with ripe citrusy fruit, quite young but should develop quickly to more complex tones. Good length in the finish.

Spicy fishcakes or deep-fried vegetables; fish with salsa

Wairau River Sauvignon Blanc 96

TDL ®

Aromatic white, fruit-driven

Minerally green fruit with a touch of smoke. Fresh, lively flavours of gooseberries and nettles, not overpowering. Good finish with plenty of lingering flavour.

Spicy fish fritters or pasta and sun-dried tomatoes

White £12 - £15

Marlborough Wairau River Chardonnay 96

TDL   ®

Full-bodied white, oak

Oaky aromas with apple and peach fruit and pepper spice, Mouthwatering fruit with a combination of ripe, honeyed flavours and refreshing citrus. Well-integrated with a touch of smoke in the finish.

Soufflé, lobster and asparagus or chicken and shrimps in coconut milk

Villa Maria Reserve Wairau Valley Sauvignon Blanc 97

Allied Drinks   ☆ ☆

Aromatic white, fruit-driven

Quite floral aromas mix with freshly picked peas, nettles and asparagus. Intense and power-ful flavours of vibrant, herba-ceous green fruit with grape-fruit acidity intertwined. Long finish.

Mixed seafood flavoured with Oriental herbs and spices or Thai food in general. Also good with chicken and sun-dried tomatoes with basil.

White £15 - £20

Corbans Hawkes Bay Private Bin Chardonnay 95

Fitzgerald   ©

Full-bodied white, oak

Intense aromas of lemon and honeyed fruit lead into cool,

well-balanced flavours. There is plenty of fruit and great complexity underneath in a classic, serious wine.

Lobster or richly cooked monkfish; chicken in cream

Wairau River Sauvignon Blanc Reserve 96

TDL   ®

Aromatic white, fruit-driven

Green fruits and garden peas on the nose. Ripe citrusy fruit with a minerally edge—could be more concentrated given the price tag.

Pasta and green vegetables or prawns and asparagus

Red £5 - £6

Cooks Hawkes Bay Cabernet Sauvignon-Merlot 95

Fitzgerald   ®

Light fruity red

Lively brambly fruit on the nose. Very approachable with soft easy fruit character.

Spicy lamb casserole or meaty pasta

Red £6 - £8

Montana Marlborough Cabernet Sauvignon/Merlot 96

Grants   ☆

Medium to full-bodied red, tannic

Slightly stalky blackcurrant aromas with undertones of nettle. Cool but ripe fruit on the palate and quite an elegant balance of tannins, acidity and fruit. Flavour develops well to richer plum and even chocolatey tastes with spice in the finish.

Versatile with most red meats but

especially good with roast lamb

Stoneleigh Vineyard Marlborough Cabernet Sauvignon 96

Fitzgerald   ®

Medium-bodied red

Blackberry and peppermint on the nose. Firm and tightly structured with rather stalky blackcurrant fruit and nice long finish.

Grilled or roast lamb; steaks

Red £8 - £10

Lintz Estate Martinborough Cabernet Merlot 95

Superquinn   ®

Medium-bodied red, tannic

Very ripe aromas of Ribena, plums and brambles, slightly herbaceous twist. Very ripe palate with soft tannins and fruit similar to the nose. Nice long finish.

Mild to medium-hot spices with lamb or beef

Morton Estate White Label Hawkes Bay Cabernet Merlot 95

Dillon   ®

Full-bodied red

Blackcurrant comes through

quite a characterful nose. Well made, very correct and balanced palate with some depth of fruit. Pleasant rather than exciting.

Simple meat casseroles, steaks and grills

Te Whetu Hawkes Bay Red 96

Allied Drinks   ®

Medium-bodied red

Good concentrated blackcurrant fruit aromas with hints of lavender and stalky backdrop. Ripe fruit flavours and nice elegant balance within a firm texture.

Irish stew or other casseroles

Red £10 - £12

Montana Reserve Marlborough Barrique-fermented Merlot 96

Grants   ®

Medium-bodied red

Toasty vanilla and ripe plums on the nose. The oak on the palate is just balanced by the fruit to give a rich, easy-drinking style with added polish.

Grilled meats, lamb and beef or liver and bacon

Portugal

Until it joined the European Union in 1986, Portugal was relatively isolated from the rest of Europe. This was in part political, in part geographic. From the point of view of its winemakers it meant that they were largely untouched by modern innovation and technology. Equally it prevented the spread of international grapes and winemaking techniques and preserved the traditional character of Portuguese wines.

Portugal's wines need a level of understanding to be appreciated. The grapes are for the most part totally different in flavour, fruit and structure. There is no similar taste to that of the Baga, Periquita or Touriga Nacional except perhaps another Portuguese grape. That extraordinary combination of acidity and toughness which characterises many of the wines is a product of climate and winemaking unique to Portugal. They are also wines intended to accompany and complement food. Given this understanding the wines are extremely rewarding; without, they will be neglected.

Membership of the EU brought an end to the monopolies of the co-ops and hence supplied the incentive to produce high quality wines. The EU also gave grants to improve and develop wineries. For the most part this has worked well. In a few cases commercial motives have led to rather bland modern wines, with the edges well-rounded but also robbed of much of their traditional character. One can detect an antipodean influence in the Alentejo and much of the South. But on the whole outsiders such as David Baverstock at Herdade do Esporão have managed to combine the best of modern expertise with the best of tradition.

Portugal's great strength is its grapes which are unique to the country and great in variety. The Port varieties of the Douro are proving capable of making good light wines also. Bairrada's Baga grape, now given less ageing in large wooden vats, has excellent fruit and a tightly-knit structure of tannins and acidity to match. In the South the inappropriately named Periquita, provides wonderfully refreshing wines, dry and firm but with wonderfully lively fruit.

Although the trend is to reduce ageing in vat, ageing in bottle is a different matter and many Portuguese wines repay keeping. Even some of the old Reserva and Garrafeira wines still around, at 10 or even 20 years old, can be bargains of the highest quality.

White £5 or less

Quinta da Aveleda Vinho Verde DOC nv

Superquinn ®

Light dry white

Green fruit and hints of sherbet aromas; fresh and lively with delicate lime fruit. Easy summer drinking.
Deep-fried fish or avocado mousse

Alta Mesa VR Estramadura 97

United Beverages ®

Light fruity white

Peach and pear ripeness on the nose. Light and stylish with lovely ripe fruit similar to the nose. Reasonable length, too.
Chicken and pepper salad, ham with melon or waldorf salad

White £6 - £8

Fiuza Chardonnay VR Ribatejo 96

Superquinn ®

Full-bodied white, oak

Lovely aromas of buttered toast and melons. Ripe tropical fruit with refreshing acidity and mineral undertones with a smoky finish.
Chicken saltimbocco, fish pie or smoked haddock tart

Albis VR Terras do Sado 96

Gilbeys ®

Light dry white

Vanilla and almond scents, quite a creamy mouthfeel with fresh acidity and citrus fruit flavours. Nice and long with character.
Spicy chicken and noodles; pasta with spinach or courgettes; simply-cooked cod or hake

João Pires VR Terras do Sado 97

Superquinn ®

Light fruity white

Floral, lemon sherbet aromas; tropical and citrus fruit flavours with fresh acidity.
Hors d'oeuvres and spicy Indian pastries

Red £5 or less

Allianca Particular DOC Dão 94

Quinnsworth ©

Full-bodied red

Typical complex Dão nose with rich fruit and earthiness. Dry and firm with rich plummy fruit flavours on the palate. Smooth texture and good length.
Moussaka, braised kidneys, stuffed shoulder of lamb

Mandos Reserva DOC Douro 96

Quinnsworth ©

Medium-bodied red

Mellow cherry and bramble nose, firm and tight with a good weight of ripe, even jammy fruits. Nice length with a touch of spice to finish.
Kidneys and bacon or pork chops

Neblina DOC Douro 95

Dunnes Stores ££

Medium-bodied red, tannic

Fruitcake, tobacco and smoke give quite a complex nose. Good weight of fruit balancing a firm structure of tannins and acidity. Nice wine.

Vegetarian dishes of lentil or beans; also pork and aubergine casserole

Caves Bonifácio VdM nv

Peter Dalton ®

Medium-bodied red

Fruit of the forest aromas with nutty overtones. Quite firm palate with good weight of ripe, spicy fruit. Long and mellow in the finish. Good value.

Bean casserole or sausages and lentils, also pork and tomato stew

Alta Mesa VR Estramadura 96

United Beverages ££

Medium-bodied red

Dark cherries and brambles with a hint of tobacco. Dry with very ripe plummy fruit. Balanced structure and refreshing bitter twist in the fruit. Very good value.

Pigeon or kidneys and mushrooms or a meat casserole

JP Barrel Selection VR Terras do Sado 92

Quinnsworth ®

Medium-bodied red

Rich fruit pudding nose with a touch of leather, dry and firm with ripe bramble fruits. Quite a bitter twist and good length.

Rice and chorizo, pepperoni pizza, well-flavoured pasta and tomato dishes

Red £5 - £6

Quinta da Parrotes VQPRD Alenquer 96

Dunnes Stores ©

Medium-bodied red, tannic

Autumn berries on the nose; firm acidity and tannin yet quite smooth-textured. Decent regional wine.

Chunky country sausages; shepherd's pie; roast pork

Red £6 - £8

Bright Brothers DOC Douro 95

Superquinn ©

Full-bodied red

Rich, mature autumnal fruit on the nose, good structure with lots of jammy, spicy fruit flavours and a smooth texture. Good combination of style and character.

Spicy sausages, pork with chestnuts, turkey stuffed with prunes

Fiuza Cabernet Sauvignon VR Ribatejo 95

Superquinn ®

Full-bodied red

Smoky blackcurrant aromas. Dry and firm but with plenty of fruit and a nice long, spicy finish.

Lasagne, meat casseroles or grilled lamb

Quinta da Alorna VR Ribatejo 94

Dunnes Stores ££

Full-bodied red, tannic

Plums and dark berry fruit with underlying aromas of tobacco and spice. Firm with dry dusty tannins but plenty of ripe fruit

Nederburg

Barton & Guestier
La passion du vin depuis 1725

LUPÉ-CHOLET

I.L. RUFFINO

CONTI SERRISTORI

BLUE NUN®

SANDEMAN
— EST 1790 —

BOLLA

MATEUS®
PRODUCED AND BOTTLED IN PORTUGAL

FOUNDED IN 1850
CARMEN

FETZER

FONTANA CANDIDA

MONTECILLO

Fine wines from Edward Dillon.

to balance. Nice weight and complexity of flavour. Long finish and real quality for the price.
Wild duck or a rich lamb casserole; venison pie

Red £10 - £12

Pegos Claros VQPRD Palmela 93
Findlater   ☆ ☆
Full-bodied red

Rich plummy fruit and spicy tobacco on the nose. Firm but ripe tannin balancing very rich fruit—plums and cherries—in a smooth, quite elegant, texture coated with fine bitter choco-

late. Long elegant finish. A lovely wine, well worth the price.
Wild duck or pheasant; pasta with hare sauce

Vila Santa VR Alentejo 96
Findlater   ☆
Full-bodied red

Bramble fruit with hints of vanilla and toffee. Fleshy, ripe fruit, fruit compote flavours with hints of bitter chocolate. Good firm structure holds everything together through a long spicy finish.
Rabbit stew or a rich chicken casserole with an olive oil-based sauce

---

Editor's Selection—Sandy O'Byrne's favourites

Sipp Mack Riesling AC Alsace 96 (France)
Shingle Peak Marlborough Riesling 97 (New Zealand)
Guigal AC Côtes du Rhône blanc 97 (France-Rhône)
Quinta da Alorna VR Ribatejo 94 (Portugal)
Saumur Champigny Dom. Filliatreau 96 (France-Loire)
Ch. Romanin AC Les Baux-de-Provence 94(France
Tioio Ribera del Duero 96 (Spain)
Pelorus Cloudy Bay 93 (Sparkling-New Zealand)
Weingut C. Schumacher Herxheimer Himmelreich
     Riesling Spätlese 97 (Germany)
Ch. Tabilk Cabernet Sauvignon 94 (Australia)
Dom. Schlumberger Les Princes Abbés Pinot Gris AC
     Alsace 96 (France-Alsace)
Taittinger Brut Réserve Champagne (France-Sparkling)

Romania

Romania is the largest wine producer in Eastern Europe and also has traditionally the biggest home market. The passage from state control to private enterprise has not been entirely smooth and investment is still badly needed.

That the country has great potential as a quality producer can be seen in the really excellent fruit produced, sometimes by relatively crude winemaking. Increasingly wineries have temperature-controlled tanks and many use specially designed rotofermenters which give the soft, fruity flavours typical of many exported wines. Ageing in large oak vats is still usual but generally it is not over-done and the fruit shines through well.

Romanian Pinot Noir was a great success on this market as it supplied rich, sweet typically Pinot fruit in a soft, approachable structure and at a very low price. Wood-aged Cabernets are balanced and quite distinctive, and Merlot rich and savoury. The whites, too, are beginning to improve.

The intrinsic quality of Romania is hardly in question, the present problem is mainly in consistency and a high rate of bottle variation. Modern bottling lines are still few and it is often at this late stage that an otherwise sound wine suffers. Time, money and confidence are needed for a country with the potential to become a major European producer.

Red £5 - £6

Dealul Mare Special Reserve Cabernet Sauvignon 95
Barry & Fitzwilliam　　Ⓡ
Full-bodied red, tannic

Good concentration of rather dusty fruit; nice weight of jammy ripe fruit on the palate with balanced tannin and acidity.
Lighter casseroles and meat pies eg navarin of lamb, steak pie

Murfatlar Cabernet Sauvignon 93
Barry & Fitzwilliam　　££
Full-bodied red

Ripe, soft fruit nose with nice weight of slightly jammy fruit on the palate. Good concentration nicely balanced by light tannin and cleansing acidity.
Chunky sausages, meatballs and Irish stew

Posta Romana Classic Pinot Noir 94

Barry & Fitzwilliam ®

Medium-bodied red

Quite rich, almost over-ripe on the nose. Dry, but with mature, ripe strawberry fruit flavour and very silky, appealing texture.
Light meat dishes, mushroom and cheese soufflé, pancakes filled with ham and cheese

Prahova Valley Reserve Cabernet Sauvignon 94

Barry & Fitzwilliam ££

Full-bodied red

Leafy blackcurrant on the nose with stalky, quite classic fruit on the palate. Well-made and balanced with a long finish.
Especially good with roast or pan-fried lamb and meat in general; also casseroles

Prahova Valley Reserve Pinot Noir 91

Barry & Fitzwilliam ££

Medium-bodied red, tannic

Nice earthy touches on the nose; dry, but with a depth of ripe fruit flavours and very well-balanced tannin and

acidity giving a soft, mellow wine with a long finish.
Strong flavours such as chicken in red wine or kidneys with cognac and cream

Red £6 - £8

Rovit Vineyards Special Reserve Pinot Noir 93

Barry & Fitzwilliam ®

Medium-bodied red

Good mix of fruit and spice aromas give an attractive nose. Dry and spicy with nice balancing fruit and refreshing acidity.
Casseroles and lighter meat dishes such as rabbit casserole; also some cheeses and cooked cheese as in cheese tart

Sahateni Vineyards Special Reserve Merlot 95

Barry & Fitzwilliam ££

Medium-bodied red, tannic

Quite rich and plummy on the nose with good weight of similar fruit on the palate and balanced tannin and acidity.
Good stews and smaller cuts of meat and some offal, also good with vegetable dishes: bean casserole, liver with red wine

South Africa

When it first reappeared on the world market, economic pressures and a backward, non-competitive industry in South Africa, made the bargain basement end of wine sales seem attractive. However, there has been a big push toward quality as well.

Apart from technology, skill and general updating of plant and technique, South African winemakers have re-discovered cooler vineyard sites. The importance of this can be seen when comparing a Sauvignon Blanc from a warm region with one from a cool climate area such as Walker's Bay. The difference is clear: clean, zippy aromatic fruit and style rather than oily grassy flavours and rather heavy-handed fruit.

Quality-driven producers such as the Meerlust Estate and Peter Finlayson, originally the winemaker at Hamilton Russell, now with his own property, a joint venture with Burgundian Paul Bouchard, Bouchard Finlayson Estate have proved that high quality brings high prices.

Finlayson has been particularly successful with Pinot Noir which challenges some of the best in the New World. But such wines are a tiny percentage of total production in a country notorious for supply problems and shortages. The best is undoubtedly only just beginning to appear and it may always be in short supply.

The lower end of the price range, however, is not a gloomy tale of bulk production. Producers like the Australian-influenced Long Mountain manage to produce excellent easy-drinking, well-priced varietals from a mixture of cool and warm vineyard sites. Traditional varieties like Pinotage with the benefits of modern technology provide ripe, juicy, easy-drinking reds at reasonable prices.

White £5 or less

Simonsig Adelblanc 97
United Beverages ®
Light fruity white
Good ripe, aromatic nose . Dry and fresh with nice fruit character. A balanced, well-made wine, very good for the price.
Good on its own or with light starters, salads etc

White £5 - £6

Cape Indaba Chardonnay 96
Barry & Fitzwilliam　　Ⓡ

Light fruity white

Very appealing fruity style with loads of melon and peach flavours. Good for the price.
Mildly spiced dishes and creamy curries of fish or chicken

KWV Gewürztraminer 95
TDL　　Ⓡ

Aromatic white, fruit-driven

Very spicy with Turkish Delight and lychee aromas. Lots of exotic fruit flavour but dry with balancing acidity. Finishes a little short but good for the price.
Small spicy foods or a salad of red peppers

KWV Sauvignon Blanc 96
TDL　　Ⓡ

Aromatic white, fruit-driven

Simple ripe gooseberry character on the nose. Good ripe fruit and crisp acidity. Straightforward and typical—good for the price
Salads of vegetables and cheese or a roasted vegetable salad

Long Mountain Dry Riesling 97
Fitzgerald　　££

Aromatic white, fruit-driven

Hints of lime and green apple on the nose. Dry with quite crisp acidity and appley fruit.
Spicy Indian pastries or kebabs of feta and sun-dried tomatoes

Nederburg Sauvignon Blanc/ Chardonnay 96
Dillon　　Ⓡ

Light fruity white

Well-made, simple and very correct wine with ripe fruit and zippy acidity.
Versatile with salads and light pasta dishes especially containing smoked foods or mild spices

Ryland's Grove Barrell Fermented Chenin Blanc WO Stellenbosch 97
Quinnsworth　　Ⓡ

Medium-bodied white with

Hints of lemon and lime marmalade on the nose. Medium weight of rather tropical fruit flavours. Good finish. A well-made wine and good value.
Vegetable-based dishes especially pastries; stir-fried fish or vegetable terrine

Simonsig Chenin Blanc 97
United Beverages　　Ⓡ

Light fruity white

Lightish nose with simple grapey, floral aromas. Similar palate, dry, soft and gulpable. A nice party or summer wine.
Very versatile party drinking especially with a big chicken curry

White £6 - £8

Boschendal Chenin Blanc 96
Grants　　Ⓡ

Light fruity white

Dry with ripe fruit, fairly well-balanced and simple. A good picnic wine.
Light, cold foods and snacks

Fleur du Cap Chardonnay WO Coastal Region 96

Febvre ®

Full-bodied white

Clean and fresh with melon and lemon fruit and some wet wool aromas. Broad melon fruit flavours with citrus acidity. Nicely balanced wine.
Fish and hollandaise sauce or a creamy pasta

KWV Chardonnay 96

TDL ®

Full-bodied white, oak

Oaky fruit aromas and a creamy, well-rounded palate with a bit of length in the finish.
Great with barbecue chicken and pork kebabs

Nederburg Chardonnay 97

Dillon ££

Full-bodied white

Waxy, honeyed tones and well-rounded, well-balanced flavours of ripe fruity and zippy lemon. Quite stylish.
Cold foods, salads—even corona-tion chicken

Niel Joubert Chenin Blanc 96

TDL ®

Light fruity white

Typical Chenin nose: wet wool with floral notes. Less reward-ing palate with simple fruit and medium weight. Balanced and well made, nevertheless.
Good choice for stuffed vegetables (not tomatoes), or light vegetable pastries

Simonsig Chardonnay 96

United Beverages ®

Full-bodied white, oak

Rich honeyed fruit and lots of oak on the nose. A big wine with ripe fruit and lots of oak. Good value.
Roast turkey or chicken with smoked bacon

Villiera Estate Blue Ridge Blanc 97

Grants ®

Light fruity white

Sauvignon predominates on the nose with fresh gooseberry aromas. Dry and well-balanced with light to medium body, good fruit and nice finish. Good value, easy-drinking.
Tomato-based starter or a mousse of smoked fish

White £8 - £10

Boschendal Chardonnay 95

Grants ®

Full-bodied white

Subtle nose followed by well-balanced palate with citrusy fruit flavours; medium to full-bodied with a touch of oak and clean dry finish.
Sauced fish, avocados and chicken salad

Mooiplaas Sauvignon Blanc 97

Findlater ®

Aromatic white, fruit-driven

Aromatic, slightly grassy nose. Quite refined and balanced on the palate with a good crisp finish. A nice wine.
Grilled or pan-fried fish—brill, bass, etc; flavoursome sauces of herbs, tomato or milder spices

Rietvallei Chardonnay WO Robertson 96

Febvre ®

Full-bodied white

Slightly under-ripe melon and lemon on the nose. Nice weight of ripe fruit; full-bodied with brisk, tart fruit finish.
Well-textured fish such as turbot in a seafood or cream sauce; or try with avocado

White £10 - £12

Plaisir de Merle Chardonnay WO Paarl 96

Dillon ®

Full-bodied white, oak

Good, quite elegant nose of honey, citrus and vanilla. Lovely complexity on the palate with good weight of fruit, well-balanced and with a long finish.
Roast chicken or creamy lobster dishes

White £12 - £15

KWV Cathedral Cellar Chardonnay 96

TDL ☆

Full-bodied white, oak

Nice mix of toasty, biscuity and tropical fruit aromas. Real depth in the fruit on the palate, perhaps lacking a little in complexity at the price but juicy and attractive all the same.
Good with spiced dishes especially satay kebabs and salmon in an Oriental marinade

White £15 - £20

Groot Constantia Sauvignon Blanc 96

Fitzgerald ☆

Aromatic white, fruit-driven

Very intense aromas of gooseberries and nettles. Glorious ripe fruit well balanced by acidity and alcohol. Long and elegant wine.
Salmon and hollandaise sauce

Long Mountain Sauvignon Blanc 97

Fitzgerald ®

Aromatic white, fruit-driven

Quite classy on the nose—ripe gooseberries with steely undertones. Nicely balanced fruit and acidity and a good weight of fruit.
Stir-fry with coriander and ginger flavours or barbecued fish and tomato salsa

Red £5 or less

Simonsig Adelberg 97

United Beverages ££

Medium-bodied red

Nice fruity, blackcurrant and raspberry aromas. Good ripe cherry fruit with some weight and an appetising touch of tannin. Quite long and very good value.
A good party wine with mixed meats and salad combinations

Red £5 - £6

Cape Indaba Merlot 96

Barry & Fitzwilliam ®

Medium-bodied red, fruit-driven

Fruit and vegetal aromas with lively, ripe cherry and straw-

berry fruit taste. Very good for the price.
Chargrilled dishes of the lighter sort, including vegetables

Cape Indaba Pinotage 96
Barry & Fitzwilliam ®

Full-bodied red, tannic

Good combination of fruit and oak on the nose. Quite a fruit bowl taste with a spicy, slightly medicinal tone. Balanced tannins add structure. A big wine and great value.
Pot roast or barbecued beef

Kumala Ruby Cabernet Merlot 97
Supervalu/Centra ®

Medium to full-bodied red

Attractive blackcurrant fruit aromas. Lean fruit on the palate but well-balanced with lean, youthful fruit character.
Red meats in general especially lamb and duck and robust stews

Long Mountain Cabernet Sauvignon 97
Fitzgerald ££

Medium-bodied red

Simple ripe fruit character on the nose. Straightforward juicy fruit flavours with balanced acidity and tannin.
Lighter meat dishes, stir-fried beef, cutlets etc

Long Mountain Merlot/Shiraz 97
Fitzgerald ®

Medium-bodied red, fruit-driven

Simple juicy berries and blackcurrant on the nose; soft and fruity with crisp acidity and a slightly burnt taste in the finish.

Medium-hot spices; pasta with some chilli; pepperoni; lamb with ginger and peppers

Nederburg Pinotage 95
Dillon ££

Medium-bodied red

Pleasant fruity nose with hints of spice. Nice balance of fruit, acidity and ripe, light tannins. Good value.
Hearty casserole of chicken and chorizo sausage or chorizo kebabs

Schoone Gevel Merlot 97
Quinnsworth ®

Medium-bodied red

Quite intense nose of baked plums. Dry with quite marked acidity and soft tannin. Lightish fruit but an easy-drinking style nevertheless
Bobotie or spicy kebabs

Red £6 - £8

African Sky Crux 95
Febvre ®

Medium-bodied red

Blackcurrant and plum aromas with a touch of woodsmoke. Nicely balanced palate, round and flavoursome.
Chicken and chorizo casserole or lamb and bacon kebabs

Bellingham Cabernet Sauvignon 96
Dunnes Stores ££

Full-bodied red

Quite complex nose. Crisp acidity, firm tannin and a good weight of fruit. Rather elegant wine for the price, with a good long finish.
Well-flavoured meat dishes, lamb steaks with herbs or beef in pastry

Bellingham Pinotage 96

Dunnes Stores ©

Full-bodied red

Loads of fruit on the nose. Full-bodied with a weight of fruit and spicy overtones. Well-balanced with good length in the finish.

Roast leg of autumn lamb cooked with herbs and garlic

Bellingham Shiraz 96

Dunnes Stores ®

Medium-bodied red, fruit-driven

Simple, fruity nose with hints of raspberry. Dry and well-balanced with direct fruitiness and savoury finish.

Spicy sausages or kebabs

KWV Cabernet Sauvignon 92

TDL ®

Medium-bodied red

Blackcurrant and oak aromas show a touch of maturity. A mellow harmonious wine with good intensity of fruit.

Fillet of lamb or duck, or guineafowl

KWV Pinotage 94

TDL ££

Full-bodied red

Big, earthy spicy nose with lots of ripe fruit aromas. Big mouthfilling wine with fruit, structure and length of finish. Super stuff!

Grilled venison steaks

Niel Joubert Cabernet Sauvignon 96

TDL ®

Medium-bodied red

Smoky blackcurrant aromas.

Well-balanced structure with soft berry fruit and underlying smoky, meaty flavours.

A very good choice for a hearty casserole of meat in wine

Niel Joubert Pinotage 96

TDL ®

Medium-bodied red

Ripe fruity, slightly spicy nose. Ripe cherry fruit with balancing tannin and good length.

Chunky, spicy sausages or kebabs

Simonsig Pinotage 97

United Beverages ©

Full-bodied red

Rich nose of cherries, cedar and spice. Quite full with loads of fruit nicely balanced by tannin. Long finish.

Robust casserole of beef or lamb with vegetables and garlic

Simonsig Shiraz 95

United Beverages ®

Full-bodied red

Punchy up-front aromas of cherry fruit with smoky, woody overtones. Dry, with balanced acidity and fruit mixed with smoky flavours. Slightly warm finish.

Stew of beef and mushrooms or barbecued or grilled meats

Tesco Beyers Truter Pinotage WO Stellenbosch nv

Quinnsworth ®

Medium-bodied red

Rich, ripe aromas of dark berry fruit with a touch of spice. Attractive flavours, ripe and jammy with soft easy-drinking appeal.

Spicy sausages, hamburgers and meatballs

Villiera Estate Blue Ridge Rouge 96

Grants   ££

Medium-bodied red

Full fruity nose with a hint of spice; nice balance—a bit like a young Rhône, good for the price.
Spicy minced meat dishes—even a not too fiery chilli con carne

Red £8 - £10

Allesverloren Tinta Barocca WO Swartland 94

Febvre   ®

Full-bodied red

Ripe brambles and plums with a hint of gaminess. Quite elegant palate with a broad expanse of rich, warm fruit, mellow and satisfying with a long finish.
Venison pie or stew

Villiera Estate Merlot 96

Grants   ®

Medium-bodied red

Subtle aromas of fruit and a touch of oak. Mellow yet quite concentrated fruit, with plumminess and a dry finish.
Grilled meats, gammon steaks and shepherd's pie

Red £10 - £12

Alto Estate Rouge WO Stellenbosch 91

Febvre   ®

Full-bodied red

Very intense and quite complex nose. Softening tannin and complex fruit with a broad mature character.
Roast rib of beef or simply cooked game

Brenthurst Merlot Cabernet Sauvignon 94

Dunnes Stores   ®

Medium-bodied red, fruit-driven

Really rich plummy and blackcurrant nose. Very good balance between acidity, ripe tannin, weighty fruit and well-integrated oak. Very well made.
This wine has the balance for quite classic food: try it with duck and blackcurrant or with medallions of beef with shallot sauce

Middelvlei Cabernet Sauvignon WO Stellenbosch 89

Febvre   ®

Full-bodied red

Lovely ripe blackcurrant fruit on the nose which rolls out in layers of flavour, ripe and juicy. Nice balance with smooth yet firm structure.
Shoulder of lamb with herbs and garlic

Plaisir de Merle Cabernet Sauvignon WO Paarl 95

Dillon   ®

Medium-bodied red

Blackcurrant and raspberry fruit follows from the nose to the palate. Dry, with balanced acidity and soft tannin. Well made, easy-drinking with simple fruit character, A touch overpriced.
Richly sauced beef or lamb

Red £12 - £15

Mooiplaas Cabernet Sauvignon 96

Findlater　　　　　　©

Full-bodied red

Autumnal fruits with a hint of smoke on the nose, quite herbal. Dry and well-balanced with impressive intensity of fruit and very long finish.
Meat, especially lamb—very good with a ragoût of kidneys

Red £15 - £20

Groot Constantia Cabernet Sauvignon 93

Fitzgerald　　　　　　®

Medium-bodied red

Blackcurrant aromas with hints of tobacco. Supple and well-balanced with quite refined fruit and a lengthy ending.
Duck breast, lamb or roast turkey

Groot Constantia Pinotage 94

Fitzgerald　　　　　　®

Full-bodied red

Rich and complex on the nose. Elegant with mouthwatering fruit and a good long finish.
Steaks and garlic butter or a casserole

Aperitifs

Wine makes a good aperitif. It stimulates the palate and prepares it for the meal, whereas spirits and other drinks dull it. Champagne and other sparkling wines are excellent icebreakers while other fresh fruity whites with lively acidity are a great and imaginative way to start.

Weingut Schneider Jesuiten Hof Kirchheimer Geisskopf Weisser Burgunder trocken spätlese 96 (Germany)
Sipp Mack Pinot Blanc AC Alsace 96 (France-Alsace)
Terre Andina Semillon 96 (Chile)
Fontana Candida Frascato Superiore 97 (Italy)
Alasia Muscat sec VdT 96 (Italy)
Chapel Hill Irsai Olivier 97 (Hungary)
Albarino Martin Codax 96 (Spain)
Anares Cava brut nv (Sparkling-Spain)
Con Class Especial DO Rueda 96 (Spain)
Pommery Brut Royal NV Champagne (Sparkling-Champagne)
Quinta da Avelada Vinho Verde nv (Portugal
Weingut C. Schumacher Herxheimer Himmelreich Riesling Kabinett trocken 97 (Germany)

Spain

If stars were awarded to countries as well as wines, Spain would certainly qualify. In an apparently very short time quality has improved beyond measure and just at the present prices are very good though this is already changing.

Rioja's early commercial success on the export market led eventually to lowering standards—over-produced and under-extracted wines with too much obvious American oak and too little real structure. But it has made a real comeback. The debate about the true character of Rioja has yielded good results and different interpretations. The wine has more intense fruit from lower yields, better integration of oak and a tighter structure from longer maceration. 1994 was a classic Reserva vintage whose wines are just appearing and will repay buying to keep as well as for current drinking.

Next door to Rioja, Navarre has made equal quality strides with some truly excellent reds. They tend to fall into two distinct styles, traditional Navarre improved by skilled vinification, such as Gran Feuda, and modern varietals, or at least Cabernet-led wines such as those of Palacio de la Vega, Guelbenzu or Ochoa. These wines have fine balance between ripe, approachable fruit with intensity of flavour, and firm structure. The best will age and gain in complexity. The most age-worthy of all, however, are to be found in Ribera del Duero, formerly associated only with Vega Sicilia and Pesquera at pretty high prices. Other wineries have followed in the high quality mould with wines which are big and bold, full-flavoured, slightly chunky and highly individual.

Rueda makes some brilliant aromatic white wines from its own Verdejo grape, often with Sauvignon Blanc and/or Viura. They are wonderfully crisp, fresh and delicious wines, still very keenly priced.

Throughout Spain winemaking has improved and there is greater selection of grape varieties to produce quality wines. La Mancha, which used to be a byword for cheap, bulk wine, now produces some really tasty reds, as does Valdepeñas in the South. Small, hardly-known regions such as Somontano are emerging, led by dedicated producers such as Enate to become the stars of tomorrow.

White £5 or less

Don Darias Vino de Mesa nv

Barry & Fitzwilliam   ®

Full-bodied white

Traditional dry, full-bodied Spanish white wine, well made and creamy with nice balance and enough acidity to be refreshing.
Especially good with spicy or garlicky food: spicy fish stew or soup or garlic mayonnaise

White £5 - £6

Marqués de Caceres DOC Rioja 97

Grants   ®

Light fruity white

Nice, gentle fruit aromas, good balance of fruit and acidity, and fresh fruit flavour. Crsip finish.
Warm, spicy chicken salad; simply-cooked fillets of seabass or seafood ragoût

Viña Marcos Viura DO Navarra 97

TDL   ®

Full-bodied white, oak

Complex aromas of toasty, nutty fruit. Mouthfilling flavours of ripe fruit with generous oak perfectly balanced. Good now and will improve.
Fresh anchovies or seabass, stuffed squid or calamary

White £6 - £8

Con Class Especial DO Rueda 96

Searson   ☆

Aromatic white

Exuberant gooseberry and lime aromas. Quite opulent style with plenty of ripe fruit, good weight and long finish. Very stylish Sauvignon.
Fishcakes, prawns in garlic or Thai-style food

Con Class Sauvignon Blanc DO Rueda 96

Searson   ££

Aromatic white

Lovely ripe, aromatic fruit aromas with good weight of lean, green fruit flavour, bracing acidity and crisp finish.
Fairly simple fish dishes; first-course salads of fennel and mixed vegetables

Hérederos del Marqués de Riscal Sauvignon DO Rueda 97

Findlater   ®

Aromatic white

Good vibrant nose of ripe green fruit. Plenty of similar fruit on the palate with balanced acidity and clean refreshing finish.
Nice refreshing wine for fish cooked with butter and herbs or for a main-course seafood salad

Mantel Blanco Verdejo-Sauvignon Blanc DO Rueda 97

Approach Trade Ireland   ©

Aromatic white

Grassy, gooseberry aromas with a hint of smoke. Ripe gooseberry and apple flavours with a touch of lime. Smoky finish works well.
Mussels with garlic butter or smoked trout mousse; also pasta with green vegetables; goat's cheese and pepper salad

Marqués de Alella Chardonnay DO Alella 96
Jenkinson ®

Light fruity white

Melon and a touch of vanilla on the nose; dry, ripe apple flavours and a hint of honey. Tangy, lemon-infused finish.
Quiche, chowder, fish in cheese sauce

Marqués de Alella Clasico DO Alella 97
Jenkinson ®

Light fruity white

Apple and gooseberry aromas. Very fresh and fruity, easy-drinking.
Light food or a mixed summer buffet

Montecillo Viña Cumbrero DOC Rioja 95
Dillon ££

Full-bodied white

Buttery aromas with melon and lemon. Medium weight with ripe peaches and melon and a touch of white pepper spice. Long, satisfying finish. Good value.
Fish or chicken pancakes; trout in pastry; baked chicken

Muga (barrel-fermented) DOC Rioja 97
United Beverages ££

Full-bodied white, oak

Toasty, buttery nose; full-bodied and rounded with oak still very obvious. Should develop beautifully. Good value.
Barbecued fish, grilled snapper or chicken kebabs

Paternina DOC Rioja 96
Barry & Fitzwilliam ®

Light fruity white

Well-balanced wine with light fruit aromas and nice creamy palate of ripe apple and lime fruit. Clean crisp finish.
Avocado mousse or guacamole; first-course vegetable salads

Raimat Chardonnay DO Costers del Segre 95
Grants ®

Full-bodied white

Rich, ripe fruit on the nose, lemon meringue pie aromas. Full and weighty with ripe, lemony fruit, quite intense and creamy with a long dry finish.
Chicken and apricots or smoked haddock and asparagus in a creamy sauce

White £8 - £10

Albariño Martin Codax 96
Karwig ®

Light dry white

Aromas of ripe honeydew melon. Dry and very fresh with the zippy taste of green apples and grapefruit. Flavour lingers well.
Sardines; avocado mousse; vegetable salads

Godello 'Guitian' DO Valdeorras 97
Approach Trade Ireland ®

Full-bodied white

Smoky, honeyed fruit, pineapple and mango with lively lemon flavour. Fresh and lingering finish.
Light creamy pasta, chicken with mango or other fruit and light pork dishes

Marqués de Murrieta Ygay DOC Rioja Reserva 91

Gilbeys ©

Full-bodied white, oak

Mature aromas of dried lemon peel and white pepper. Dry and very nutty with lemony acidity. A distinctive style but excellent.
Garlicky fish soup or stew; seafood curry

Torres Waltraud Riesling 97

Molloy's ®

Aromatic white

Delicate floral aromas with a citrus hint. Dry with mouthwatering acidity cutting right through melon and green apple fruit. Full and smooth with a long finish. Should last well.
Creamy fish dishes or onion tart

White £10 - £12

Enate Chardonnay DO Somontano 96

Febvre ©

Full-bodied white, oak

Honeyed bouquet with oaky, nutty fruit. Dry and broad with hazelnut and apple flavours, lemon and pepper coming in at the end. Needs time, but a good wine.
Richly sauced fish including lobster or turbot with avocado sauce; duck with peaches

White £12 - £15

Enate Chardonnay DO Somantano 95

Dunnes Stores ©

Full-bodied white, oak

Smoky citrus fruit on the nose with vanilla and slightly honey

tones in the background, Big and mouthfilling with oak and spice mingling with ripe fruit. Quite a powerhouse, with a long finish, too.
Works best with robust, well-flavoured foods, barbecued fish or chicken, creamy pasta with bacon, mushrooms etc. or with an excellent smoked fish pie

Godello 'Guitian' oak-fermented DO Valdeorras 96

Approach Trade Ireland ®

Full-bodied white, oak

Clean, lime fruit aromas. Delicate, floral fruit flavours. Fresh and crisp with spicy white pepper on the finish.
Fishcakes, skate wings or cold salmon

White £15 - £20

Chivite Colleccion 125 DO Navarra 94

TDL ®

Full-bodied white

Melon, honey and olive oil on the nose; flavours of lightly toasted hazelnuts and delicate fruit in a well-balanced wine with a lot of finesse.
Roast veal or chicken; turkey or monkfish with a cream sauce

Red £5 or less

Agramont Garnacha de Viñas Viejas DO Navarra 95

Dunnes Stores ©

Medium-bodied red

Very ripe, baked fruit aromas with lovely weight of ripe plum and spicy dried fruit on the palate. Satisfying flavours with a hint of cherry in the finish.

Lovely with chunky spicy sausages—Merguez—or even venison

Coto del Varal DO La Mancha 95

Quinnsworth   ®

Medium-bodied red

Jammy nose with a slight peppery tone. Easy-drinking, fruity style with nice balancing acidity. Fine at the price.
Bacon and mushroom kebab; olive bread; marinated chicken wings or drumsticks

Don Darias VdM nv

Barry & Fitzwilliam   ®

Medium-bodied red

Lots of brambly fruit on the nose; soft and rounded palate with a good weight of dark berry fruit. Dry finish.
Pizza, pasta or bacon

Roblejano VdM nv

Gilbeys   ®

Light fruity red

Ripe, rather jammy nose. Easy-drinking, ripe fruit on the palate and clean, short finish. For the price you can't go wrong.
Spicy pizza, garlic mushrooms

Red £5 - £6

Agramont Merlot/Tempranillo DO Navarra 96

Dunnes Stores   ®

Medium-bodied red

Spice and ripe autumn fruit on the nose. Spicy plums, rounded and appealing with an appetising dry finish.
Liver and bacon or well-flavoured minced meat dishes

Agramont Tempranillo DO Navarra 96

Dunnes Stores   ££

Medium-bodied red

Sweet, inviting fruit aromas and lovely ripe jammy fruit, berries and cherries, on the palate. Soft and rich and great value.
Baked ham or a spicy vegetable casserole

Agramont Tempranillo/ Cabernet Sauvignon Crianza DO Navarra 94

Dunnes Stores   ££

Medium-bodied red

Forest fruits and vanilla on the nose. Concentrated berry fruit on the palate offset by peppery spice. Well-balanced with a long finish.
Turkey or chicken wrapped in bacon or ham; couscous

Berberano Tempranillo DOC Rioja 96

Quinnsworth   ©

Medium-bodied red

Great fruit on the nose! Strawberries, cherries and a touch of vanilla. Soft, fruity toffee and vanilla-style Rioja but well-balanced within the style. Good price.
Rich chicken, peppers and rice casserole or stuffed turkey

Bodegas Piedemonte Tinto DO Navarra 96

Findlater   ££

Medium-bodied red

Nice spicy aromas with ripe fruit underneath. Concentrated and rich with plummy fruit and spice and a herbal twist creeping in at the end. Lovely mouthful!

Lamb casserole cooked with paprika or aromatic spices

Conde Bel Rioja DOC Rioja 96
Jenkinson ®

Medium-bodied red

Fruit compôte on the nose; soft and easy-drinking now. Good value.
Goes well with mildly spicy food, including Chinese duck or more simply a salt beef sandwich

Faustino VII DOC Rioja 96
Gilbeys ££

Medium-bodied red

Soft and fruity, easy-drinking with a little length. Great value.
Pasta and bacon or with ham

Gandia Hoya Valley Cabernet Sauvignon 93
Barry & Fitzwilliam ®

Full-bodied red

Good blackcurrant aromas. Well-structured with ripe fruit, full, rounded body and long finish.
Lamb chops or a steak; not too robust casseroles of meat

Gandia Tempranillo Hoya Valley DO Utiel-Requena 92
Barry & Fitzwilliam ®

Medium-bodied red

Loads of soft ripe fruit on the nose; mouthfilling plum and ripe berry fruit with a nice dry bite.
Baked ham or ham steaks; mixed grills

Gran Feudo Crianza DO Navarra 94
TDL ©

Full-bodied red

Lovely nose with blackcurrant

fruit, tobacco and spices. Full-bodied with rounded, ripe fruit and nice baláncing tannin.
Lamb, meatballs or baked ham

Marqués de Aragon Old Vine Garnacha DO Calatayud 97
Searson ®

Medium-bodied red

Lively red fruit aromas and vibrant cherry and redcurrant flavours right through the palate. Big and mouthfilling with generous alcohol and a sharp twist in the finish.
Pasta and chorizo sausage or baked aubergines with olives and cheese; also good with lamb casseroles

Marqués de Griñon Durius VdM 96
Fitzgerald ®

Medium-bodied red

Chocolatey fruit on the nose. Broad spicy, brambly palate—very ripe and quite vigorous in taste. Long finish.
Barbecued lamb or chunky sausages; also good with shepherd's pie

Vega Ibor DO Valdepeñas 93
Approach Trade Ireland ®

Medium-bodied red

Nice brambly, fruitcake nose with a touch of chocolate. Good ripe fig and raisin fruit character. Good value.
Roasted vegetables or stuffed aubergines, also herby lamb

Viña Albali Cabernet Sauvignon DO Valdepeñas 93
Superquinn ®

Medium-bodied red, tannic

Quite dark, ripe fruit coming through on the nose with a hint of rubber. Well-rounded flavours of dark plummy fruit, nice balanced tannins and long finish. Very good value.

Great with meatballs or hamburgers; also with Irish stew or lamb casserole

Viña Albali DOC Valdepeñas Gran Reserva 89

Superquinn   ®

Medium-bodied red

Quite pronounced nose with dark, plummy fruit, spicy wood and vanillin tones. Some complexity also in taste— mature fruit, integrated oak and spice nuances. Long finish. Great value

Lamb kebabs cooked on rosemary twigs or a mushroom risotto

Vina Marcos Tempranillo DO Navarra 97

TDL   ®

Medium-bodied red

Lovely blackberry jam aromas with very appealing fruit compote richness in flavour and some toffee in the finish. Typical and good value.

Spicy vegetable casserole or pasta

Red £6 - £8

Anares DOC Rioja 95

Allied Drinks   ®

Medium-bodied red

Hints of chocolate and spice on the nose. Quite meaty palate with concentration of dark, ripe fruits. Very dry finish.

Robust casseroles

Cune Rioja DOC Rioja 95

Findlater   ££

Medium-bodied red

Plummy, meaty aromas with

hints of ripe strawberry. Well structured. Spicy with a good weight of fruit and nice length. Good value, too!

Chicken cooked in wine orrabbit stew

Finca Resalso (Emilio Moro) DO Ribera del Duero 96

Approach Trade Ireland   ☆

Full-bodied red, tannic

Deep, dark plummy aromas. Mouthfilling, chunky wine with loads of character. Warm, rich fruit and obvious tannins— very big and satisfying and will get better. Great value.

Roast beef, saddle or leg of lamb or roast leg of pork; also game casserole and hard English cheeses

Gran Feudo Reserva DO Navarra 94

TDL   ®

Full-bodied red

Ripe berries and plums with a definite hint of chocolate on the nose. Relatively full with lots of plummy fruit and spicy wood influences. Firm tannin. Good traditional style.

Robust meat casserole or lentils and chorizo

Marqués de Cáceres DOC Rioja 94

Grants   ®

Medium-bodied red

Quite complex nose of red berries, oak and leathery tones, which turns into a well-structured meaty palate, typical of Rioja.

Game pie or braised pheasant

Marqués de Griñon DOC Rioja 96

Fitzgerald ®

Medium-bodied red

Lovely ripe strawberry fruit with hints of vanilla, a touch acidic just now but will balance with a little more time.
Nice with pork chops or Irish stew

Monasterio de Tentudia Vino de Extramudara 92

Leinster Merchant Wines ®

Medium-bodied red, tannic

Ripe, almost dried fruits on the nose. Nice balance of baked plum flavour, tannin and weight. Very Spanish and very nice.
Rabbit or chicken casserole with peppers and sausage or a risotto of mushrooms and black pudding

Montecillo Viña Cumbrero DOC Rioja 95

Dillon ®

Medium-bodied red

Elegant, spicy red berry fruit. Soft tannin and oaky finish—the style which makes Rioja so popular.
Hearty casseroles of beef or lamb

Múrice Crianza DOC Rioja 94

Greenhills ££

Medium-bodied red

Inviting nose of sweet, ripe fruit and vanilla tones—typical Rioja. Rounded palate with great depths of fruit and spice that go on and on. Excellent value for money.
Roast ham or a smoky, wine-rich casserole

Palacio de la Vega Crianza DO Navarra 94

Fitzgerald ☆

Full-bodied red

Pronounced aromas of ripe dark fruit, vanilla and a hint of burnt rubber. Mouthfilling flavours of raspberry, damson and fig-type fruit. Big and beautiful and lasts well. Excellent value.
Perfect with a robust vegetable couscous or roast or grilled lamb

Palacio de la Vega Merlot DO Navarra 95

Fitzgerald ®

Medium-bodied red, tannic

Slightly earthy plummy fruit with a meaty edge. Rich cherry fruit is balanced by tannin to give a well-rounded flavoursome wine with a nice long finish.
Bean stew or beef in Guinness

Petit Caus DO Penedès 96

Approach Trade Ireland ®

Medium-bodied red

Ripe blackcurrant with spicy overtones. Well-balanced with a nice weight of ripe curranty fruit and a dry finish.
Lamb shanks or a winter casserole

Piedemonte Crianza DO Navarra 94

Findlater ®

Full-bodied red

Baked, spicy plums on the nose and similar ripe, almost dried, fruit on the palate with spicy wood undertones. Full and rounded.
Dark, rich winter stews

Pozuelo Crianza DO Yecla 92

Grants ©

Full-bodied red

Quite complex mix of fruit and wood on the nose which follows to a palate of soft fruit and spicy wood. Quite firmly structured with good length in the finish.
Pot roast or braised poultry or lamb especially with mushroom and herb flavours

Principe de Viana Merlot DO Navarra 96

Febvre ®

Medium-bodied red, tannic

Plummy chocolatey aromas, touch of cakemix. Well-rounded with a good weight of generous fruit supported by tannin and alcohol.
Pork casserole cooked with wine and dried fruits

Raimat Abadia DO Costers del Segre 95

Grants ©

Full-bodied red

Lots of blackcurrant fruit aromas on the nose: full-bodied, chunky wine with blackcurrant fruit mixed with smoky, spicy flavours and firm structure.
Char-grilled and barbecued meats—not too spicy flavours, though

Ramón Bilbao Crianza DOC Rioja 95

Approach Trade Ireland ☆

Full-bodied red

Blackcurrant aromas mingle with tobacco and rubber, quite complex. Well-structured palate with good weight of ripe fruit and nice spicy length.

Richly cooked poultry: turkey steaks with port, apple and bacon, guineafowl and mushrooms

Ramón Blibao Monte Llano DOC Rioja 96

Approach Trade Ireland ®

Medium-bodied red

Sweet, baked fruit aromas with weight of ripe fruit on the palate, Nice spicy edge and refreshing acidity. Good value.
Black pudding, bacon or salted beef

Rioja Bordón Crianza DOC Rioja 95

Jenkinson ®

Medium-bodied red

Good on the nose and well made but a little short on fruit and weight.
Nice with a pork casserole or even a chunky club sandwich

Vina Mara DOC Rioja Reserva 94

Quinnsworth ®

Full-bodied red

Strawberries, plums and damsons on the nose with a vanillin twist. Rounded and fruity with spicy plum flavours and balanced acidity.
Lamb casserole or lamb shanks cooked in beer

Red £8 - £10

Campillo DOC Rioja 93

Barry & Fitzwilliam ££

Medium-bodied red

Lovely, intense aromas of strawberries and oak following on the palate which is well-structured and balanced. Hard to beat for quality and value.
Roast pheasant or medallions of beef with mushrooms

Chivite Reserva DO Navarra 93

TDL   ®

Medium-bodied red, tannic

Ripe and plummy on the nose with a hint of burnt caramel. Well-structured with firm tannin and full body; damson-type fruit with pepper spice.
Lamb steaks or roast leg of lamb, especially served with beans; also good with robust meat casseroles

De Muller Merlot DO Tarragona 96

Karwig   ®

Medium-bodied red, tannic

Earthy, jammy plums on the nose. Quite dry on the palate with noticeable tannin but also a weight of ripe fruit. Attractive.
Very good choice for a bean stew, with or without meat, also good with carbonade and other warming casseroles

Marqués de Griñon Colleccion Personal DOC Rioja Reserva 93

Fitzgerald   ☆

Full-bodied red

Textbook Rioja Reserva from the weight of rich, brambly fruit to the balanced oakiness and the long, lingering finish.
Try this one with the very best black pudding you can find

Muga DOC Rioja Reserva 94

United Beverages   ®

Full-bodied red

A traditional Reserva with wild herbs and oak aromas and dense fruit and oak flavour. Complex and good.
The oaky flavours are good with rich sauces with beef or lamb, or even pheasant

Negre Scala Dei DO Priorat 97

Karwig   ®

Medium-bodied red, tannic

Spicy cherries on the nose with slight herbal twist. Good weight of fruit with nice light tannins.
Flavoursome dishes such as hearty pasta, chicken, rice and chorizo casserole

Palacio de Valdeinfante (Gran Reserva) VdT Barros 92

Leinster Merchant Wines ®

Medium-bodied red

Lots of ripe, almost jammy fruit on the nose with a touch of spice. Medium weight with plenty of fruit and flavour.
Cold, salami-types meats or spicy sausages; good for a barbecue

Paternina Crianza DOC Rioja 94

Barry & Fitzwilliam   ®

Full-bodied red

Brambly, slightly earthy nose. Good weight of fruit on the palate with nicely balanced structure. Ripe and sweet with oaky spice.
Lighter casseroles, roast stuffed chicken, baked ham

Rioja Bordón DOC Rioja Reserva 91

Jenkinson   ©

Full-bodied red

Lots of ripe vanillin fruit; beautifully balanced with excellent structure.
Quail cooked with mushrooms; grilled, glazed poussins

Siglo DOC Rioja Reserva 87
Superquinn ©
Full-bodied red

Quite mature vegetal aromas with sweet berry fruit and spice. Mellow, complex palate, still firm with spicy tones developing into rich, complex, fruit flavours. Quite delicious and a real bargain.
Wild duck and port or pheasant and mushroom pie or a lamb casserole

Tioio DO Ribera del Duero 96
Jenkinson ☆
Full-bodied red

Nice complexity of plum and blackcurrant fruit and spice aromas. Complexity also on the palate with ripe blackcurrant, mocha and earthy influence. Very long and satisfying.
Beef en croûte or roast fillet, or with a farmhouse Cheshire

Red £10 - £12

Emilio Moro Crianza DO Ribera del Duero 95
Approach Trade Ireland ☆
Full-bodied red, tannic

Cherries and blackcurrants on the nose with a spicy edge. Great concentration on the palate with rich fruit to offset firm tannin. Mouthfilling and velvety right through a long finish.
Particularly good with game— saddle of venison or roast wild duck

Florentino de Lecanda DOC Rioja Reserva 89
Approach Trade Ireland ©
Full-bodied red

Lovely mature nose of ripe, sweet fruit with a touch of wet leather aroma. Quite a complex palate with spicy oak and very ripe fruit. Good concentration and length.
Pheasant pie or casserole, mushroom risotto, turkey

Ijalba DOC Rioja Reserva 93
Greenhills ©
Full-bodied red

Complex and restrained on the nose. Quite youthful but well-balanced with plummy fruit and oak flavours in a tight structure. Expensive but good.
Braised lamb shanks

Marqués de Griñon Dominio de Valdepusa Petit Vero 95
Fitzgerald ®
Full-bodied red, tannic

Dark and spicy with a curious mix of violets and rubber on the nose. Full and rich in the mouth with deep fruit flavours similar to the nose. Firm but balanced tannin; chewy, satisfying and long.
Confit of duck or a hearty mixed meat stew

Marqués de Griñon Dominio de Valdepusa Cabernet Sauvignon VdM Toledo 96
Fitzgerald ®
Full-bodied red, tannic

Ripe concentrated nose of blackcurrants and figs. Velvety palate with good intensity of blackcurrant fruit married with oak. Substantial amounts of tannin are well balanced by the fruit. Excellent example of a Spanish Cabernet which should also last well.
Well-flavoured rack of lamb with a herb and garlic crust or tapenade

Marqués de Griñon Dominio di Valdepusa Syrah VdM Toledo 95

Fitzgerald ®

Full-bodied red

Ripe, dark berry aromas with a touch of tobacco and peppery spice. Really ripe fruit, intense bramble, damson and plum flavours well supported by alcohol. Not for the faint-hearted.

Needs robust, chunky flavoursome food, especially venison or T-bone steaks

Muga DOC Rioja Gran Reserva 89

United Beverages ®

Full-bodied red

Chunky rather than elegant but with a good weight of plummy, blackberry fruit and well used oak.

Robust, flavoursome casserole of beef, lamb or game

Palacio de la Vega Cabernet Sauvignon DO Navarra 93

Fitzgerald ®

Full-bodied red, tannic

Lots of blackcurrant aromas. A big, mouthfilling, mouthwatering wine with rich, ripe black-currant fruit and structuring tannins and acidity.

Lasagne, moussaka and other chunky meat dishes

Red £12 - £15

Campillo DOC Rioja Reserva 90

Barry & Fitzwilliam ☆

Full-bodied red

Sweet fruit with a touch of

mature gaminess on the nose. Soft, supple style with lovely weight of fruit.

Guineafowl cooked with wine and bacon, or even Christmas turkey

Chivite Coleccion 125 DO Navarra Gran Reserva 92

TDL ®

Full-bodied red, tannic

Earthy nuances mix with ripe berry fruit aromas. Layers of fruit on the palate, plummy and quite chocolatey in flavour with supporting tannin and alcohol. Spicy and long in the finish. Good if expensive.

Roast pheasant or even tradtional turkey

Conde de Valdemar DOC Rioja Gran Reserva 91

Febvre ©

Full-bodied red

Complex nose with plummy fruit aromas mingling with leather, spice and tar. Opens up in the glass. Lots of vanillin oak on the palate with rich plummy fruit; balanced and long. Should last well, too.

Game such as roast pheasant or pheasant with mushrooms, also turkey stuffed with prunes or spatchcocked quail

Enate Reserva Cabernet Sauvignon DO Somantano 93

Dunnes Stores ©

Full-bodied red

Mature gamey bouquet and mellow flavours of mature fruit and oak. Complex and interest-ing with layers of oaky spice especially in the finish.

Simply roasted pheasant or roast beef or lamb

Faustino I DOC Rioja Gran Reserva 91

Gilbeys ☆

Full-bodied red

Ripe, dark fruit aromas follow to the palate. Good fruit developing quite complex mature nuances.

Braised poultry or rabbit, or fillet of beef

Florentino de Lecanda DOC Rioja Gran Reserva 87

Approach Trade Ireland ®

Full-bodied red

Lots of oak on the nose with violet and dried fruit aromas. Well-balanced palate with a good concentration of fruit backed by oaky spice. Soft and velvety, a Rioja in traditional style with a long finish.

Roast lamb or turkey

Imperial DOC Rioja Reserva 91

Findlater ®

Full-bodied red

Rioja's stylish, elegant side with spicy, oaky fruit in perfect balance.

Chicken or turkey cooked with a mushroom or herb sauce

Imperial DOC Rioja Reserva 91

Findlater ©

Aromaticwhite, fruit-driven

Lots of clean, fresh fruit on the nose; really bracing, mouthwatering palate with lime and bitter orange conserve set against honeyed ripeness. Long opulent finish.

Food with plenty of flavour, fish and light meats or pork; Thai-style curried fish or chicken, stir-fry pork or angelhair pasta with sundried tomatoes, roasted peppers and chilli

Marqués de Cáceres DOC Rioja Reserva 90

Grants ®

Full-bodied red

Textbook Reserva: spicy with loads of fruit and well-structured oak.

Roast lamb or beef or a leg of pork

Marqués de Murrieta Ygay DOC Rioja Reserva 92

Gilbeys ©

Full-bodied red

Well-balanced sweet fruit and vanillin oak. Plenty of character and well-priced.

Baked ham or corned beef!

Monte Real DOC Rioja Reserva 91

Barry & Fitzwilliam ®

Full-bodied red, tannic

Meaty and mature on the nose. Lovely balance of ripe fruit, softening tannins and lively acidity.

Risotto of wild autumn mushrooms

Paternina DOC Rioja Gran Reserva 89

Barry & Fitzwilliam ®

Full-bodied red

Intense aromas of ripe strawberries, rounded and complex with beautifully elegant fruit. Well worth the price.

Tart of pheasant and potatoes

Red £15 - £20

Bodegas y Viñedos Alion DO Ribera del Duero 94

Mitchell ☆

Full-bodied red

Lovely ripe berry fruit on the nose; intense dark fruit flavours with complex spice. Full and well-rounded with a long stylish finish.
Roast beef and lamb, hard cheese, game pie

Campillo DOC Rioja Gran Reserva 88

Barry & Fitzwilliam ☆ ☆

Full-bodied red

Super aromas of ripe, sweet fruits with a hint of caramel picking up the oak. Well-balanced and complex mingling of fruit, spice and emerging gaminess for those prepared to pay!
Try this with chicken and truffle and never mind the expense!

Emilio Moro DO Ribera del Duero Reserva 94

Approach Trade Ireland ®

Full-bodied red, tannic

Deep, rich plummy fruit with cedar and cigar box aromas, Very big with firm tannic structure but plenty of supporting fruit which needs a year or two. Should be beautiful.
At present benefits from roast meats, rare beef, venison etc and mild to medium hard cheeses

Viña Turzaballa DOC Rioja Gran Reserva 85

Approach Trade Ireland ®

Full-bodied red

Richly spicy nose with blackcur-

rant fruit. Plenty of concentrated fruit and spice flavour with little sign of its age. Good if expensive.
Roast meats and poultry: chicken and truffles or lamb en croûte

Viña Turzaballa DOC Rioja Gran Reserva 81

Approach Trade Ireland ®

Full-bodied red

Mature complex aromas. Quite elegant palate with well-developed fruit flavours, dried fruit, spice. Long finish.
Simply cooked game or ragoût of wild mushrooms

Red £20 - £25

Baron de Chirel DOC Rioja Reserva 92

Findlater ☆ ☆

Full-bodied red

Complex, developed aromas. Well-structured, traditional Rioja with a beautiful balance of ripe, sweet, earthy fruit fusing with spicy oak and mature flavour. One of the best.
Roast pheasant or guineafowl

Jean Léon Cabernet Sauvignon DO Penedès Gran Reserva 79

Molloy's ☆ ☆

Full-bodied red

Very mature, complex nose with spice and dark chocolate aromas. Really warm, layered palate, smooth and chocolatey with a long warming finish.
Leg of lamb cooked over charcoal; pheasant

Red £30 - £35

Bodegas y Viñedos Vega Sicilia 'Valbuena' DO Ribera del Duero 93

Mitchell ©

Full-bodied red

Quite restrained on the nose; meaty and well-structured with layers of dark fruit and spice. A good wine with real classic style but expensive.
Roast venison or venison steaks, beef with a wine, port or mushroom sauce; hare

Rosé £5 - £6

Chivite Gran Feudo DO Navarra 96
TDL ££
Ripe strawberries come through on the nose. Flavours of ripe soft fruits with crisp acidity and short but dry finish. Good value
Couscous salad or warm Mediterranean vegetables

Rosé £8 - £10

Enate Rosado Cabernet Sauvignon DO Somontano 96

Febvre ®
Ripe but quite restrained berry fruit aromas. Opulent strawberry fruit flavours, lively and juicy yet not too obvious and with good balancing acidity. Well-balanced, appealing style.
Mediterranean-type appetisers with anchovies and olives or anchovy pastries

United States

After a racing start, the recent history of Californian wine has had its share of problems. Phylloxera attacked a great number of Napa vineyards which were considered protected by a subsequently unreliable rootstock. A number of short vintages followed in the midst of a replanting programme in many of the vineyards. Add to that competition from cheap wine from South America, and the ever-present anti-alcohol lobby, 'the Surgeon General warns etc' and it is not a happy picture.

However, things have improved. Phylloxera has done its worst and the vineyards have been replanted. 1997 produced a huge, high quality crop, and Beringer won a formidable battle to be allowed to put the beneficial properties of wine on the label along with the health warnings.

In the meantime, quality has improved. There has been significant taming of styles, and though the wines are still big they are more often beautiful as well. Less oak and alcohol has made a marked difference to Chardonnay in particular and many are now subtle and quite Burgundian in character.

As far back as 1983, vineyards were divided into AVAs—American Viticultural Areas and since then delimiting has become more and more specific. Most of the smaller producers, of which California has a great number, make only a few wines which do indeed closely reflect their geographic origins.

Outside California, the 'wine state', Oregon and Washinton are producers of small quantities of exciting wines, including top notch Pinot Noir and some really stylish classic Cabernet.

California

White £6 - £8

Fetzer Echo Ridge Fumé Blanc 96
Dillon ®
Aromatic white
Rather slow, green fruit nose, slightly citrusy. Quite spicy fruit, chunky rather than zippy. Clean and balanced in the finish.
Creamy pasta with pancetta; mussels with cream and saffron; chicken with a cream sauce

Talus Califorrnia Chardonnay 95
Barry & Fitzwilliam ££
Full-bodied white, oak
Rich honeyed fruit on the nose with pronounced oakiness.

Mouthfilling concentration of fruit and oak, smoky and spicy flavours which linger endlessly. Not subtle but generous and well made.
Pasta and creamy sauces; chicken and pork dishes; turkey and ham

Vendange California Chardonnay 96

Barry & Fitzwilliam   ®

Full-bodied white

Ripe, spicy nose with lively palate of citrus fruit and bracing acidity. Quite spicy in the finish.
Vegetable pastries or vegetarian burgers; also crisp prawn toasts

White £8 - £10

Gallo Sonoma Sonoma County Chardonnay 95

Fitzgerald   ®

Full-bodied white, oak

Oak dominates the nose just about balanced in the taste by lots of ripe tropical fruit. If you like positive use of oak, this is a good example of the style.
Needs quite strong flavours and works especially well with smoky, chargrilled food

Sebastiani Sonoma County Chardonnay 95

Barry & Fitzwilliam   ☆

Full-bodied white, oak

Quite elegant complexity on the nose, smoky and biscuity aromas with subtle richness. Full-flavoured with great concentration of fruit and tightly-knit, well-integrated structure. Long and satisfying.
Lobster in a rich sauce or farm chicken with truffle oil; also fish gratin

Stratford California Chardonnay 96

Barry & Fitzwilliam   ®

Full-bodied white, oak

Oak predominates on the nose, balanced by good fresh fruit and ripeness on the palate. Good weight and length on finish if not especially concentrated.
Needs rather well-flavoured food with rich sauces or olive oil to offset the oak: fish en croûte with a creamy sauce, rich pastas or ham steaks with cream and celery sauce

White £10 - £12

Beringer Vineyards Napa Valley Fumé Blanc 96

Allied Drinks   ®

Full-bodied white, oak

Aromas of buttery, toasty Chardonnay jump from the glass. Round and soft on the palate with some rich, buttery fruit appearing from behind the oak. Balanced acidity and some length. Good example of a rich, oaky Chardonnay and well-priced.
Good with a deep-dish creamy chicken pie or go really over the top and serve it with lobster Mornay

Sequoia Grove Carneros Napa Valley Chardonnay 95

Findlater   ®

Full-bodied white, oak

Rather understated nose, honeyed with citrus tones. Refreshing acidity and ripe apple-type fruit and a touch of vanilla spice. Good balance in the finish.
Chicken, turkey and light meats

White £12 - £15

Beringer Vineyards Napa Valley Chardonnay 96
Allied Drinks ☆

Full-bodied white, oak

Lovely buttery nose, quite stylish with ripe fruit aromas in the background. Balanced palate with enough fruit for quite a bit of oak. Full and elegant with good weight and a long finish.
Gratin of (proper) smoked haddock or chicken with saffron

Caymus Vineyards Barrel Fermented Napa Valley Sauvignon Blanc 95
Mitchell ®

Aromatic white, oak

Oak dominates the nose along with gooseberry-tyoe fruit aromas. Broad, full, slightly oily palate with persistent oak. Apple fruit with honeyed tones and length. Good example of the broad, soft side of Sauvignon.
Grilled or barbecued fish such as salmon, also asparagus with hollandaise sauce

Gallo Sonoma Laguna Ranch Vineyard Chardonnay 96
Fitzgerald ☆

Full-bodied white, oak

Rich oakiness and ripe buttery fruit give quite a complex style with plenty of weight and long flavour.
Home-made fish pie, farm chicken or old-fashioned lobster dishes

Robert Mondavi Napa Valley Fumé Blanc 96
Febvre ®

Aromatic white, fruit-driven

Lots of ripe gooseberry aromas on the nose with a touch of boiled sweets. Lemon and citrus flavours—simple and easy to drink.
Barbecue food: fish and poultry kebabs

White £15 - £20

Hagafen (Kosher) Napa Valley Chardonnay (barrel fermented) 95
Mitchell ®

Full-bodied white, oak
Subdued aromas of honey and vanilla—butterscotch sauce. Ripe fruit with firm structure and balanced acidity. Refined, elegant and pricey!
Creamy chicken dishes with lobster and richly cooked prawns

Rutz Cellars Quail Hill Russian River Valley Chardonnay 95
Mitchell ☆ ☆

Full-bodied white, oak

Complex nose with aromas of tropical fruit, oak, smoke and spice. Big firm structure supported by lots of fruit: passionfruit and kiwis with a flavour which goes on and on. Serious stuff!
Good with creamy chicken, turkey and with elegant pastas

White £25 - £30

Byron Estate Chardonnay 94
Febvre ®

Full-bodied white, oak

Big complex nose with melon and lemon fruit and hints of vanilla. Full palate with smoky tones lurking behind melon fruit. Broad and long. Expensive.
Roast or baked chicken or turkey

Red £5 - £6

Glen Ellen Proprietor's Reserve Cabernet Sauvignon 95

Grants ®

Medium-bodied red, fruit-driven

Ripe blackcurrant on the nose and plenty of similar fruit flavour. Nice, refreshing acidity sets off the rich fruit.
Pasta or pizza or a stir-fry of meat

Glen Ellen Proprietor's Reserve Merlot 96

Grants ®

Medium-bodied red

Light, ripe soft fruit with a touch of strawberry character. Soft, supple wine though balanced. Very easy-drinking.
Versatile with lighter meats and meat dishes, especially cold meals and picnic fare

Inglenook Estate Cellars California Cabernet Sauvignon nv

Dillon ©

Full-bodied red

Aromas of ripe currants and bramble fruit carry through to the palate to give a young but richly flavoured wine with a depth of fruit and balanced structure. Very good value.
Steaks, lamb, meat kebabs

Vendange California Red 96

Barry & Fitzwilliam ®

Medium-bodied red, fruit-driven

Berry fruit aromas and ripe, juicy, berry fruit on the palate. Soft and easy-drinking, well made.

Meatloaf, pasta and meatballs or hamburgers

Vendange Zinfandel nv

Barry & Fitzwilliam ££

Full-bodied red, fruit-driven, tannic

Impressively complex nose with rich fruit aromas mixed with spice and caramel. Quite liquoricey with good balance of fruit and ripe tannin. Pleasantly dry in the finish.
Strong and spicy flavours such as olive and anchovy pizza or hamburgers and relishes

Red £6 - £8

Ernest & Julio Gallo Turning Leaf Cabernet Sauvignon 95

Fitzgerald ®

Full-bodied red, fruit-driven

Ripe cassis aromas. Lots of immediate fruit with lively acidity. Rather stalky character mid-palate with some length in the finish. Fine for the price.
Meat loaf or lasagne

Ernest & Julio Gallo Turning Leaf Merlot 96

Fitzgerald ®

Medium-bodied red, fruit-driven

Very rich on the nose with really meaty aromas coming through. Good intensity of fruit with balanced acidity and soft tannins. Very rich, chocolatey character to the fruit—trying to out-Pomerol Pomerol but fine in its own over-the-top way.
This could overshadow a lot of foods: a good match with beef and red peppers or with a barbecue

Fetzer Eagle Peak Merlot 96
Dillon   ®

Medium-bodied red

Aromas of spicy plums give a
ripe, sweet nose with hints of
eucalyptus. Fruit on the palate
is leaner though still quite
rounded. Soft in the finish yet
clean.
*Versatile with mixed and cured
meats; poultry and pasta with meat
and tomatoes; works with mild to
medium-hot spices.*

Fetzer Zinfandel 95
Dillon   ®

Full-bodied red, fruit- driven

Lots of plummy and rich, baked
fruit aromas, rounded and
mellow with plummy fruit and
soft tannin. Rather spicy finish.
*Spicy and sweet flavours and
relatively robust food, also roast
vegetables or casseroles; ribs with
barbecue sauce, kebabs with sweet
peppers*

Talus Cabernet Sauvignon 94
Barry & Fitzwilliam   ©

Full-bodied red, fruit-driven,
tannic

Lovely spicy aromas with rich
baked fruit. Dry and well-
structured with plenty of fruit,
firm tannins and good weight,
Quite robust and chunky with a
nice dry finish.
*Steak and grilled meats or beef in
pastry*

**Vendange Cabernet Sauvignon
95**
Barry & Fitzwilliam   ®

Medium-bodied red, fruit-
driven

Vibrant berry and currant fruit

aromas; loads of ripe berries on
the palate yet dry with a clean
refreshing finish.
Grilled lamb chops or kebabs

**Wente Vineyards Cabernet
Sauvignon 95**
Dunnes Stores   ®

Light fruity red

Ripe, almost sweet, berries on
the nose; lots of lively summer
fruit flavours in a very refreshing wine for easy drinking.
*Quite spicy stir-fried food and
casseroles with spices*

Wente Vineyards Zinfandel 96
Dunnes Stores   ®

Full-bodied red, fruit-driven

Lots of ripe blackberries on the
nose; big and mouthfilling with
spicy, peppery fruit. Nice
balance of fruit, tannin and
acidity.
*Robust, spicy and sweet flavours,
Chinese beef with plum sauce, roast
bacon with fruit chutney*

Red £8 - £10

**Beringer Harmonie Red Table
Wine 95**
Allied Drinks   ®

Medium-bodied red, fruit-
driven, tannic

Brambles and berry fruit
aromas; deep blackcurrant and
bramble fruit flavours. Well-
balanced with a nice bite of ripe
tannin and a long dry finish.
*Roast beef and lamb or a winter
stew*

**Ernest & Julio Gallo Turning
Leaf Zinfandel 93**
Fitzgerald   ©

Full-bodied red, fruit-driven

Lovely ripe, sweet fruit aromas with a touch of spice. Blackcurrant and mixed spices dominate the palate with nice balance of tannin, acidity and alcohol to support the flavours.

Spicy flavours especially from zippy barbecue marinade and relishes: venison sausages, grilled lamb with mustrad and soy

Ernest and Julio Gallo Sonoma County Pinot Noir 95

Fitzgerald ®

Medium-bodied red, fruit-driven

Rather lean nose with hints of summer fruit. Good weight on the palate with ripe fruit, spicy and soft with balancing acidity.

Chunky venison sausages

Gallo Sonoma Sonoma County Cabernet Sauvignon 92

Fitzgerald ☆ ☆

Full-bodied red

Intense aromas of earthy blackcurrant with definite hints of eucalyptus. Mouthfilling style, but well-balanced with excellent weight of complex fruit flavour. Should develop further over one or two years.

Lamb steaks and chargrilled meats in general especially barbecued butterfly leg of lamb

Geyser Peak Cabernet Sauvignon 96

Peter Dalton ®

Full-bodied red

Ripe, rich nose with plums and blackcurrant and a hint of eucalyptus. Dry and well-rounded with good concentration of ripe fruit flavour.

Meat casseroles or charcoal-grilled meat

Geyser Peak Merlot 95

Peter Dalton ®

Medium-bodied red

Slightly green on the nose though with plummy fruit underneath. Soft, rounded and very supple with juicy fruit and a touch of spice.

Marinated, grilled tuna steak

Sebastiani Sonoma County Cabernet Sauvignon 94

Barry & Fitzwilliam ☆

Full-bodied red, fruit- driven

Blackcurrant aromas with vanilla and spice. Big, brash flavours of fruit and oak, brambles and spice with great length. Blockbuster style but none the worse for it.

Char-grilled meats, especially T-bone steak

Sebastiani Sonoma County Zinfandel 96

Barry & Fitzwilliam ©

Full-bodied red, fruit- driven

Quite strong blackcurrant aromas with subtle spice. Good weight of fruit, deep rich blackcurrant and blackberry flavours along with warm aromatic spiciness. Long and delicious in the finish.

Well-flavoured meats, especially chargrilled, and more robust stir-fry dishes: grilled steaks with mustard glaze, stir-fry beef with red peppers and black bean sauce

Stratford California Cabernet Sauvignon 95

Barry & Fitzwilliam ☆

Full-bodied red, fruit-driven

Complex mingling of ripe fruit and oak on the nose. Dry, with tannins balanced by plenty of ripe soft fruit. Delicious and mouthfilling with flavours that go on and on.
Good rich meat casserole: beef or lamb cooked with wine and aromatics

Wente Vineyards Charles Wetmore Reserve Cabernet Sauvignon 95

Dunnes Stores ☆

Full-bodied red, fruit-driven

Complex nose—aromas unfold slowly. Very intense fruit on the palate woven around spicy oak. Big and mouthfilling with lovely complexity and warm toasty character. Long finish, too.
Rack of lamb or roast duck with fruit stuffing

Wente Vineyards Reliz Creek Reserve Pinot Noir 95

Dunnes Stores ®

Medium-bodied red, fruit-driven

Rich spicy fruit on the nose, just a touch vegetal. Medium weight, quite spicy with loads of slightly jammy fruit and crisp acidity.
Cold meats and chutney or barbecued poussin

Red £10 - £12

Beringer Vineyards Zinfandel 94

Allied Drinks ©

Full-bodied red, fruit-driven

Deep plummy, spicy nose with quite a bit of wood showing. Well-structured with spicy plummy fruit. Firm, but with a weight of baked fruit flavour and a spicy, bitter twist on the finish.
Traditional turkey or rabbit with peppers and spicy sausage

Seghesio Sonoma Zinfandel 96

Findlater ☆

Full-bodied red, fruit-driven

Wonderful fruitcake aromas along with deep intense fruit. A firmly structured wine with mouthfilling fruit and spice— rich and ripe—offset by oak. A big but well-balanced wine with a very long finish.
Mild to medium spices and robust rather than rich meat dishes; roasted vegetable gâteau, beef with a spicy crust

Wente Vineyards Crane Ridge Reserve Merlot 95

Dunnes Stores ©

Full-bodied red, fruit-driven

Berries and redcurrants on the nose with lots of juicy fruit flavour. Quite rich and developed fruit which yields more as the wine opens in the glass. Delicious and well made.
Beef steaks with porcini, roast pork with dried fruits

Red £12 - £15

Flora Springs Sangiovese Napa Valley 96

Mitchell ©

Full-bodied red, fruit-driven

Black cherries and chocolate with hints of vanilla on the nose. Mouthfilling with flavours similar to the nose. Soft and rounded with a rich cherry flavour lingering through the finish.

Magret of duck with a fruit sauce or beef with soy and ginger

Gallo Sonoma Frei Ranch Vineyard Cabernet Sauvignon 94

Fitzgerald ©

Full-bodied red, fruit-driven

Lovely fruity nose with a touch of spicy new oak. Loads of fruit with balancing tannins and alcohol. Delicious length in the finish. Expensive but good.

Excellent wine for steaks and roasted ribs of beef

Gallo Sonoma Frei Ranch Vineyard Zinfandel 95

Fitzgerald ©

Full-bodied red, fruit-driven, tannic

Quite a bit of oak on the nose with ripe fruit also; deep, rich palate with plenty of ripe berry fruit and firm tannin. Very long, spicy finish.

Robust meat dishes and strong flavours— venison casserole, aubergine and mozzarrella pizza

Robert Mondavi Coastal Pinot Noir 96

Febvre ®

Medium-bodied red

Quite vegetal on the nose with bramble and damp leaf aromas. Lots of flavour with ripe berry fruit and elegant balanced structure. Quite classic.

Game and fruit combinations such as pheasant with blackberries or wild duck and peaches

Rutz Cellars Russian River Valley Pinot Noir 95

Mitchell ®

Medium-bodied red, fruit-driven

Ripe, rich nose of cherries and strawberries. Well-balanced palate with long, quite spicy finish. Good example of the fruit-first style of New World Pinot.

Spices—with chicken or salmon

Red £15 - £20

Alban Vineyards Reva Edna Valley Alban Estate Syrah 93

Mitchell ©

Full-bodied red, fruit-driven, tannic

Ripe blackberry nose with lots of peppery spice. Big and meaty with firm tannins and plenty of fruit. Will develop further and gain in richness.

Beef or game eg venison, pheasant with rich sauces

Beringer Napa Valley Cabernet Sauvignon 95

Allied Drinks ®

Full-bodied red, fruit-driven

Quite a stalky, oaky nose with blackcurrant fruit aromas. Well-balanced with concentrated fruit and ripe tannins. Full and long.

Magret of duck with a dark wine and fruit sauce

Beringer Vineyards Knights Valley Meritage 93

Allied Drinks ☆

Full-bodied red, fruit-driven

Very intense nose with shades of mocha and spicy, rich fruit. Full, layered palate with plummy, chocolatey fruit. Spicy, rich and long.
Beef ribs and roasted vegetables or a soy-glazed fillet

Beringer Vineyards Napa Valley Cabernet Sauvignon 94

Allied Drinks ®

Full-bodied red, fruit-driven

Intense blackcurrant nose with smoky, cedary aromas. Deep, full palate with firm tannin and plenty of fruit.
Lamb casserole or lamb steaks

Ernest and Julio Gallo Sonoma Northern Sonoma Merlot 93

Fitzgerald ®

Medium-bodied red, fruit-driven, tannic

Fragrant, quite stylish, nose with slowly emerging ripe fruit. Youthful palate with dominating tannin and good underlying fruit. Promises well.
Mixed grill or a casserole of lamb

Hagafen (Kosher) Napa Valley Cabernet Sauvignon 95

Mitchell ®

Full-bodied red, fruit-driven

A big wine with powerful aromas of oak and blackcurrant fruit, mouthfilling, complex fruit flavours and a long finish.
Beef and lamb, especially charcoal grilled

Seghesio Vitigno Toscano Alexander Valley Sangiovese 95

Findlater ©

Full-bodied red, fruit-driven, tannic

Pronounced aromas of wood, fruit and spice. Firm tannin and balanced bramble fruit flavours. Spicy overtones give a nice edge. A mouthfilling wine which should develop further but it's expensive.
Casseroles of meat and grilled steaks, chops etc

Sequoia Grove Napa Valley Cabernet Sauvignon 95

Findlater ☆

Full-bodied red, fruit-driven

Intense aromas of aromatic blackcurrants. A big, powerful wine with soft berry fruit overlaid by meaty savoury tones. Quite classic in style—cool and refined with a long finish.
Roast leg of lamb marinated with herbs and mustard; char-grilled steaks

Red £20 - £25

Caymus Vineyards Napa Valley Cabernet Sauvignon 94

Mitchell ☆ ☆

Full-bodied red, tannic

Beautiful, quite classic nose of blackcurrant, spice and tobacco. Very full-bodied; firm tannins well cloaked by mouthfilling fruit and oak flavours which linger into a long elegant finish.
Rack of lamb or magret of duck

Hagafen (Kosher) Reserve Napa Valley Cabernet Sauvignon 90

Mitchell ®

Full-bodied red

Intense and complex on the nose—quite unusual aromas. The palate has ripe fruit and smoky, vegetal flavours. Full-bodied and relatively complex: big in every way, including price!
Sauced meat dishes or winey casseroles

Rutz Cellars Dutton Ranch Russian River Valley Pinot Noir 95

Mitchell ®

Medium-bodied red, fruit-driven

Quite smoky, gamey nose. Good weight and well-balanced structure with concentrated spicy fruit and quite a long finish. Quite pricey.
Game, especially pheasant and quail

Red £25 - £30

Robert Mondavi Oakville Cabernet Sauvignon 95

Febvre ®

Full-bodied red, fruit-driven

Ripe and complex fruit with a slightly medicinal edge. Big and well-structured but with a weight of ripe fruit. Not subtle but good and well-made of the style.
Lamb steaks or a robust meat casserole

Washington

White £8 - £10

Ch. St Michelle Chardonnay 95

United Beverages ☆

Full-bodied white

Attractive mixture of zingy citrus aromas and soft lactic nuances with a hint of smoke. On the palate ripe, buttery melon-type fruit is balanced by crisp acidity. A wine with good weight and some length.
A fine piece of turbot with a cream sauce or a seafood pasta

Columbia Crest Cabernet Sauvignon 94

United Beverages ®

Full-bodied red, fruit-driven

Lots of cassis on the nose. Rich and ripe, well-balanced with soft ripe tannins and good weight of fruit. A bit one-dimensional but nice.
This would take quite a spicy casserole or stir-fry of beef

Red £10 -£12

Ch. St Michelle Cabernet Sauvignon 93

United Beverages ☆

Full-bodied red, fruit-driven

Quite a complex nose of blackcurrant and cedar. Firm palate with ripe but cool blackcurrant fruit and elegant, well-balanced structure. Very stylish with a long finish.
Rack of lamb or magret of duck with shallot sauce

Quarter bottles

These are a new addition to the wines covered in *The Best of Wine in Ireland.*

The quarter bottle has made a very big difference to the quality of wine available in pubs and bars. They are simple to handle and supply wine in consistently good condition. The range of wines has increased with France, Spain, Italy and most New World countries represented.

The wines themselves vary considerably in quality; it seems that technology may still have something to learn about consistency in this size. However, many proved very satisfactory, providing good fruit and balance. A few, notably from Spain and France, were very attractive indeed.

White wines

Argentina

Trapiche Sauvignon Blanc 97
United Beverages   ®
Very ripe, gooseberry pie aromas with a touch of peardrops. Rounded, soft palate with nice light fruit and crisp acidity to make it refreshing.

Australia

Sacred Hill Colombard/ Chardonnay 97
Febvre   ®
A touch of Chardonnay character on the nose, more lemon meringue than citrus, aromas which follow also to the taste.

Chile

Santa Carolina Sauvignon Blanc
TDL   ®
Gooseberry fruit on the nose;

off-dry style with crisp tangy green fruit and refreshing finish.

Valdezaro Chardonnay Maule Valley 97
Barry & Fitzwilliam   ®
Citrusy nose with reasonable weight of fruit on the palate and in the finish.

Valdezaro Sauvignon Blanc Maule Valley 97
Barry & Fitzwilliam   ®
Clean, fresh nose with grassy, slightly floral aromas, zesty and young. Dry, with plenty of crisp, green fruit and a touch of spice to pep up the taste. Lasts well.

France-Bordeaux

Calvet Sauvignon Blanc AC Bordeaux 96
Grants   ®
Citrusy, lemon- peel aromas with green apple fruit flavours. A dry, fresh mouthful.

Ch. Bel Air AC Bordeaux 96
Febvre   ®
Nice aromas of ripe apple and gooseberry fruit. Quite full and creamy in the mouth with good weight of green fruit flavour. Nice glass of wine.

France-Burgundy

Cuvée Les Loups VdT nv
Findlater   ®
Stewed apples on the nose with rather sweeter apple flavours; good concentration.

France-Languedoc

Antonin Rodet Chardonnay VdP d'Oc nv
Febvre   ®
Rather buttery, appley nose; good weight of soft buttery fruit with refreshing citrus acidity.

Le Séjour VdP d'Oc nv
Allied Drinks   ®
Fresh, leafy nos. Dry palate with attractive melon-like fruit and balanced acidity.

Les Fumés Blanches VdP d'Oc nv
Febvre   ®
Clean, fresh nose *with* lemon peel and slightly honeyed fruit aromas. Ripe fruit on the palate and a twist of white pepper. Well-balanced, off-dry style.

France-Loire

Barton & Guestier AC Muscadet de Sèvre-et-Maine nv
Dillon   ®
Lightly aromatic nose. Dry with a minerally edge. Crisp finish. Light and simple.

Justin Monmoussean AC St-Nicholas-de-Bourgueil 95
Febvre   ®
Light aromas of green apples, slightly sherbety. Dry and crisp on the palate with fruit similar to the nose. Clean finish.

Les Maitres Goustiers Muscadet de Sèvre et Marne nv
Febvre   ®
Fresh and clean with light fruit and lively acidity.

Remy-Pannier Blanc de Blancs VdT nv
Barry & Fitzwilliam   ®
Lemony nose with a hint of peardrops. Fresh, mouthwatering fruit, lively and citrusy in character. Well-balanced with moderate acidity and crisp finish.

Spain

Paternina Rioja DOC 96
Febvre   ®
Rather floral ripe fruit on the nose, apple and melon-type fruit on the palate. Light and refreshing.

Paternina Blanco Seco DOC 96
Febvre   ®
Lemony aromas on the nose, dry palate with medium acidity and appley fruit. Simple and quite nice.

USA California

Fetzer Sundial Chardonnay 95
Dillon   ®
Citrusy aromas with fresh, appley fruit on the palate which finishes dry and clean.

Glen Ellen Proprietor's Reserve Chardonnay 96
Grants   ®
Quite buttery on the nose; balanced fruit and acidity in the taste with some length to a clean finish.

Red wines

Australia

Hawkes Run Shiraz nv
Allied Drinks   ®
Smoky and spicy aromas dominate giving quite a lean nose. Ripe fruit on the palate with firm tannin and decent body. Finish lasts well.

Chile

Santa Carolina Cabernet Sauvignon
TDL   ®
Blackcurrant aromas, mellow and rich palate of brambly, dark fruit. Very pleasant.

Valdezaro Cabernet Sauvignon 96
Barry & Fitzwilliam   ®
Very rich boiled sweets and caramel on the nose. Very soft palate with cassis-like fruit, low acidity and tannin.

France

Chantelle des Vins Red nv
Febvre   ®
Ripe raspberries and cherries on the nose with a touch of bubblegum sweetness. Tastes of juicy, jammy raspberries. A fresh, fruity quaffer.

Cuvée de la Reine VdT nv
Barry & Fitzwilliam   ®
Smoky, spicy aromas on the nose. A bite of tannin and plenty of stalky blackcurrant fruit; appetisingly dry.

Pierre Jean Cabernet Sauvignon VdP des Côtes de Gascogne
Febvre   ®
Rich cherry fruit on the nose, slightly jammy aromas; fruity palate with some length.

Pierre Jean Merlot VdP des Côtes de Gascogne 97
Febvre   ®
Raspberries and plums on the nose and also in the taste. Good fruity character and relatively firm tannin.

France-Bordeaux

Ch. Bel Air nv
Febvre   ®
Rich, fruity nose, flavours of black cherries backed up by firm tannin. A big wine in a little bottle!

France-Burgundy

Cuvée Les Loups VdT nv
Findlater   ®
Light and fruity with hints of canned strawberry aromas. Soft and easy-drinking with a twist of pepper.

France-Corsica

Laroche Pinot Noir VdP de l'Ile de Beauté 96
Allied Drinks   ®
Summer berries and brambles on the nose which persist also in the taste. The palate fills out a

Chapel Hill

BALATONBOGLÁR
Estate Bottled

CHARDONNAY
OAKED

DRY WHITE QUALITY WINE – SZÁRAZ FEHÉR MINŐSÉGI BOR

Produced and bottled by : Balatonboglár Winery, Hungary

PRODUCE OF HUNGARY

12.0% vol   75 cl ℮

MICHEL LYNCH

BORDEAUX
APPELLATION BORDEAUX CONTRÔLÉE

12% vol.   **1994**   750 ml

MIS EN BOUTEILLE PAR C.M.G.C. A 33290 FRANCE
PRODUCT OF FRANCE

L. 9401

Le BORDEAUX de Jean-Michel CAZES

bit to a kind of tart plummy fruit and quite mouthfilling weight.

France-Languedoc

Barton & Guestier Cabernet Sauvignon VdP d'Oc nv
Dillon ®
Rich, cherry fruit nose. Balanced taste with ripe, soft fruit. Fruity and easy-drinking.

Calvet Merlot VdP d'Oc 96
Grants ®
Ripe, brambly nose; lots of rich, soft, baked fruit flavours but also a nice bite from dry tannins and a firm finish.

Le Séjour VdP d'Oc nv
Allied Drinks ®
Ripe berry fruit aromas with plenty of juicy blackcurrants and ripe plums in the taste. Well made, quite full-bodied.

Reine Pédauque Cabernet Sauvignon VdP d'Oc nv
Barry & Fitzwilliam ®
Fruit aromas mix with some vegetal character on the nose. Dry, quite appetising taste with a bit of length.

France-Loire

Remy-Pannier Rouge de Rouges VdT nv
Barry & Fitzwilliam ®
Clean, fresh fruity aromas. Light with lots of fresh soft fruit. Summery and easy to drink.

France-Rhône (South)

Barton & Guestier AC Côtes du Rhône nv
Dillon ®
Attractive nose with ripe berry

aromas. Dry with lots of fruit— ripe rasberries and strawberries. Some weight in the mouth and decent, dry finish.

Dom. Notre Dame des Paillères AC Côtes du Rhône 96
Febvre ®
Ripe blackcurrant and black- berry aromas. Ripe chewy fruit on the palate, backed by firm tannin and plenty of alcohol. Well made with quite a long finish.

Dom. Notre Dame-des-Paillères AC Côtes du Rhône 97
Febvre ®
Nice mouthful of ripe berry fruit with a touch of cherry, dash of spice and clean dry finish.

France South-West

Pierre Jean Merlot VdP Côtes de Gascogne 97
Febvre ®
Lots of red berries on the nose; ripe, juicy style—very lively and refreshing with plenty of fruit.

Italy

Botter DOC Valpolicella nv
Barry & Fitzwilliam ®
Baked plummy fruit on the nose. Good fruit palate— ripe and quite concentrated.

Colli di Catone DOC Montelpulciano d'Abruzzo 96
Febvre ©
Brambly fruit on the nose with a touch of spice. All red berries and ripe brambles in the taste. A fruity number with weight and length too.

South Africa

Drostdy Hof Cape Red 97
Febvre ®
Ripe, summer fruit nose with a hint of plummy richness. Lots of fruit also on the palate—jammy raspberries and strawberries. A well-made, delicious, easy-drinking wine.

Spain

Cune Rioja DOC 93
Findlater ®
Cherry and strawberry aromas; soft fruits also on the palate. Ripe and balanced.

Gran Feudo Crianza 94
TDL ®
Dark fruit aromas, soft and mellow flavours with good fruit concentration and a hint of liquorice.

Gran Feudo Reserva 92
TDL ®
Ripe blackcurrants and a touch of mint in the aroma, mellow, rich and ripe. A delicious glass of wine.

Paternina Rioja DOC 95
Febvre ®
Vanilla and strawberry on the nose; juicy and refreshing with a nice, soft, rounded structure and spicy finish.

Rioja Bordón Crianza DOC Rioja 95
Jenkinson ®
Ripe, gamey nose and similar flavour of ripe fruit and punchy spice.

Señorio de Nava DO Ribera del Duero nv
Febvre ©
Plums and chocolate on the nose; good warm, mouthfilling wine with lots of taste. Rich, ripe fruit and earthy finish

USA California

Fetzer Valley Oaks Cabernet Sauvignon 95
Dillon ®
Inviting aromas of Ribena-type blackcurrant fruit. Ripe fruit flavours with balancing acidity. Quite a charmer.

Estate Cellars Inglenook Cabernet Sauvignon nv
Dillon ®
Rich 'cake mix' nose; rather tinned fruit in taste, but soft and easy.

Glen Ellen Proprietor's Reserve Cabernet Sauvignon 95
Grants ®
Red berry aromas with plenty of fruity taste and balanced acidity. Quite drinkable.

Vendange Autumn Harvest Cabernet Sauvignon nv
Barry & Fitzwilliam ®
Plenty of fruit character on the nose. Ripe, fruity taste with balanced acidity and some length.

Sparkling wines

As we edge towards the end of the millennium, Champagne has become a focus as never before. Since the slump in the early '90s when the Champenois got a much needed jolt and lost most of their export market due to rising prices and lowering quality, standards have greatly improved. Champagne has no business to be inexpensive or even value for money in its pricing. But it must deliver quality which in Champagne terms means finesse, elegance, complexity and a long, long taste. At its best Champagne is like no other sparkling wine on earth.

The wines of Champagne showed extremely well in this year's tastings. They were riper and more mature than usual thanks to a number of good harvests, a commitment to quality and the use of older wines for blending the NVs.

Though I cannot think of anything other than Champagne for 2000, there are alternatives for various festive occasions which make a lot of sense. Good Champagne should be treated like a fine wine, and really tasted in a way that it never is. The quality of other sparkling wines is very good and at half the price of NV Champagnes are perfect icebreakers and for pouring into partygoers. New World sparklers have the advantage of more fruit and often a higher dosage than Champagne which makes them easier to drink without food.

The question of Champagne and food is important. Although usually drunk on its own—or quite incongruously with Christmas or wedding cake—it matches certain foods very well. The long aftertaste of a good Champagne means that it suits strong food tastes and spices. It cuts nicely through Sushi and smoked salmon and is even a good partner for fish'n chips. More full bodied Pinot Noir dominated wines can match game especially eaten cold.

Champagne

White £10 - £12

Grandin Brut nv
Febvre ®

Aromas of toast and roasted almonds, slightly steely. Crisp, green apple fruit and a dry finish. Good value.

White £15 - £20

Bernard Depoivre Brut nv
Bubble Brothers ®

New-mown grass combines with honey, nuts and toast to give a complex nose. Plenty of green fruit flavour with creamy texture, crisp acidity and a nice long finish.

Canard-Duchêne Brut nv
TDL ☆

Light but elegant nose, a bit fuller in taste. Well-sustained mousse and clean finish. Fair value.

Heidsieck Monopole Blue Top Brut nv
Allied Drinks ☆

Full, rich, ripe fruit aromas showing also in the taste. Good quality and excellent value.

J.M. Gremillet Brut nv
Allied Drinks ®

Light, clean nose and simple fresh fruit flavours. Soundly made and relatively good value.

Jean de Praisac Brut nv
Molloy's ®

Yeasty bready aromas and quite lively in the glass. Light, fresh and fruity with melon flavours. Easy-drinking and good value.

Jean-Claude Vallois Assemblage Noble Blanc de Blancs Brut nv
Bubble Brothers ®

A very fine mousse which persists well after pouring, Honey and raspberries on the nose with a touch of toasted almond. Dry and crisp with a good weight of green apple fruit and a refreshing finish.

Marie Stuart Brut 1er Cru nv
Wines Direct ®

Layers of aromas of oily lambswool; apple, citrus and marmalade flavours expand in the mouth and finish well.

Mountaudon Brut nv
Mitchell ®

Lemony, yeasty aromas with a bit of toast in the background. Dry, yeasty and fresh with youthful green fruit. Simple, light bubbles.

Pierlot Fils Grande Réserve Brut nv
Bubble Brothers ®

Lots of honey on the nose and biscuity aromas; nice mousse though it should hold better. Typical Pinot raspberries following through in a dry finish.

Princesse de France Grande Réserve Brut nv

Bacchus ®

Wet wool, together with toast and almonds on the nose. Very dry with crisp acidity and crunchy apple fruit.

White £20 - £25

Bernard Gentil Réserve Brut nv

Bubble Brothers ®

Tropical fruits on the nose echoed by melon, crisp apple and subtle, honeyed flavours giving a complex palate. An elegant mousse and lasting flavour give a very pleasant wine with a long finish.

Billecart Salmon Brut Réserve nv

Brangan ☆ ☆

Beautifully balanced, elegant Champagne from the creamy mousse to the long lingering finish. Good weight of complex, restrained biscuit, fruit and nut flavours.

Bricout Brut nv

Greenhills ®

Biscuit, melon and citrus fruit aromas. Dry with zippy acidity and citrus, appley fruit. Dry, very clean finish.

De Venoge Cordon Bleu Brut Select nv

Bacchus ®

Buttery biscuits with apple aromas. Lively, crisp and clean with green apple fruit. Mouthfilling creaminess and length.

Lanson Black Label Brut nv

Adams ☆

Tantalising, endless streams of tiny bubbles then aromas of ripe fruit with nutty, biscuity tones—Lincoln creams from one enthusiastic taster. Dry, very fresh palate; ripe fruit cut through with acidity and a long finish.

Laurent-Perrier Brut nv

Gilbeys ☆ ☆

Rich and toasty aromas; the richness follows through to the taste which has hints of mocha and cherry character. Refreshing with very long finish.

Moët et Chandon Brut Imperial nv

Dillon ®

Minerally nose with underlying aromas of marzipan and green apples. Bone-dry with crisp apple fruit. A shy personality, beginning to evolve in the finish.

Pommery Brut Royal nv

Grants ☆ ☆ ☆

Pale, lively mousse and elegant floral nose of apple blossom and sweet pea. Creamy and mouth-filling with ripe, mature fruit. 'Scrummy!' and 'Heavenly!' to two tasters.

White £25 - £30

Deutz Brut Classic nv
Febvre ®
Subtle aromas of biscuits, honey, ripe fruits. Dry and crisp with a palate of apricot and other honeyed fruits in a delicious creamy texture. Full, ripe and complex with a longlasting finish.

Jean-Claude Vallois Blanc de Blancs Brut 90
Bubble Brothers ®
Rich nose of butter, honey and almonds. Very lively with ripe but subtle flavours of melon, apples, pears. Elegant, with a lot of finesse.

Joseph Perrier Cuvée Royale Brut nv
United Beverages ®
Honey, nuts, lemon and lime all combine on the nose; refreshing and lively with ripe flavours of honeyed autumn fruit and nuts. Long and dry in the finish.

Pommery Brut 91
Grants ☆ ☆
Fine, mature threads of bubbles. Dry toast, honey and jasmine aromas give a mature, complex nose. Dry and richly satisfying with silky, creamy texture and nutty fruit. Long, complex finish.

Taittinger Brut Reserve nv
Febvre ®
Floral, tropical fruits— passionfruit and mango— come through on the nose. Bone-dry with a lively mousse and flavour dominated by Granny Smith apple tastes. Long and dry in the finish.

Veuve Clicquot Ponsardin Brut nv
Findlater ®
Long, luxurious columns of bubbles. Ripe aromas of red apples and citrus fruits. Crisp, fresh palate developing a rather rich, tropical fruit character with balancing acidity. Cream and honey on top.

White £30 - £35

Alfred Gratien Brut nv
TDL ®
Yeasty, even vegetal, on the nose, more fruit on the palate; quite fresh with decent length.

De Venoge Blanc de Blancs Brut 90
Bacchus ☆ ☆
Elegant nose with buttered toast and summer fruits. Lovely ripe palate with strawberries, raspberies and creamy nuttiness in the flavour. Complex and long and worth the price.

Moët et Chandon Brut Impérial 92
Dillon ☆
Sparkling
Assertive bouquet of butter, nuts and biscuits with well-integrated fruit. Similar full-bodied palate with bready,

biscuity tastes and sharp fruit. Very long finish. A beautifully crafted wine.

White £35 - £40

Billecart Salmon 'Cuvée Nicolas Francois' Brut 90

Brangan ☆☆☆

Intense layered and subtle bouquet of strawberry and marzipan. Full, complex mouthful of golden apple and almond fruit in a creamy mousse. Very long, elegant finish. Well worth its price.

White £60 and over

Cuvée William Deutz Brut 90

Febvre ☆☆

Buttered toast, almonds and ripe fruit on the nose. Lovely elegant wine with an endless, lively mousse. Dry, creamy and complex with toast, biscuits, strawberries.

Dom Pérignon 90

Dillon ☆☆

Subtle, full nose with butter and ripeness dominating. Great elegance mixes with loads of ripe fruit in a creamy texture. Very long and impresssive in the finish.

Taittinger Comtes de Champagne 89

Febvre ☆

Beautiful mousse rising end-lessly in the glass; developed aromas of honey, butter and apricots. Dry and nutty with great elegance and balance. A real beauty.

Rosé £15 - £20

Comte L. de Ferande Brut Rosé nv

Dunnes Stores ££

Lovely strawberries and cream on the nose and similar fruit taste with a refreshing clean finish. If Champagne can be good value this is it!

Rosé £20 - £25

Delbeck Brut Heritage Rosé nv

Mitchell ®

Light aromas of red berry fruit and similar palate with modest berry fruit flavours. A sound example.

Rosé £25 - £30

Lanson Brut Rosé nv

Adams ®

Light, fruity aromas with simple fruity taste. Refreshing, with a clean finish and some length.

Rosé £30 - £35

Laurent Perrier Rosé Brut nv

Gilbeys ®

Vigorous fine bubbles and aromas of raspberries and red berries. Dry with balanced acidity and good weight of berry fruit flavour. Subtle and elegant.

Rosé £35 - £40

Möet et Chandon Rosé Brut nv

Dillon ©

Ripe fruit aromas of cherry and strawberry and rich fruity flavours which are lingering, moreish and delicious. Expen-sive but worth it !

Sparkling

White £5 - £6

Tesco's Australian Sparkling Chardonnay Brut nv (Australia)
Quinnsworth ®
Nice persistent sparkle and aromas of bread dough and biscuits. Dry with crisp green apple acidity and yeasty flavours, a touch floral, too. Excellent party bubbly at a good price.

White £8 - £10

Blaners Brut AC Blanquette de Limoux nv (France—Loire)
Wines Direct ®
Lovely peach and apricot on the nose with a touch of honey. Mouthfilling mousse which holds up well, Plenty of fruit and a clean dry finish. Good value.

Jacob's Creek Sparkling Chardonnay/Pinot Noir nv (Australia)
Fitzgerald ®
Ripe fruit aromas mixed with honey and toast. Lots of fruit and rich flavour on the palate.

Orlando Carrington Brut nv (Australia)
Fitzgerald ®
Melon, honey and lemon sherbet aromas. Very fruity, simple and refreshing.

Mondoro DOCG Asti nv (Italy)
Grants ®
Light and grapey with attractive medium-sweet flavours.

Codorníu Cuvée Raventós Cava Brut nv (Spain)
Grants ®
Lively in the glass with lots of tangy, juicy citrus fruit flavours; slightly toasted in the finish.

Tesco's Cava Brut nv (Spain)
Quinnsworth ®
Drifting bubbles and pleasant aromas of ripe, red apples which follow to the palate. Nicely balanced acidity and a touch of yeast. Decent Cava.

White £10 - £12

Anares Cava Brut nv (Spain)
Allied Drinks ☆
Very appealing nose with creamy fruit aromas. Fresh fruity and clean flavours. Very attractive Cava.

Clover Hill Tasmania 93 (Australia)
Dunnes Stores ®
Lovely, lively mousse with fresh, attractive fruit aromas and mouthfilling apple and citrus fruit in a creamy texture.

Gratien & Meyer Brut AC Saumur nv (France—Loire)
Gilbeys ☆
Typical Chenin nose of honey, lemon and toast. Lively, refreshing and fruity flavours. Very moreish indeed!

Orlando Trilogy Brut nv (Australia)
Fitzgerald ☆
Sparkling
Classy, biscuity nose with melon-type fruit aromas. The palate is fresh and clean with a decent length.

Seaview Brut nv (Australia)
Findlater ££
Touch of marzipan on the nose, also ripe fruit aromas; lively and fresh with ripe fruit and crisp finish. Great value.

White £12 - £15

Hardys Nottage Hill Sparkling Chardonnay 96 9
Allied Drinks ®
Fresh and clean with lovely ripe apple aromas and deliciously fresh, rounded, easy flavours.

Seaview Pinot Noir/Chardonnay Brut 94
Findlater ££
Really ripe summer fruit nose with a touch of toasted almond. Lovely balance of fresh fruit, lively acidity and long, creamy finish. Elegant for the price.

Rotari Brut (Mezzacorona) DOC Trento nv (Italy)
Mitchell ®
Elegant appearance and quite pleasing green fruit and grassiness on the nose. Dry, with very green fruit and bracing acidity.

Parxet Cava Chardonnay DO Alella nv (Spain)
Jenkinson ®
Lots of yeast aromas with rather toasted flavours of dried fruit. Quite full and rounded with good sparkle.

White £15 - £20

Pelorus Cloudy Bay 93 (New Zealand)
Findlater ☆ ☆
Rather deep, luminous gold with steady streams of tiny bubbles. Developed mature nose: yeast and oakiness with underlying mushroom aromas. Dry with satisfying honeyed oiliness, quite earthy palate. Tasted against Champagnes it did better than most!

Red £8 - £10

Seppelt Dry Sparkling Shiraz 93 (Australia)
Dunnes Stores ®
Really rich cassis and Ribena on the nose with a weight of berry fruit flavour. Off-dry but with enough acidity to carry the fruit. Great with really hot chilli and Szchen food.

Rosé £8 - £10

Orlando Carrington Brut Rosé nv (Australia)
Fitzgerald ®
Light, fruity nose; rather rich, tinned strawberry fruit—a touch cloying—with a fairly dry finish. Good soft style of pink sparkler.

Rosé £10 - £12

Seaview Brut Rosé nv (Australia)
Findlater ®
Attractive ripe berry fruit on the nose; fruity, soft palate with ripe strawberries and balanced acidity.

Sweet wines

Until a few years ago sweet wines were rather out of fashion, due mainly to a proliferation of bad examples. However, they are returning to favour and are a lovely and special way to end a memorable meal.

A few new styles of sweet wine have recently appeared. From the New World there are late-harvested Rieslings and botrytised Semillons as well as Muscats. These have loads of super-ripe fruit and clean refreshing acidity, sometimes a bit one-dimensional but always well-made.

Tokay, the wine of kings and king of wines, is returning to quality and popularity as Hungary revitalises its industry. These famous wines are complex and elegant and still relatively inexpensive. Other unusual bargains are the delicious aged Muscats of Setúbal in Portugal and a number of lesser-known sweet offerings from Italy.

Fortified Muscats from the South of France, such as Muscat de Beaumes de Venise, are well known. Liqueur Muscats from Australia have just appeared. These are dark, rich and chocolatey, and totally intoxicating. Banyuls in the Roussillon area is also a slightly different sweet wine, made from the red Grenache grape and aged in wood. It is Port-like though not so strong, and the classic choice with chocolate.

£6 - £8

Fonseca Alambre Muscatel de Setubal 91 (Portugal)
Gilbeys ☆
Fruit and nuts on the nose, sultanas and figs; lots of weight with big mouthfilling dried fruit flavours. Long finish.

MezzaCorona Moscato Giallo 96 (Italy)
Mitchell ®
Very light and fresh with lovely sweet grapey fruit and lively freshness. Not super-sweet, very easy-drinking and attractive.

Mick Morris Rutherglen Liqueur Muscat nv (Australia)
Fitzgerald ®
Liqueur fruits and nuts dominate the nose. Warm and liqueuer-like on the palate with loads of dark dried fruit, raisins and chocolate flavours. Long in the finish and well priced.

£8 - £10

Cave des Vignerons de St Jean de Minervois AC Muscat St-Jean de Minervois 94 (France—Languedoc-Roussillon)
Searson ££
Ripe apricot and peach fruit

with honeyed tones; quite luscious on the palate but with beautifully clean fruit flavours running right through to a refreshing finish.

Dom. Parcé VDN AC Muscat de Rivesaltes nv (France—Languedoc-Roussillon)
Wines Direct ®
Lovely nose of sweet jam, honey and ripe fruit. Acidity balances the sweetness and flavour lingers well.

James Halliday Griffith Botrytis Semillon 95 (Australia)
Findlater ☆
Intense honeyed citrus fruit with heady botrytis aromas. Great concentration of ripe, ripe fruit, honey and marmalade flavours with cleansing acidity and a long finish.

Penfolds Magill Tawny (Liqueur) nv (Australia)
Findlater ®
Deep rich raisiny aromas; very concentrated dried fruit flavours—prunes and figs, with spicy nuances and warm lingering finish.

£10 - £12

Ambeille Banyuls Perlé VdM nv (France—Languedoc-Roussillon)
Mitchell ©
Rich fruit aromas on the nose with a weight of ripe, dark cherry flavours. Spicy flavours and alcohol give a lingering warmth with enough acidity to balance.

Cormòns Isonzo Vendemmia Tardiva DOC Friuli 96 (Italy)
Select Wines from Italy ©
Honey and ripe apricots

dominate the nose. Lovely, ripe tropical fruit flavour and refreshing acidty. Long finish.

Cormòns Passito di Cormòns VdT 95 (Italy)
Select Wines from Italy ®
The nose has a touch of walnut and dried fruits; similar rich dried fruit on the palate with acidity to balance. Long enough in the finish.

Domaine Brusset VDN nv (France—Rhône (South))
Mitchell ®
Typically oxidised aromas coming off the nose; sweet, complex palate with grape and raisin fruit and warm alcohol showing through.

Leone de Castris Negrino Aleatico Dolce DOC Salice Salentino Rosso 92 (Italy)
Select Wines from Italy ®
Ripe nose of plums and chocolate. Good rich flavours and balanced acidity; slightly short finish.

Terre di Brognoligo Cecilia Beretta DOC Recioto di Soave 93 (Italy)
Mitchell ©
Developed honeyed nose with layers of yeast and slightly oxidised aromas. Sweetness offset by caramel and spice influences with good length in the finish. Different and well made.

Zagara (Marchesi di Barolo) DOCG Moscato d'Asti 97 (Italy)
Select Wines from Italy ®
Rather sherbety nose which follows through to the palate of sweet, sweet apple. Nice, refreshing acidity to finish.

£12 - £15

Ch. de la Peyrade AC Muscat de Frontignan nv ((France—Languedoc-Roussillon)
Brangan ☆
Delightful nose of exotic fruit and Turkish Delight. Full, rich fruit on the palate—lychees, rosewater, mangoes with clean, balancing acidity to keep it fresh. Long, delicious finish.

Dom de la Rectorie 'Cuvée Parcé Frères' AC Banyuls 96 (France—Languedoc-Roussillon)
Brangan ☆
Plummy and rich on the nose with huge weight of plum and cherry fruit flavours. Warming alcohol and fresh acidity give a good balance and the flavours linger well.

Domaine Coyeux AC Muscat de Beaumes-de-Venise 95 (France—Rhône (South))
Findlater ®
Lovely rich, honeyed Muscat nose, full and rich with lots of grapey, orangey fruit flavour and a long, warm finish. Enough acidity to prevent cloying.

Fischer Eiswein 92 (Austria)
TDL ©
Complex honey, tropical fruit and obvious botrytis on the nose. Elegant, balanced palate with honeyed fruit and long luscious finish,. Great value.

Fischer Trockenbeerenalese 95 (Austria)
TDL ©
Very concentrated tropical fruit and honey aromas. Quite a lot of finesse on the palate with elegant, honeyed fruit and clean, fresh acidity. Long finish. Good value.

Sipp Mack Gewürztraminer Vendange Tardive Cuvée Lucie-Marie AC Alsace 94 (France—Alsace)
Mitchell ☆
Elegant floral, rosewater aromas with a spicy, rich edge. Restrained yet quite sweet on the palate with honeyed exotic fruit and a very clean, dry finish with white pepper spice. Long and stylish.

£15 - £20

Ch. de Fesles AC Bonnezeaux 94 (France—Loire)
Superquinn ©
Pure honey on the nose with underlying peach and apricot fruit. Very rich and luscious palate, apricots, peaches with a touch of orange zest and bathed in honey. Good balancing acidity kicks in to a clean, refreshing finish.

Domaine du Mas Blanc AC Banyuls 95 (France—Languedoc-Roussillon)
Wines Direct ®
Plummy fruit aromas combine with fruitcake and raisins. Similar layers of rich spicy fruit on the palate with tingling alcohol in the finish. Delicious.

Tokaji Aszú Oremus Puttonyos 5 93 (Hungary)
Mitchell ®
Honey and syrup on the nose; very rich palate with huge concentration of intriguing fruit, cut through with fresh orange peel flavour. Long and warm. Fascinating and delicious wine.

£20 - £25

**Weingut Johanneshof
Dirmsteiner Mandelpfad
Gewürtztraminer eiswein QmP
89** (Germany)
Octavius ®
Lovely rich honey and tropical
fruit on the nose with a touch of
spice and flowers. Excellent
balance of fruit and acidity and
rich, spicy exotic flavour.

£25 - £30

**Herxheimer Himmelreich
Scheurebe Eiswein QmP 90**
(Germany)
Mitchell ☆ ☆
Lovely nose of apricots, honey
and peaches. Long, sweet,
luscious flavours and balancing
acidity. A complex, hedonistic
treat.

Importers of listed wines

Adams Vintners Ltd, 1 Charleston Rd, Dublin 6 Tel (01) 496 3866 Fax (01) 496 0186
Wines are widely available.

Allied Drinks Limited, Windsor Hill House, Glounthaune, Co. Cork, Tel (021) 353 438 Fax (021) 354 362 JFK Road, JFK Industrial Estate, Dublin 12 Tel (01) 450 9777 Fax (01) 450 9699
Wines are widely available.

Approach Trade Ireland, Ltd, South Quay, Carrick-on-Suir, Co. Tipperary Tel (051) 640 164 Fax (051) 641 1580
Wines are available direct and also from
Don Angel, 7 D'Olier St, Dublin 2 Tel (01) 679 3859
Karwig Wines, Carrigaline, Co. Cork Tel (021) 372 864
Quay St Wine Bar, Galway, Tel (091) 565 662
Patrick Egan, Liscanor, Co Clare Tel (065) 81430

Bacchus Wine & Spirit Merchants Ltd Unit T.28 Stillorgan Industrial Park, Blackrock, Co Dublin, Tel (01) 294 1466 Fax (01) 295 7375
Wines available from off-licences and wine merchants.

Barry & Fitzwilliam Ltd, Glanmire, Cork Tel (021) 821 555 Fax (021) 821 60450 Dartmouth Square, Dublin 6 Tel (01) 660 6984 Fax (01) 660 0479
Wines are widely available.

Brangan and Company Ltd 7 Deerpark Avenue Dublin 15 Tel and Fax (01) 821 4052 email: brangan.wines@indigo.ie
Wines are available from off-licences and wine merchants.

Bubble Brothers, 43 Upper John St, Cork Tel and Fax (021) 552 252 (01) 672 5777
Wines are available direct

Burgundy Direct 8 Monaloe Way, Blackrock, Co. Dublin Tel (01) 289 6615/ 288 6239 Fax (01) 289 8470
Wines are available exclusively through Burgundy Direct Mail.

Peter A. Dalton Food & Wine 'Loch Grein', Ballybetagh, Kilternan, Co. Dublin. Customer enquiries: Tel (01) 295 4945 Fax (01) 295 4945
Wines are available from off-licences and wine merchants.

Edward Dillon & Company, 25 Mountjoy Square East, Dublin 1 Tel (01) 836 4399 Fax (01) 855 5852
Most wines are widely available but some only from specialist outlets.

Dunnes Stores, Head Office, 67 Upper Stephen Street, Dublin 8 Tel (01) 475 1111 Fax (01) 475 1441
Wines are only available from Dunnes Stores.

Febvre & Company Limited 15-17 Maple Avenue, Stillorgan Industrial Park, Blackrock, County Dublin Tel (01) 295 9030 Fax (01) 295 9036
Most wines widely available but some only from specialist outlets.

Findlater (Wine Merchants) Ltd. The Harcourt Street Vaults, 10 Upper Hatch Street Dublin 2 Tel (01) 475 1699 Fax (01) 475 2530
Wines are widely available.

Fitzgerald and Co Ltd, 11-12 Bow Street, Dublin 7. Tel (01) 872 5911 Fax (01) 872 2809
Most wines are widely available and others only from specialist outlets.

Gilbeys of Ireland, Gilbey House, Belgard Road, Dublin 24 Tel (01) 459 7444 Fax (01) 459 0188
Wines are widely available.

Grants of Ireland Ltd, St Lawrence Road, Chapelizod, Dublin 20 Tel (01) 626 4455 Fax (01) 626 4680
Wines are widely available.

Greenhills Wines & Spirits, Aisling House, Shanowen Road, Santry, Dublin 9. Customer enquiries Tel (01) 842 2188 Fax (01) 842 2455
Wines are widely available.

Jenkinson Wines, 4 Sylvan Lawns, Kilcoole, Co Wicklow Tel (01) 287 3533
Wines are widely available.

Karwig Wines, Kilnagleary, Carragaline, Cork Tel (021) 372 864 Fax (021) 372 864
Wines available from off-licences and wine merchants.

Koala Wines, 25 Seatown, Dundalk, Co Louth Customer enquiries Tel (08) 016937 52804 Fax (08) 016937 52943
Wines are widely available.

Leinster Merchant Wines, The Barn Store, Loughanure, Clane Co. Kildare Tel (045) 868 425 Fax (045) 861 441
Wines available direct

Mitchell & Son, 21 Kildare Street, Dublin 2 Tel (01) 676 0766 Fax (01) 661 1509 54 Glasthule Road, Sandycove, Co Dublin Tel (01) 230 2301 Fax (01) 230 2305
Wines are available only from Mitchells Wine Shops or through the Internet at http://indigo.ie/~mitchell.

Molloy's Liquor Stores, Head Office, Block 2, Village Green, Tallaght, Dublin 24 Tel (01) 451 5544 Fax (01) 451 5658
Wines are available only from branches of Molloy's Liquor Stores, or through the Internet at www.liquorstore.ie.

Octavius Wines, 23 Grattan St, Sligo, Tel (071) 71730 Fax (071) 70483
Wines are available exclusively through this outlet.

Quinnsworth Tesco, Gresham House, Marine Road, Dun Laoghaire, Co. Dublin Tel (01) 280 8441 Fax (01) 280 0136
Wines are available only from branches of Quinnsworth Tesco only.

Searsons Wine Merchants, 6a The Crescent, Monkstown, County Dublin, Tel (01) 280 0405 Fax (01) 280 4771

Wines are available only from Searsons Wine Merchants.

Select Wines from Italy Ltd, 12 Balally Close, Dundrum, Dublin 16 Customer enquiries Tel (01) 294 2858 Fax (01) 294 2858

Superquinn, Sutton Cross, Sutton, Dublin 13 Tel (01) 832 5700 Fax (01) 832 6544
Wines are available only from branches of Superquinn.

SuperValu Centra, Head Office, Tramore Road, Cork Tel (021) 803 00 Fax (021) 313 621
Wines are available from branches of SuperValu-Centra.

Taserra Wine Merchants, Hogan House, Grand Canal Street, Dublin 2 Tel (01) 490 0537 Fax (01) 490 4052
Wines are widely available.

TDL, 47-48 Pearse Street, Dublin 2 Tel (01) 677 4381 Fax (01) 677 4775
Wines are widely available.

United Beverages, Finches Industrial Park, Long Mile Road, Dublin 12 Tel (01) 450 2000 Fax (01) 450 9004
Wines are widely available.

Wines Direct, Lisamate, Irishtown, Mullingar, Co Westmeath, Tel 1800 579 579 Fax (044) 40015
Mail Order

Index of listed wines